Peter FitzSimons was raised 80 kilometres north of Sydney, After six years of boarding at Knox Grammar School in Sydney, he went to America for one year on an exchange scholarship and returned to get an Arts degree from Sydney University.

In 1984, he played one game for the Wallabies against a Fijian provincial side, before heading off to Europe for the next five years to play rugby in Italy and France, and to begin his writing career. While in France, he had the honour of being officially rated the no. 1 second-rower in the country and was asked by French coach Jacques Fouroux to naturalise so as to play for the national XV.

FitzSimons declined, and returned to Australia in 1989 to force his way into the Wallabies, going on to play seven Tests. This was followed by a brief appearance for the World XV against the All Blacks in 1992, just before he retired from rugby at all levels — bar after-dinner speaking, where he remains one of the busiest in Australia.

As a journalist, FitzSimons has been full-time with *The Sydney Morning Herald* since 1989 and has been writing a regular column for the *London Daily Telegraph* since 1991. He also worked for four years as a reporter with Channel Nine and now works as a panellist with the Fox Sports pay-television service in Australia, appearing on their "Back Page" program.

Married in 1992, he lives with his wife Lisa Wilkinson and their three children in Sydney and is now the author of thirteen books in all. In February of 1996, Stephen Jones — the noted rugby writer for Britain's *Sunday Times* — released his own list of the 20 best rugby books ever written. FitzSimons was the only author to appear on the list twice, for *Basking in Beirut* and for his best-selling biography of the 1991 Wallaby World Cup Winning captain, *Nick Farr-Jones*. He has also since released the biography of the 1999 Wallaby World Cup Winning captain, *John Eales*.

Peter FitzSimons

The Rugby War

HarperSports
An imprint of HarperCollinsPublishers

While every effort has been made to contact the copyrightholders of photographic material contained in this work, the publisher welcomes any information in relation to missing credits or acknowledgments.

Harper*Sports*
An imprint of HarperCollins*Publishers,* Australia

First published in Australia in 1996
This edition published in 2003
by HarperCollins*Publishers* Pty Limited
ABN 36 009 913 517
A member of the HarperCollins*Publishers* (Australia) Pty Limited Group
www.harpercollins.com.au

HarperCollins*Publishers*
25 Ryde Road, Pymble, Sydney, NSW 2073, Australia
31 View Road, Glenfield, Auckland 10, New Zealand
77–85 Fulham Palace Road, London, W6 8JB, United Kingdom
2 Bloor Street East, 20th Floor, Toronto, Ontario M4W 1A8, Canada
10 East 53rd Street, New York NY 10022, USA

National Library of Australia Cataloguing-in-publication data:

FitzSimons, Peter.
  The rugby war.
  Updated ed.
  Includes index.
  ISBN 0 7322 7882 1.
  1. Rugby Union football. 2. Rugby Union football – History. I. Title.
796.333

Cover photo courtesy of Getty Images
Cover and internal design by Gayna Murphy, HarperCollins Design Studio
Printed and bound in Australia by Griffin Press on 79gsm Bulky White

6 5 4 3 2 1   03 04 05 06

Contents

For my children,
Jake Raymond, Louis McCloy
and Billi Maria Sofia FitzSimons

Introduction

Whenever a definitive history of the rugby union game is written, 1995 will forever stand out as a year of extraordinary change.

After the code had lived on a diet of fresh air and love for well over a century, it was the year that three major national Rugby Unions of the southern hemisphere signed a deal with a massive media corporation guaranteeing them over half a billion American dollars in return for a decade's worth of television rights. In reply, an organisation called The World Rugby Corporation launched a stunning counter-coup, contracting most of the planet's best players from all the major Unions to an alternative competition set up on a *global* basis.

It was, as a consequence, the year of the Rugby War ... When the War was over, the International Rugby Football Board — nominally the game's ruling body, even if Missing In Action throughout — formalised the already apparent. They announced that the code would henceforth abandon its famous amateur ethos and instead embrace outright professionalism.

My aim with this book when I was writing the first edition in late 1995 and early 1996, was to tell how all of the above happened, and *why* it happened. Before beginning to write the account, I had no doubts at all as to the rights and wrongs of the Rugby War. Too easy. The "establishment" was 100 per cent right, and the "rebels" were every bit as wrong, plus a bit more besides. The more I researched, though, the more I realised that it was not so simple.

Rather than a parable with a clear moral to the story, the fight between The World Rugby Corporation and the national Rugby Unions around the world was a clash of generations, of footballing ideologies, of one set of business interests against another. Most of all it was about a violent difference of opinion between revolutionaries, as to what form the revolution should take.

Aux armes, citoyens!

It did, of course, get very bitter, and with that in mind when first approached to write the book I refused outright on the grounds that I had no stomach to delve into the still gaping wound that the War had wrought on the game's soul. But after a chance breakfast meeting in Newcastle, Australia, with one of the movers and shakers of The World Rugby Corporation in Michael Hill, I came to two conclusions while driving back to Sydney Town.

Firstly, it was too absorbing a story not to be told. And secondly, there actually were two sides to it — meaning that the inexplicable behaviour of some of my close friends in the Wallabies was suddenly more comprehensible.

With the latter particularly in mind, I hoped, with all humility, that the book would help to heal the wound that was still weeping at the time I released it.

After all ...

"Rugby people is good people", as an old Italian second-rower once told me. The Rugby War saw very good people on both sides of the barricades, many of them close compatriots before it all started.

In terms of the structure of the book I framed the account in rough, though not strict, chronological order of how things unfolded. I did not always name names. True, it was occasionally unwieldy to be describing someone as "a prominent British rugby coach", instead of simply stating his name, but there is another basic rule that I followed.

Generally, no one's name appeared in the book unless it was already a matter of public record that they had been involved, or, though they hadn't yet been named, they were happy to acknowledge their part in proceedings.

Now, eight years on, I have kept to that same principle. In no way, shape, sense or form did I want this book to be seen as a "witch-hunt". For starters, that would have implied massive wrongdoing on one side or another. And while at the War's height both sides accused the other of engaging in massive skulduggery, for what it's worth, I found very little.

In terms of actually writing the beast, I'd like to particularly thank all those people who gave me their account of what happened. I was most grateful at the time to the men of The World Rugby Corporation for granting me careful access to their side of the story, even when they knew that when the fight was at its height I was as bitterly critical of them as anyone. And I remain thankful since.

I also appreciated the attitude of such people as Rod McCall, Sean Fitzpatrick, Laurie Mains and Phil Kearns who were candid about what they did and why they did it, and were happy to answer most questions I had.

Finally I thank again my wife, Lisa, who was extremely supportive throughout the writing process — not only doing an enormous amount of skilled editing, but also managing to keep our two sons away from the study when Daddy was banging away on the "puter".

Which was most of the time.

Why have I released this new edition? Because it is far and away, of the thirteen books I have written, the one that has generated most interest, and, since the time I wrote it Rugby has grown exponentially. Though I was conscious at the time I was writing it that I was documenting an important event in the history of rugby, the passage of the years has confirmed that it really was *the* seminal event, the key bridge between two entirely different eras.

Peter FitzSimons.
Sydney, July, 2003.

Author's note

For the sake of simplicity, I have taken liberties in the names used to describe four institutions. While the International Rugby Football Board has of course the initials IRFB, people in the rugby world invariably call it the "IRB". I use that term throughout.

Ditto, the Australian Rugby Football Union, which is known to all and sundry as the ARU or simply the Australian Rugby Union. Double ditto The World Rugby Corporation, or TWRC, which I have also standardised to WRC, the common usage of the time.

News Limited Australia is a division of News Corporation International. To avoid confusion I have, in both quotes and text, changed all references to News Limited to News Corporation.

In terms of research I found, needless to say, the output of journalists from around the globe helpful in understanding how the whole story fitted together. An article written in New Zealand's *Metro* magazine, by Tom Hyde, was extremely helpful in my basic research as to what happened in that country.

Equally, in France, I found Richard Escot's book, *Rugby Pro Histoires Secrêtes*, useful to understand at least the basic mechanics of what went on there.

In February 1996, Peter Jenkins of *The Australian* newspaper, put out a seven-part series on the whole affair, and I was able to firm up from his writings particular episodes that I was still foggy on.

Finally I ripped off the title of the third chapter, *Wheeling, Dealing and Mealing*, from a newspaper clipping that I've since lost.

Chapter one
In the beginning

Kerry Packer was not well pleased.

It was in the late afternoon of Friday, March 31, 1995, and in the space of a day, the man touted as "Australia's richest man" had seen one of the most lucrative sources of revenue for his media conglomerate come under unprecedented attack.

"Super League" — a naked attempt by the corporate forces of Rupert Murdoch to take over the Australian domestic rugby league competition — had been launched.

Right at Kerry Packer.

The night before, News Corporation had launched a full-scale legal assault designed to break the ties that bound the players and the clubs to the Australian Rugby League's competition. That very afternoon, the story had got out that "the players were going". Players like Bradley Clyde — perhaps the most admired rugby league forward in captivity — were apparently going to be offered salaries of up to 700,000 Australian dollars a year, three to four times what they had been earning previously.

Intelligence was already flowing into Packer's Park Street head-quarters in Sydney that players like Clyde might merely be at the pointy end of a whole battalion of regular rugby league players who would soon be offered similar multiples of their previous salaries. Almost before Packer's very eyes, a sporting competition that his television network had helped to build up, that had delivered consistently enormous ratings and advertising revenue for the previous four years, appeared to be on the edge of dissolving.

What the *hell* was going on here?

It was all about the emerging pay-television market in Australia, where two major consortiums were getting ready to go to air by the end of 1995 and were urgently looking for "product" that would make the population keen to subscribe with them.

In NSW and Queensland — where 52 per cent of Australia's high-spending 18–35 male population lives — rugby league was far and away the most valuable televisual product of all. In those climes there simply wasn't a single sport more major-league than rugby league as a "driver" of subscriptions.

The Optus Vision pay-television consortium was aligned with Packer, while Foxtel was in the Murdoch camp. Foxtel was extremely keen to broadcast league, but found its way blocked because Packer held both free-to-air and pay-television rights to broadcast the Australian Rugby League's competition right up until the turn of the millennium.

Well, if Murdoch couldn't televise the ARL's competition, he'd bloody well start his own.

And now it was on. That Friday was the beginning of a blitzkrieg campaign of a venom and fire-power the like of which had never been seen in Australian sport or even *business* — and the border between the two was continuing to blur with every passing hour.

In defence against Murdoch's charge, Packer was even then organising his side of the corporate battle to unlock the coffers and put into the war effort many millions of dollars with which he could hopefully retain the loyalty of the players.

Beyond this, in terms of defending his position, Packer could also claim at least tenant rights on the moral high ground — in that he had a valid contract with the ARL, an organisation of close on 90 years standing.

He also had what remained of the status quo to lean on, as there was enormous resistance from much of the rugby league public to the whole concept of Super League and he had ... he had ... well, what else did he have to defend himself with?

It was time to talk to key advisers and business associates equally keen to thwart Murdoch's move — and one of the many calls put in that afternoon from Packer's offices went to David Gonski, a principal of the business advisory firm Wentworth Associates. Gonski had been a great help to Packer many times in the past and he just might be of help on this occasion too.

Not that rugby league football was David Gonski's forte. As a matter of fact, on his way out the door he asked his partner and friend, Geoff Levy, to tell him again, "Is a football oval or round?"

Gonski was kidding, of course, but he really wasn't sure of his ground when that ground was full of massive men running into each other, all for the sake of a bit of pumped-up leather. Gonski suggested to Levy that he might like to give the matter some thought over the weekend, to see if he might come up with something to counter the Super League threat.

A tiny seed had just fallen on some extremely fertile soil.

For Levy, matters of football were every bit his thing. The South African-born lawyer loved everything about it — rugby union, to be precise — and had played it since the age of six in the back-blocks of the veldt, up through the South African school system and onwards through the army.

Even after Levy had arrived in Australia in 1981 as a 21-year-old — with $800, one suitcase full of clothes and another with books — he had continued to play rugby at the sub-district level. He had even represented Australia in rugby at the Maccabi games held in Israel in 1985, "but only because there were only 20 people who turned up to the selection trials".

So it was that the young lawyer retired for the weekend to his home in Sydney's Eastern suburbs, and turned the whole problem of Super League over in his head.

"What was clear to me from the beginning," he recalls now, "was that it was crazy to think that league was an important 'product' anywhere outside New South Wales, Queensland and a few other parts of the world. It wasn't really international at all, while rugby, I knew for a sure and certain fact, went all over the planet."

Following this line of thinking, Levy came up that weekend with an idea that was the rough equivalent of the Russians' famous tactic against the advancing French army of Napoleon in the campaign of 1812 — that is, abandon Moscow all but entirely and then swoop down from the hills to crush them later, when the French were starving, cold and tired.

In this instance, Levy's idea was for the Packer camp to switch their attention to rugby union. Maybe it was time to set the genuinely worldwide game up on a truly professional basis and then return to choke the living daylights out of Murdoch's rugby league which, by comparison, was quite simply a piss-ant parish-pump game.

In Levy's words, "It was time that rugby union became a big boys' sport. I thought if the elite level of the game could be set up into one professional worldwide competition, then it would be unstoppable."

He mulled it over the whole weekend long, becoming progressively more enthusiastic about the concept.

The beat went on. Over this same weekend, revelations of the extent of Super League continued …

Saturday morning brought the stunning confirmation that many of rugby league's "superstars" really had signed overnight, including many of the Australian Test side, the Kangaroos.

Sunday morning, more of the same … One by one, then two by two, then drove by drove, the cream of rugby league playing talent was being picked off for Rupert Murdoch's "rebel" competition.

By Sunday afternoon, at half-time of the game between Manly and the Gold Coast, a clearly shocked Australian Rugby League Chairman, Ken Arthurson, addressed the crowd and plaintively asked into the microphone, "Who *are* these people?"

Mr Arthurson, meet Rampagin' Rupert Murdoch, the media magnate out of Adelaide, via America — 175cm tall, and weighing in at some $US15.5 billion. With a reach that extends from Los Angeles in the East to Los Angeles in the West, he's got a right hook that has already pulled in soccer in Britain and the National Football Conference in America, both of which now appear on his television outlets. Just the previous February, Rampagin' had been voted the most powerful man in world sport by the influential American magazine *Sports Illustrated*. And it was said then, as it is said now, that most of the pin-stripe brigade around the world go belly-up and want their tummy tickled at the mere mention of his name.

Well, not Geoff Levy. Not by a long shot.

On the Monday morning Levy made his way past yet more newspaper billboards in Sydney's Martin Place blaring the very latest in extraordinary Super League recruitments — "SUPER LEAGUE BONANZA!" "MORE SIGNINGS!" — and thence up to his offices in the MLC Centre, where he unveiled his concept to David Gonski.

Gonski gave the barest minimum of encouragement that Levy needed to go ahead, and with that Levy phoned up Kerry Packer's right-hand man on all things concerning his business interests, Brian Powers.

Powers, an American with a background in international merchant banking, listened intently to what Levy had to say, and then after a few questions, rejoined by saying, "Why don't you put a paper together on it and send it over?"

Levy did just that, and got the paper to Park Street on the same day. Within 48 hours he had his answer.

"What they told me," Levy recalls, "is that the concept is great, but the implementation is impossible. They said, 'you'll have problems with all the Rugby Unions, problems with the players, problems with the whole culture, but if you can get to another step come and talk again'."

Another step. That meant a rather more detailed plan, together with some evidence that the plan had at least reasonable expectations of succeeding.

Levy says, "I knew I needed to get someone involved who knew the whole rugby world intimately, but who was not officially involved with it and wouldn't have to put it through all the committees."

He knew just the man. Ross Vincent Turnbull — a former Wallaby Test prop. Levy had worked with Turnbull extensively in the mid-eighties when Turnbull had been Chairman of the NSW Rugby Union, and Levy had been engaged as a legal-cum-business adviser to get that Union out of the deep financial mire in which it had become bogged.

A lot of people, true, had severely blamed Turnbull for all those financial problems, but Levy had never been of their number.

"I've always thought that blaming Ross for all that was very unfair," he says, "and it was never a factor in our friendship."

Far from it. To Levy's mind, Turnbull was perfect for the project at hand. Described by a long-time acquaintance as having "more front than the Sydney Opera House", Turnbull in person is an ebullient and engaging sort of fellow who manages, whatever his circumstances at the time, to always give the impression that he has just personally banked a million dollars in cash.

There is a natural optimism about him, a refusal to ever be weighed down by hassles — of which he has had at least his fair share throughout his rugby administrative and business career — and, most importantly for the purposes of Geoff Levy, he was renowned for being unstoppable.

Once embarked upon a project, Turnbull simply ploughs on regardless, up hill, down dale, across rivers and through swamps if necessary. To stop "Mad Dog", as he was known in the rugby ranks in his playing days, one has to either physically man-handle him from the tractor, or throw the keys down a rabbit burrow. And even then ...

Levy was decided. He called Ross Turnbull at the office where he sometimes worked as an independent consultant for the Ernst & Young accounting firm, and spoke with restrained excitement.

"Ross, I'm thinking of trying to set up a kind of international Super League for rugby union, which would still keep rugby's culture and traditions together," is the way Levy says he began describing his broad concept.

Would Ross like to help work out the nuts and bolts of it?

Would he what!

"Geoff," Turnbull exulted in that initial conversation, "this is my *destiny*. This is what I was BORN to do!"

He liked the idea. Turnbull promised he'd get on to it right away and get back to Levy as soon as he'd nutted out some sort of basic proposal.

That evening, while Turnbull was driving his Mercedes-Benz through the William Street tunnel that lies just on the eastern edge of Sydney's Central Business District, the car-phone rang.

It was Levy.

"Ross, have you got anything yet?"

"Steady on, Geoff, steady on. Of course I haven't got anything substantial yet ...

"But I'm working on it."

And he really was. That same afternoon, Turnbull had put in a call to the well-known Sydney sporting identity, David Lord, the only person to ever have attempted mounting something like this.

In 1983 Lord had launched, and then had to abort, "The World

Rugby Championship", involving 200 of the top players around the world who were to be paid around $A180,000 to play in a round-robin tournament involving the eight leading rugby nations.

Turnbull told Lord that he would like to look at the blueprints of Lord's scheme, and if he and his associates liked what they saw and went on to use it, "there could be a quid in it for you".

The following day Turnbull did look at Lord's plan, but didn't like it on two counts. Firstly, the said blueprint set up a structure that did not include in any way the national Unions around the world, meaning the Unions would inevitably become implacable enemies against them throughout.

And secondly, Lord's scheme wasn't all-encompassing. With only eight nations involved, it hardly covered the world in the way that Turnbull and Levy had in mind. The concept that Turnbull was already warming to would include all the national Unions and leading provincial Unions around the world, and have them as part-owners of a competition which would be set up on the American model of professional sporting franchises.

"The thing that rugby officials do well is put on good rugby games," the former Wallaby prop says now, "and what they do badly is run the business side of things. Business knows how to make money, but has no idea how to put on good rugby games. I wanted a structure where you'd get the best of both worlds."

Turnbull had no compunction whatsoever about heading off in a direction that would take rugby away from its famed ethos of amateurism, which, though it had become shaky and a little sickly in recent years, still existed.

"What was also obvious to me was that with Super League on the boil," Turnbull says now, "things had to change for rugby and change very quickly. They either had to go fully professional immediately to counter Super League, or they would finish up slowly withering on the vine."

Of course, it wasn't just Turnbull who realised this …

Far to the east, in the Land of the Long White Cloud that is New Zealand, the newly-installed Chairman of the New Zealand Rugby Football Union, Richie Guy, was sitting in his office at the Union's headquarters in Wellington. A former All Black prop and now farming man from Waipu in New Zealand's North Island, Guy turned his head and his telephone to the problem at hand — just as many rugby administrators were doing at that very moment throughout Australasia.

Since rugby league's very beginnings it had fought a long-running guerilla war against the amateurs of rugby union. For the last century or so, the monied war-lords of league had made an art form out of periodically tearing down from the hill-tops on hit-and-run raids, where they lured away whichever union player took their fancy with promises of enormous amounts of moolah.

For just as long, the war had been more or less manageable, with rugby union able to hold most of its favoured players with the persuasive argument that rugby was the *truly* international game which offered the best benefits overall. If it was money you were after, no other game anywhere offered even half the contacts with the rugby-mad business community, and let's not forget the honour and glory, the glory and honour, the honour and glory.

This Super League thing, Richie Guy concluded, was something else again. Even run-of-the-mill rugby league players were being offered up to four times more than they'd been earning previously, and it simply didn't bear thinking about what some of his star All Black players might now be offered to defect.

Actually, they were already getting paid to a certain extent. The best of the All Blacks that year could expect around $NZ130,000 through endorsements and promotions — raised largely through the marketing of the All Black name — but that was clearly not going to be enough any more.

"I think we realised immediately," Guy says, "that we had to give the All Blacks *vastly* larger incomes. The first provisional figure we talked about was another five million dollars to protect the All Blacks and obviously the protection needed to be much wider than just the national team, so we started thinking we would need to initially target 150 players, to have them getting a good income too. The question I was thinking a lot about then, was where would we get the money from?"

Funny he should say that.

At that time, around and about him in other sections of New Zealand rugby, as well as "over the ditch" in Sydney, quite a few people were going flat-out tackling that very problem.

Among them was the well-known former Australian flanker, Simon Poidevin. Though his autobiography of the late 1980s had been famously entitled, *FOR LOVE NOT MONEY*, he now clearly realised that love alone was never going to be enough to hold the line in the brand new sporting age into which rugby was heading.

Poidevin, a successful stockbroker, was like many Wallabies of his generation in that while he may have barely made a single solitary cent out of his rugby specifically from playing, he nevertheless had business contacts around the world that would be the envy of a Lear Jet salesman.

One of these contacts was with the now London-based Sam Chisholm. Chisholm was the head of all Rupert Murdoch's global television operations outside of the USA — making him inarguably the most powerful television executive in the world.

The two had got to know each other in the mid-eighties at a time when Poidevin was the strike-weapon of choice for the Wallaby back-row and Chisholm was the undisputed king of Kerry Packer's Channel Nine television network.

Since that time Poidevin had gone on to rack up a total of 59 Tests before retiring at the end of 1991, while the New Zealand-born Chisholm had fallen out with Packer but prospered with Murdoch.

Poidevin phoned Chisholm at his BSkyB offices at Isleworth in

London in that first week of April, and wondered out loud why on earth News Corporation wouldn't be interested in getting involved in the *truly* international football game of rugby union.

"'We're one step ahead of you, Simon,'" Poidevin remembers Chisholm replying in his distinctive voice of fine gravel sliding down a tin roof. "'I think you should get in touch with [News Corporation's Australian boss] Ken Cowley and see if we can't do something about this.'"

A small parenthesis here. There were other contacts between the rugby world and Murdoch's News Corporation around this time.

In that same week, and apparently independent of the Poidevin/Chisholm phone conversation, one of the senior officials in the Australian Rugby Union, Dick McGruther, took a call from David Smith, one of the senior executives of News Corporation's Australian division.

The call was to say, in McGruther's words, "That, just because we have signed with rugby league doesn't preclude us dealing with other sports. When you've got something that you want to put to us, don't forget, the door is open."

Smith also called the chairman of the NSW Rugby Union and a director of the ARU, Ian Ferrier, with exactly the same message.

Overall, it is not clear whether News Corporation had rugby in its sights all along. But there was an obvious paradox in that the corporate force causing the ruckus in the first place was the very same corporate force to which the rugby administrators would turn to save the code.

Such was the tenor of the times, such was the enormous power of Rupert Murdoch's devastating right hook.

Close parenthesis.

R ichie Guy asked for the players' attention. He was standing in the President's Room of the Otago Rugby Union headquarters in Dunedin, before assembled All Blacks and other leading players, who had finished playing a short time before in the annual North/South selection trials.

"And so ... the main thing," Richie Guy said when he got to the point, "is that you all realise that we're very aware that the Super League people will be making some attractive offers to a lot of you, if they haven't already. But what we want from you is two or three months grace to organise ourselves, and I think we'll be able to come back to you with an attractive offer on our own account. Please don't sign any contracts meantime."

Guy also had brief meetings with three separate All Blacks and asked them to each come back to him within a couple of days with a figure of how much extra guaranteed money they thought would be needed on an annual basis to "protect the All Blacks".

(He shortly had his answer. One player said $NZ100,000; one said $150,000 and the other had a range from $80,000 for "past-it" players like himself, up to $150,000 for the superstars.)

R oss Turnbull busily worked away, mostly in the front study of his Bellevue Hill home. Writing, scratching out provisional plans, redoing them and starting again.

As a backdrop to the work, he was surrounded by the book-lined walls, one entire section of which is stocked solid with rugby books — while the other shelves carry various tomes about such heavyweight historical figures as Richard Nixon and Napoleon Bonaparte. Ironically, in terms of what would later happen in the Rugby War, one whole shelf of Turnbull's study groaned under the weight of books about Rupert Murdoch.

("I'm a very great admirer of Murdoch's business acumen," says Turnbull simply, "and always have been.")

He ploughed on. At one moment, with a map of the world before him, Turnbull might imaginarily create a professional rugby franchise in say, Los Angeles, and then, thinking better of it, scratch that out and put it in Dallas instead.

So did the brave new world of professional rugby form up beneath his flying fingers.

Every now and then he'd make or take a call, and then get back to it. More coffee, more rough diagrams. A bit of a chat with his young wife, Susie, to see what she thought about it — she liked it! — then back to it again. A quick trip into town to consult with Levy and then he'd bury himself in it once more.

The plan that emerged was a system of three separate competitions, or "conferences" as he called them, in play around the world over roughly the same calendar season, from March through to the end of October.

Such a system would entail the northern hemisphere rugby players playing through their summer, but it would allow a world champion to be produced every year — both at a provincial and at a national level.

How could such a system get around the obvious difficulty that weak rugby nations, like the United States or Japan, could never hope to beat a New Zealand or Australian team in a genuine world championship?

Problem? What problem, officer? Ross Turnbull fixed it with a few strokes of his pen. Built into his plan was that those contracted players who didn't make the cut of being among the best 30 players in one market, like Sydney, would have to be available to move to another market, like New York — where they would definitely be needed to bolster the side's strength. In this way, the standard of competition could be evened up around the world and every franchise would have at least a fighting chance of becoming world champion.

Instead of the status quo, which was a mosaic of hotchpotch matches played between nations around the world — all coming together only once every four years for the World Cup to produce a champion — the game would be properly internationalised, with a veritable World Cup being held throughout the year, every year.

Turnbull's "vision", as admirers came to call it, rested on two planks.

1. The Unions really did have to remain involved. The leading provincial representative teams around the world would be owned and run by franchises, which in turn would be 50 per cent owned by the Rugby Unions. These Unions would be granted half-ownership, right from the beginning, of fully professional teams.

    Though there was no expectation that these Unions would come on board voluntarily, Turnbull argued strongly that, "If we cut their water off, as in the players, they'll have no choice but to come with us."

2. The players themselves would have to be the "drivers" of the revolution, enticed into pushing it by their belief in the concept, and more particularly by the enormous financial rewards they would enjoy by playing in a truly international and professional competition. If they stood as one, and demanded it, then the Unions which were in existence to represent *their* interests would simply have no choice but to fall into line and embrace the concept.

Turnbull kept at it, trying to get it all to a point where he could show Levy the model and have it stand up to the high level of scrutiny that gentleman was sure to apply …

Chapter two
Setting up

It was time for the Unions to get serious in beating back the threat of the Super League. At 9am, Saturday, April 8, on the top level of the Australian Rugby Union headquarters at 12 Mount Street, North Sydney, a secret meeting was held. The invitees were drawn from both Australian and New Zealand rugby circles together with their corporate advisers.

They included such people as NSWRU Chairman Ian Ferrier, ARU Chairman Leo Williams, ARU Director Dick McGruther, ARU President Phil Harry and Chief Executive Officer Bruce Hayman, Deputy Chairman of the NZRFU, Rob Fisher ... and so on. Simon Poidevin also attended, asked along by Ian Ferrier after the NSWRU Chairman had learned of Poidevin's conversation with Sam Chisholm.

All participants had been told not to speak to anyone about it, but to come along to discuss what steps rugby should take to protect itself from the incursions of Super League.

The boardroom of the ARU is extremely spacious, with wonderful views of the Sydney Harbour Bridge and surrounding harbour, and up on the wall the usual collection of famous photos from generations of Wallabies past. The centre of this room is dominated by an enormous set of tables set up, appropriately in this instance, in the classically defensive circular wagon-train fashion.

The mood was a curious combination of light, as many old friends greeted each other around the table, and dark, as everyone equally realised the purpose for which they were gathered was a serious one.

Leo Williams chaired the meeting, and opened the floor to suggestions as to how they should best go about countering the threat posed by Super League.

Initial discussion focused on the need to come up with money to "protect" rugby union players from league. Just who was going to pay the big bucks needed though? The obvious answer was one or other of the television moguls, ever and always the sugar-daddies of the modern sporting era.

"What became apparent as the meeting progressed," Phil Harry remembers, "was that international representative rugby as it stood was not much of a television product. For the purpose of building a product — the way rugby league had created the annual State of Origin series in Australia — rugby union was too *ad hoc*.

"This country tours one year, somebody else tours another. We realised we needed to put something in there that was consistent and repetitive, so that a prospective backer could have a longer-term involvement, knowing exactly what was going to happen each year."

As it happened, what the New Zealanders had to bring to the table was something that *prima facie* looked like the very thing — a proposal by Sky Television (NZ) to establish a professional competition between the six leading rugby provinces from New Zealand and the two best teams from Australia.

It was Rob Fisher — an affable lawyer with a long background in rugby who was also the Deputy Chairman of the NZRFU — who put this proposal forward.

"I'd very quietly cleared it with Sky beforehand," Fisher recalls, "telling them this was too good an opportunity to miss. We'd had a lot of discussions about it earlier in the year, and this was an obvious time to present it to the Australians to see what they thought."

Not much, as it turned out. Capitalised at some $NZ20 million a year over three years, the calculations were that this would raise only some $50,000 a year per player. As far as the Australians were concerned, this proposal was almost immediately put on the back-burner as a serious option on the grounds that it simply would not generate enough money to keep the Super League wolves from the door; that it allowed for only two Australian provincial teams; and, more importantly, it did not include any of the South African provinces.

In the words of Phil Harry again, "Whatever kind of competition we came up with, if it was going to have the proper international flavour, then it was equally obvious that South Africa had to come into the picture."

And that really was obvious. As a land of rugby nutters — at least within the white population — South Africa had recently emerged from some two decades of international sanctions, and had already made an enormous impact on the international sporting stage. Importantly for this meeting, South Africa is also in the southern hemisphere, meaning there would be no problems in forming a competition within the same seasonal time span. *Plus* the South African rugby folk were monied ...

While places like Western Samoa and Fiji, for example, were nearby rugby strongholds, they did not boast populations that could contribute a lot of money back to the television overlords who were going to have to buy this product. That said, Phil Harry acknowledges there was no discussion whatsoever at this meeting of widening the concept of a professional rugby competition to the rich rugby nations of the northern hemisphere.

"There was simply no time," he says, "to get something like that together when you're dealing with all the committees. We had to do it *quickly*, and with Australia, New Zealand and South Africa being both strong financially and strong on the ground in rugby terms, we could sit down together and mash something out in a weekend."

After the meeting cooled to the Sky New Zealand proposal, talk turned to the subject of Rupert Murdoch's News Corporation — and the fact that it boasts a television empire which stretches around the world to much the same extent as the rugby game itself — which is to say *right round* the world.

It was Simon Poidevin who broached the subject first, suggesting that instead of Murdoch being the enemy on this occasion — the Super League move initiated by the media mogul's organisation was, after all, the cause of this crisis meeting — he might be converted into a friend.

After some three hours of discussion, the meeting broke up with the resolve to ...

1. Look at exactly what the "Perfect Rugby Product" consisted of, in terms of the kind of regular competition between Australia, New Zealand and probably South Africa, which would most appeal to prospective buyers.
2. Make formal contact with News Corporation and determine just what level of interest they really had.
3. To work, at both the NSW and Queensland levels, towards making a very quick announcement that "amateurism as a concept was outmoded". This was deemed necessary to free the administrators' hands to do what was necessary to "save rugby", and to send a clear signal to the players that rugby union really was taking serious measures to keep them with the game and stop them going to rugby league.

Ross Turnbull was done. It had been a long haul, and he'd seen one or two sunrises that he otherwise wouldn't have expected to, but he now had a neatly typed document setting out the basics of his plan. Details could be added later.

On the morning of April 12, only a week or so after he'd begun the project, he showed it to Levy in his office. Levy went through it quickly, quietly, with just the odd question here and there.

In the end, he leaned back and gave his pronouncement ...

"I like it."

He still had a few queries, though. One of these was, how do you keep it quiet? Turnbull's plan was to sign players up on the quiet, and then only unveil it to the rugby authorities when a "critical mass" had been reached, when they would simply have no choice but to embrace the concept. But, Levy wanted to know, would the players keep their mouths shut?

On this count Turnbull had no worries whatsoever, explaining to Levy, "Don't worry, you can count on rugby people to keep their silence. It's part of their make-up."

He then reminded Levy of the rugby man's concept of "The Tour Secrets Act".

The essence of this mythological Act is that "what goes on tour *stays* on tour" — that whatever high jinks, low acts, and back-lot forwardness occurs while overseas, the firm rule is that such things are never spoken about once everyone returns home, unless with a member of the team who was on the same tour. As silly as such a rule might sound to outsiders, it has real teeth with rugby players.

For the purposes of Ross Turnbull it was firm evidence that rugby players knew how to keep their mouths shut.

Together, he and Levy began to fine-tune the concept.

Late that afternoon, just a kilometre or so from where Turnbull and Levy had met, two printed pages spat out of the fax machine in the Sports Department at *The Sydney Morning Herald*.

Pandemonium throughout. Hold the front page, wipe the back page. Start again. News that major Rugby Unions like NSW and Queensland were formally abandoning the principal plank on which the game was built — amateurism — was big news indeed.

The fax began:

RUGBY IS NO LONGER AMATEUR

In response to increasing speculation about the future of rugby at international and provincial level, the chairman of the New South Wales Rugby Union, Mr Ian Ferrier, said in Sydney today:

"The board of New South Wales Rugby Union, at its meeting on Monday, 10 April, 1995, passed a resolution recognising that, 'Rugby is no longer an amateur sport...'"

It would be a long night for the staff at *Herald* Sports, while over the road at Ian Ferrier's business premises, things were calm.

The job had been done two nights before when the decision had been taken at the board meeting of the New South Wales Rugby Union, which had been held just two days after the meeting at the ARU's offices. In the words of Ferrier, "It meant that to hold the players, we in rugby no longer had to fight with both hands tied behind our back."

It was time. Levy and Turnbull had been refining the plan for a few days, checking whether their financial estimates all stacked up, whether the provisional figures they'd put against income from television rights, from merchandising and ticket sales for their new competition, really would give them an enormous profit at the end of the day.

Revenue would be produced from marketing rights, merchandising rights, ticket sales, catering rights and most particularly television rights (not including pay television rights). Their estimation was that this would produce $US209.17 million in the first year.

Yes, true, their estimation was also that it was going to *cost* $US229.12 million in that first year, but a large part of that was going to be one-off start up costs. Their figures also showed that by the second year they would have turned the corner to make a $US44.93 million profit and the same for the third year. All up, after three years, WRC would be $US70 million ahead!

There, in a nutshell, were the figures that the world's first truly professional rugby competition was hopefully going to be built upon.

Now they felt it was time to send the whole thing over to Kerry Packer's headquarters.

In pushing the scheme into Kerry Packer's orbit, they had one clear thing in their favour. Pretty much of all the people in the *world*, Packer knew better than anyone that such a thing could be done, if enough energy and money were put towards it.

For it was Packer himself who in 1977 had succeeded in launching "World Series Cricket" — in essence a hijacking of international cricket for his own corporate purposes. To do it, he had relied on the simple expedient of paying Test players no richer than the dirt they played on, up to five times what they had been receiving from their national cricket boards. The whole thing had obviously turned out well, with both Packer and the players enriched by the exercise.

It's fairly safe to say that cricket, too, had benefited, though the purest of the purists — who to this day say "it's just not cricket" — still dispute it.

Yet, when essentially the same exercise was being proposed for rugby union — and at a time when it was being done to him in rugby league — Packer remained to be convinced. After Packer's advisers had closely examined Turnbull's plan, Levy received Packer's verdict over the phone from the man he and Turnbull had been primarily dealing with, Nick Falloon, one of Packer's leading financial experts. That verdict, according to Levy, was along these lines:

"Look, we've got the Super League fight going on, we're flat out fighting in court trying to get the [rights to run] the Sydney Casino back to us, and while we really think it's a brilliant idea and good for the sport, we don't want to be seen to be at the front of all that.

We don't want to be involved in it unless you get to a point where you've got the players. If you can get to a point where you can get the players, well, we might be prepared to come and back the players. But the players have got to really want to do it and be united."

John Singleton listened intently. He and his visitor were in the principal's office of John Singleton Advertising Agency, with panoramic views of Sydney's Darling Harbour spread before them, and on the walls all around, myriad memorabilia of great Australian sporting stars.

The visitor was Geoff Levy, one of the valued directors of Singleton's board, and a personal friend. But this wasn't the Geoff Levy he was accustomed to.

This was an animated Geoff Levy, an almost un-lawyerly one, speaking with enormous passion about this rugby concept he'd come up with which he thought not only had the potential to revolutionise rugby worldwide but also made very good business sense.

They made a curious pair, the knockabout genius ad-man and the rather intellectual and usually reserved lawyer, sitting in this high-rise office, while beneath them the traffic of Sydney hummed past on the highways and byways of the metropolis.

Singleton sat there as a million dollar advertising man *and* a former suburban rugby player. He'd made his fortune through his renowned understanding of the Australian "ocker" psyche, coming up with campaign after campaign that managed to press all the right buttons in average Australians so that they would reach for their credit cards to buy whatever product he was flogging.

And while the smallish and impeccably turned out Levy was about as far from this kind of "knockabout bloke" as it was possible to get, Singleton still valued highly Levy's corporate advice.

Speaking of which, Levy had some pretty strong corporate advice on this occasion too, and was now getting to the point.

"So what we need, John, is some 'seed money', for the project, so we can go overseas and test our assumptions, to see if it is as good as we think it is."

Singleton did in fact like the idea and, as Levy recalls, commented that in all of their long friendship, "He'd never seen me get so passionate about anything. If I was this keen about it he'd better back it."

"I said to him, 'All I want to do is raise a few hundred thousand dollars to do a bit of research. I want to do a trip around the world and see all the moguls. I want to test the waters.'"

Singleton, a gambler by nature, agreed to put some money towards it, in return for a share of the action if it got up. Turnbull and Levy were even then in the process of forming a company called TWRC Pty Ltd — short for the rather grandiosely titled, The World Rugby Corporation — and in return for his money Singleton would receive a certain percentage of the company's shares.

Singleton also suggested that if Levy was looking for other people to put in "seed money" he should give Jack Cowin of the hamburger chain, Hungry Jack's, a call. Cowin already had a major sponsorship interest in Australian basketball, and might well be attracted to something like this too, he said.

As was the way of the Rugby War, with most involved already connected in some fashion before it began, Levy already had a business relationship with Cowin. They both sat on the board of the television network Channel Ten, and got on well.

It was all starting to take shape. Cowin had come to the party in terms of providing seed money, meaning Turnbull and Levy could start checking their passport expiry dates, and inquiring about visas in preparation for the overseas expedition.

And someone else had joined the team. Michael Hill was Turnbull's great friend and former partner in the legal practice *Turnbull & Hill* which the two had started in Newcastle in the late sixties.

Hill had just the background that Turnbull and Levy needed in this exercise. Not only was he a former New South Wales cricketer, but he was one of the founding directors of the Newcastle Knights rugby league club — meaning he knew what it was to build a sporting organisation from the ground up — *and* he had been involved as a lawyer with the World Series Cricket revolution.

Best of all, he was keen.

"I thought if it came off," says the laid-back Hill, "it would be good for rugby and very lucrative for all involved. I might say, though, that when I started out, when Ross and his wife would ask me what chance the whole thing had of succeeding, I'd tell them, 'no better than a one in 20 chance.'"

Another day, another secret meeting.

This one was in the Holt Street offices of Ken Cowley, the boss of the Australian division of News Corporation, on the morning of April 19.

It was to be the first formal contact between Rupert Murdoch's organisation and the rugby union authorities. It had emanated from the decision on April 8 to formally approach News Corporation to see if they might be interested in buying the rights to some kind of regular rugby competition between provincial teams from the three most powerful rugby nations on earth.

But, and it was a big "but" under the circumstances, this meeting took place without the knowledge of the Australian Rugby Football Union Chairman, Leo Williams.

The reason why Williams was excluded while nominally less powerful officials "picked the ball up and ran with it", is not possible to tie down solid.

Around the table then were the silver-sideburned and patrician Cowley himself, ARU President Phil Harry, Simon Poidevin, NSWRU Chairman Ian Ferrier, with his Queensland counterpart, John Breen ... and a TV rights expert, Ian Frykberg.

Frykberg was there as the Chief Executive of Communications Services International (CSI), a London-based international brokerage house for television rights which had long had contracts in place with the Australian, New Zealand and South African Rugby Unions to negotiate their overseas television rights for them.

The meeting did not take long. According to Simon Poidevin, it was, "A general discussion of how News Corporation could best get TV product out of rugby union."

At its conclusion, the softly spoken and very precise Cowley confirmed that his company was interested in buying the rights to rugby, but said that specific negotiations over TV rights would have to go through Sam Chisholm in London, as what they were talking about was definitely in Chisholm's province as manager of Murdoch's worldwide television operations.

It was obviously premature to hold serious negotiations yet, he said, as there was still nothing definite that the Unions had to sell. But perhaps they could talk again when there was a definite rugby product that could be valued.

Ian Ferrier concluded on the ARU side of things by saying that they would try and get back to Cowley with the product by early July at the latest.

Thanks for coming, and see you later.

On the pavement outside News Corporation's headquarters, Simon Poidevin and Ian Frykberg had a brief conversation.

Both thought the meeting had gone very well, with Frykberg particularly gung-ho. It was his feeling, as Poidevin recalls, that if the rugby union authorities could get a detailed plan to News Corporation as quickly as possible — and if it could be a lot quicker than July that would be much better — then real headway could be made in securing some sort of deal.

An indication of the "rogue" nature of the meeting though, came in a furious memo that was sent out to directors of the ARU by its Chairman, Leo Williams, that very afternoon.

At the end of the memo, Williams wrote:

*I have just learned that a meeting took place this morning
(Wednesday) involving Phil Harry, Ian Ferrier and John Breen
(all officials of the ARU) and Ken Cowley (News Ltd), Ian Frykberg
(CSI) and Simon Poidevin (?).*

*It is clear we have people going in all directions ignorant of the
sensitivity of our position and not prepared to disclose their activities —
not for the first time.*

On a Monday, April 24, at around 1pm, Wallaby coach Bob
Dwyer sat in Geoff Levy's office and looked across the meeting
room table at both Turnbull and Levy.

Dwyer, himself a businessman, had come to the meeting at the
behest of one of Geoff Levy's close friends, David Shein, of a
technology company called Comtech. Dwyer, Levy and Shein all sat
on the board of Comtech, though Levy and Dwyer did not know
each other well at this time.

After a few pleasantries, Levy got to the point.

"Look, Bob," the lawyer remembers telling him, "we're looking
at doing something that will put international rugby on a sound
business footing, will be really good for the game, and we want to
talk to you about it, but we will want you to sign a confidentiality
agreement first. Would you mind?"

Dwyer did mind. He declined to sign any such agreement, saying
"I've got obligations to the Australian Rugby Union and whatever
you tell me you've got to assume I'm going to tell them."

Levy decided to take his chances anyway, holding back on most
of the detail of what they were planning, but still sounding the
national coach out about his opinion on whether or not the players
would be interested.

Dwyer recalls his reply: "I didn't say 'The players are a certainty
to be in.' I said, 'I think the players would be interested.' I said,

'I think the players would definitely be interested for that sort of money.'"

A notation in Ross Turnbull's diary further fills out the substance of the meeting:

"Dwyer said the boys would like to stick together and play rugby with their mates. They didn't want to be playing rugby league, they needed to be paid but it was not as much as we had budgeted, it was a different budget to what we had. Contact could be made through the coaches, most of whom he knew ..."

And so on. They left it at that.

The plans of the nascent World Rugby Corporation moved ahead. To do this trip properly, the trio wanted to be totally professionally prepared, and one of the things they organised quickly was a formal brochure setting out exactly what the World Rugby Corporation was all about, how it would work, be financed and so forth.

"*The WRC*," it explained on its very first page, "*will be the controlling body of the world organisation for professional rugby. It will initially own all the commercial rights and entitlements to the WRC and its franchised areas, being all television rights (both free-to-air and pay-for-view), all marketing and merchandising rights, and all other revenue areas, including corporate sponsorships and ticket sales ...*"

As Levy, Turnbull and Hill started to put the pamphlet together, there was one thing they decided to emphasise in particular — that while their concept might appear to be an abrupt departure from the unbroken line of tradition that gives the rugby game so much of its charm, it was in fact the code's best chance of prospering in the brave new world of sport it was heading into.

With this in mind, a passage given some prominence in the document read thus:

"*It is an important aspect of the objectives of WRC that the traditional rugby ethos and spirit be maintained. Accordingly, the WRC structure provides for the traditional authorities (national, state, provincial, club, schools, juniors and referees) to be maintained and to continue to act as a feeder system for professional rugby. This will be achieved by a process that will enable representation by the traditional rugby authorities through the WRC structure."*

Disingenuous? Levy says not. "We really did think this was the way to go. We genuinely felt that apart from being good business, it would be the best thing for rugby, and the Unions would *have* to come on board."

This theme that the traditional authorities would eventually fall into line, come what may, was one that the WRC would hammer into the players' heads throughout — and it was to prove extremely persuasive in gaining their allegiance.

Levy put the question to Turnbull at least once, though. Given the part of the plan that relied on the Unions being a part of the scheme, was it possible that they should approach them *immediately*? Wasn't it at least a possibility to show them the plans, convince them of its feasibility — nay, *desirability* — and see if a lot of obvious unpleasantness could be avoided?

"Ross was convinced that it just wouldn't work if we did it like that," Levy recalls. "He said the only way it could possibly work was if there was overwhelming force upon the Unions, if they had no direction to turn but to embrace our concept."

For all the seeming Machiavellian nature of such a plan, Levy is careful to note that his friend actually spoke of his erstwhile colleagues in quite generous terms.

"Ross said to me, 'You are dealing with good men, honest men,'" Levy says. "'They are men who believe what they're doing is right and they're *rugby men*. However, they do not have the wit or the will to embrace revolution, or change things. They have demanding full-time jobs themselves and they don't have the time for change at this level, or the inclination to make those changes, quite frankly.

"'The status quo is quite comfortable for them. They are treated like royalty wherever they go in the rugby world, because they run it.'"

There is something lonely about empty rugby stadiums. They are made for *people*, lots of people, both on the field and off, and without them they invariably look forlorn and bereft. Ballymore, the Queensland Rugby Union ground near the centre of Brisbane, was just such a place in the last few days of April, and every now and then, during a break in work, the Executive Director of the NSWRU, David Moffett, would look at the empty oval and wonder just what kind of encounters would be taking place there in the future.

For, as a matter of fact, within the stadium offices where the headquarters of the QRU are situated, he was engaged in working out that very thing. In the company of his Queensland counterpart, Terry Doyle, and the Chief Executive Officer of the ARU, Bruce Hayman, Moffett was working out just what the Perfect Rugby Product they were hoping to sell actually consisted of.

"It was a long process, but very interesting," says Moffett. "It took us two days to work it all out, but essentially what we were doing was elucidating just what the model of the PRP actually looked like — as in what 'windows' of the season we would play in, how many teams would participate from each of Australia, South Africa and New Zealand, when the finals would be held, and all the details that went with all of that."

The model they came up with was, at the provincial level, a "Super 12" competition, consisting of five sides from New Zealand, four from South Africa and three from Australia. That competition would start in early March and go through till the finals in late May, whereupon each nation would have six weeks to host the usual incoming tours from the northern hemisphere, and then in July the model called for each nation to play in a tri-series — two Tests apiece against the other two. With minor overlapping, the schedule also allowed for South Africa's Currie Cup and New Zealand's National Provincial Championship to be played out in full at the conclusion of the Tests.

"And that was it," says Moffett. "I guess in many ways it sounds simple now, but there was a lot of to-ing and fro-ing to get to that point."

Far to the south-east of them, the New Zealanders were engaged in exactly the same exercise. Led by Dave Galvin, who was the head of the Tours Committee, and with input from such people as Richie Guy and Rob Fisher, the New Zealanders came up with three possible competition structures — one of which looked very like the Australian option, except that it had 16 teams instead of 12.

One way or another, the southern hemisphere was getting closer to actually having something to sell.

In South Africa all was quiet on the Western Front, at least insofar as possible repercussions on the local scene from what was happening in far-off Super League.

"There was a little bit of news here and there about it," recalls Dan Retief, the lead rugby writer for South Africa's *Sunday Times*, "and one or two Springboks who said they'd been contacted, but it was no particular big deal."

What was a big deal was the coming World Cup, now only a month away, when all the rest of the rugby world would be descending on South Africa to do battle for the right to be crowned World Champions. Already enthusiasm for the event — and the chances of the Springboks to be so crowned — was building to that hallowed state so beloved by sports journalists, "fever pitch".

In their regular training camps around the veldt, the Springboks worked assiduously away, entirely unaware of just how very high the highs and low the lows would be for them in coming months ...

Turnbull got through to Simon Le Bon quickly, as always. The British pop star and the former Wallaby had met, of all places, hiking up mid-sized mountains in America, and had kept in touch since.

Turnbull told the front man for Duran Duran that he needed help. He was shortly going to be in Britain and he needed to get in touch with Richard Branson — the famously entrepreneurial boss of Virgin Records — as well as a few other business people whom he thought Simon might have contacts for.

He outlined what WRC was all about, and Le Bon waxed enthusiastic. According to a note in Turnbull's diary, which chronicles the fact that he rang at 9.35pm Sydney time on May 3, Le Bon's reply was succinct.

"Look, Roscoe," Turnbull jotted down as a summation of the Englishman's response, "I'm with you. Many of us believe rugby in Britain will disappear up its own arse unless something is done."

Something was done. Le Bon came good with Branson's number and Turnbull called him a short time afterwards (although he declines to divulge just what Branson's reaction was). Of course, Turnbull made many other contacts with various rugby and business people around the world in those early days of May, setting up for the coming trip.

He called Greg Norman's manager, Frank Williams, to see if the great golfer might like to be involved at some level, perhaps as an investor. He called Tony O'Reilly, the former Irish winger and now head of the enormous Heinz company, who, according to Turnbull, "was very supportive". He called literally dozens of his rugby contacts around the world, to carefully ascertain the lie of the land in each country insofar as it touched on the relationship between rugby and business.

All up, Turnbull was well satisfied. True, they'd already had one setback when the Optus Vision pay-television outlet had knocked them back after expressing initial interest, but that was not a big deal really. Turnbull felt strongly that that was nought but a hiccup, and now everything seemed to be starting to fall into place. Turnbull felt he was already laying secure foundations for a strong international WRC structure.

On the morning of Sunday, May 7, an interesting array of people sat around the living room of Geoff Levy's palatial house, as his four children and wife, Deborah, said their goodbyes — the two boys off to soccer games and the two girls out for a drive with their mother.

Apart from Levy, Ross Turnbull and Michael Hill, John Singleton was there together with Jack Cowin from Hungry Jack's. The Australian coach, Bob Dwyer, was also in attendance, as was Jeff Miller, the recently retired Queensland and Australian flanker.

While Singleton and Cowin had agreed to put money into WRC, which would go towards financing the first sojourn overseas, Dwyer and the former Wallaby were there on different missions.

Miller had been asked down from Brisbane by Turnbull, simply because he was highly respected by all the current players. The meeting wanted from him two things: his assessment of the feasibility of their plans from a player's point of view, and his commitment to tell a couple of the key Wallabies, with Dwyer's blessing, that they shouldn't go to Super League because this was in the wind and could very well get up.

And the reason for Dwyer's presence?

"I was very concerned that the Australian Rugby Union be involved in this whole thing," the former World Cup-winning Wallaby coach says, "and I wanted to know just what the state of play was."

Had he been free of all obligations, Dwyer says he might have been tempted to embrace WRC more fully, but, "At the end of the day I felt that I could not walk away from a group of people [in the Union] who had placed some faith in me at that point in time."

Both Dwyer and Miller pushed the point that the Unions should be told, and Miller, particularly, was very dubious about speaking to any of the Wallabies without that commitment. Dwyer was also not sure, for his part, that he wanted anything at all to distract from the Wallabies' focus in this crucial lead-up to the World Cup in South Africa.

"But anyway," Dwyer takes up the story, "eventually they convinced us that, 'Look, what harm can this possibly do? All we are doing is saying to these guys, there is a potential for an alternative which would allow you to stay in the game — don't jump now.'"

Of a like mind, Miller finally said, "Okay, I will do it." He agreed to talk to some of the most vulnerable Super League targets in the Wallabies — the famous young centre pairing Jason Little and Tim Horan were the most obvious ones — before the team left, but he added, "I am not interested in being involved in any way, shape or form unless the administration is involved."

Both Dwyer and Miller were then and there wrestling with the dilemma that literally hundreds of rugby people would be grappling with over the next few months of the Rugby War.

That was: what was the *right* thing to do? Do you back the Union mother body that has nurtured you all these years, or do you embrace a bold new concept that you're told might develop into the best thing that ever hit rugby union?

Well, maybe they could do both. In the words of Jeff Miller, "They were absolutely clear that the Unions were going to be involved, it was just that it wasn't then. When the whole thing was better structured, they would take it to them."

So it was all systems go. Convinced that their concept was good — and hoping that both rugby players and business people around the world would embrace it eagerly once they got a good look at the concept — Levy, Turnbull and Hill had even then packed their bags and were ready to head to the USA that very night on their first international jaunt to test the strength and marketability of their concept.

On that very same Sunday, at that very same hour, back closer to the centre of Sydney, at the Parkroyal Hotel at The Rocks, a meeting was being held between leading officials and the chairmen of the three national Unions concerned — Richie Guy from New Zealand, Dr Louis Luyt from South Africa, and Leo Williams from Australia.

(Williams had re-established control of the Australian end of the process at this stage, after attending a brief meeting two days previously with Ken Cowley and Phil Harry.)

The issue of this meeting was to determine whether or not Dr Luyt would agree to try to sell to News Corporation the competition that the other two Unions had come up with. And that he would agree was never taken for granted ...

Dr Luyt is a formidable man by any measure, not at all averse to being *disagreeable*, and there was no telling how he was going to react. As a man who had made his millions, perhaps *billions*, of South African rand out of hard-nosed dealings in such varied products as fertiliser and beer, he is a man who doesn't particularly mind saying "no" to whomsoever he damn well likes.

But on this occasion ...

"Okay ..." said Dr Luyt after the presentation was done, "let us see if Mr Murdoch likes this as much you do ... but you have my commitment that we will back it."

While the Sky proposal from out of New Zealand still had a faint pulse at this stage — "we had to keep it alive in case Murdoch fell through," recalls Rob Fisher, who was also at the meeting — there was equally no doubt that the best product to sell was one with all three Unions involved.

At the conclusion of the meeting, Richie Guy and Fisher said that they would be going to meet with Ken Cowley the next day and would show him the version of the Perfect Rugby Product that they had come up with. Now, for the first time, they really had something to show News Corporation, and with the endorsement of the

South African Rugby Football Union, no less, who would provide both their national team and their leading provincial teams to take part in the three-nation competition they wanted Murdoch's crowd to buy.

For the rest of that day and early the next morning, Guy and Fisher worked at the ARU offices in Mount Street, refining their proposed competition structure and working it all up into one presentably professional document.

This meeting with Cowley had been arranged by Kevin Roberts — the head of the massive New Zealand brewery concern Lion Nathan, chief sponsors of the All Blacks. Roberts and Cowley had had many telephone conversations over the previous few weeks on this very subject, during which Roberts had pushed the desirability of News Corporation "getting the All Blacks on board".

Roberts had also advised Richie Guy and Rob Fisher on just how they should approach the whole deal, all-important negotiating strategies included. To go to Cowley's office they would leave from Roberts' Sydney headquarters and return there when it was over.

Why was Roberts so heavily involved? For purely personal reasons, he says, which had *nothing* to do with the interests of Lion Nathan.

"Lion Nathan's policy," he says firmly, "is that we don't have one. Our policy is that 'you guys sort this out amongst yourselves, we are just sponsors and we have no say in the running of the game'."

As an aside, though, he can't help but noting, purely as a matter of interest, that, "Beer sales are linked directly to rugby success. When the All Blacks do well we sell more Steinlager. That is just a fact of life. And when we beat the Wallabies we sell even more, because people are excited, they go out and the whole spirit of the place lifts up."

Who knows how much beer might be drunk if the All Blacks were to sign a massive deal with Murdoch and head off into a glorious future?

Cowley liked it. Maybe he even liked it a lot. At the very least, in a phone conversation he had with Kevin Roberts, shortly afterwards, he pronounced himself "very impressed".

Which is exactly what Guy and Fisher were counting on.

"I think Cowley felt, after seeing the document," recalls Fisher, "that rugby had really got its act together now. Here are three of the major rugby nations all agreeing to play this Tri-series and he said that it was now clearly ready to go to the next stage and be dealt with by Chisholm in London. Immediately."

TAXI!

Within days the two New Zealanders were on their way, ready to meet Chisholm in the company of officials from the Australian Rugby Union, and the ubiquitous Ian Frykberg, who had been monitoring progress closely.

Chapter three

Wheeling, dealing and mealing

They were off. Turnbull, Levy and Hill. Their mission, if they decided to accept it, was to determine whether or not what they'd been talking about for the previous month was mere fantasy or if it had a real chance of working. Crucial to this would be the world television industry demonstrating that it would indeed be interested in such a concept.

They flew out of Sydney Airport on the night of Sunday, May 7, up at the extreme pointy end of the plane — Ross, for one, only ever travelled business class, at worst. Their first stop was Dallas, Texas, where the annual conference of the international cable television industry was being held over three days.

The Dallas conference is basically a hawking bazaar where executives from around the world buy and sell pay-television "products". Arriving on May 8, the trio quickly moved through a series of meetings, unveiling just enough of their concept to gauge the level of interest of the international consortiums. And that level of interest would be ...

"Extremely high," says Levy flatly. "The reaction was simply fantastic, from everyone we talked to. They all loved the idea and wanted to know more about it."

In that first day in the United States, the trio gave presentations to no fewer than four international television companies, and Turnbull concurs with Levy's viewpoint that "each one was a great success".

There was, however, at least one of these meetings where the reaction was, in reality, not as fantastic as they might have perceived.

David Dodds, an Australian who is the Vice-President of the American cable conglomerate Prime International, was one of the television people who had been approached, and he remembers the meeting well.

"I was at the Loews hotel in Dallas with my colleagues on the night of May 8," Dodds recounts, "and we'd been asked to meet with Ross Turnbull. We were talked to by Geoff Levy, who painted a very sketchy illustration of what they were trying to do."

It was all about a "global" rugby competition, Levy told them.

"The reason they wanted to speak to us," Dodds recalls, "knowing that we were operators with Australis pay-television sports channels in Australia, was to see if we'd be interested in getting involved at some level.

"We said 'well, certainly we would be prepared to have a look at it but we would want to clearly have a look at a business plan' and they undertook that they would get back to me."

When they'd gone, one of Dodds' colleagues turned to him and asked what he thought of the whole presentation.

"'Well, I don't want to sound like a smart arse,'" Dodds says he replied, "'but I'd be surprised if we ever hear from them again.'"

And they never did.

Perhaps, though, the reaction of this particular group was an exception. For all three of the travelling Australians maintain that the general reaction to their spiel was extremely positive.

From the cable conference, the trio headed to New York, where they had a similar round of meetings starting with one of the biggest Sports conglomerates of all, the American ESPN network.

It was time to talk serious turkey.

The first top-ranking executive of the network they met with, Andrew Brilliant, listened to their spiel for only long enough to determine what it was that they had come to sell, before he took them to meet another executive in a nearby office.

He began to introduce them to the second executive, Mark Rielly, thus: "These guys have come to talk to us about setting up a world rugby competition ... "

"Rugby ...?" Levy remembers Rielly exclaiming, as he warmly shook their hands. "I *play* rugby. I love rugby. Rugby is played in 116 countries around the world, it has about one million players and an expected television audience of around 2.3 billion in the next World Cup and ... "

And so on.

"It was just unbelievable," Levy recalls, "how this top-line American television executive was an absolute rugby enthusiast."

The bottom line?

"They said, 'sight unseen, we will back it for one year,'" Levy recalls. "'We'll give you all the production facilities in America, we'll put it on our alternative sports channel, ESPN2, and, if everything works out, then, out of every three minutes of advertising, we'll give you a minute you can give to your sponsors.'"

True, they offered not a jot of money, but it was extremely encouraging. On their way down in the lift, Ross Turnbull was waxing jubilant.

"I think we've got us a deal here!" he said to his two companions.

"There's never a deal until it's *documented*, Ross," replied the far more cautious Levy. But he too was extremely happy at the reaction they were getting.

Not that everything went smoothly, for all that. Two such strong personalities as Turnbull's and Levy's were always going to have clashes on occasion and one of these occurred a little later in the foyer of the famous Blackrock building, the massive headquarters of the CBS television network in New York. The issue was just how much of the specifics of the plan should be revealed — Levy was always worried that if the networks knew too much they could simply run with the idea, and have no further need for them.

After emerging from a meeting with an Executive Vice-President of CBS, Levy forcefully told both Turnbull and Hill that they should be a lot more circumspect when it came to giving out details. Turnbull — as he is wont to do when vigorously verbally engaged — made a "shoo"ing motion with his left arm, telling Levy he was barking up the wrong tree, and that he should calm the hell down.

It was enough for Levy.

"Don't wave your arm at me, Ross!" he exploded. "Don't *ever* wave your arm at me. I'm out of this project, I won't be involved any more. I'm going home on Tuesday!"

Turnbull kept at him anyway, waving his left arm relentlessly, continuing to tell Levy to calm down, even as their two voices inevitably became more heated and began to echo around the foyer.

As the two became progressively more upset — there in the very public foyer of a major American corporation — Michael Hill took a couple of steps backward. Partly, perhaps, it was a natural inclination to retreat from the heat, and partly a simple desire to disassociate himself from such an embarrassingly public altercation. It was the sort of "blue" you'd need Henry Kissinger to sort out and, as a matter of fact … there he was now!

Henry Kissinger *hisself*, with briefcase, walking into CBS headquarters and looking warily at the two shouting Australians as he passed. Turnbull, a devoted Americanophile to beat them all, caught sight of the former American Secretary of State mid-sentence and suddenly stopped speaking, though his waving left arm took a couple of moments longer to lose power.

The exceedingly dry Hill's summation of the whole episode? "As big a blow-up as it was, I don't think it will feature in Kissinger's memoirs."

Not that Levy's anger lasted long. It never did. By that evening the lawyer had entirely regained his equanimity, so much so that Turnbull had no compunction about coming up to Levy and Hill in the bar of the Plaza Athenee hotel, where they were staying, and saying, "Good news, guys — I've got a friend who's got some tickets to see the Knicks playing the Pacers in the play-offs."

So Turnbull went to see the Knicks play. Sure, it turned out that the former rugby prop's "good news" extended to only one ticket — for him. But that was just Ross. Levy and Hill went to see "Miss Saigon" instead.

A phone call to Phil Harry. In his ARU offices at North Sydney. Did Harry know that Ross Turnbull had been spotted at a television convention in Dallas trying to flog a new concept for rugby and the word was he'd moved on to New York?

No, but thanks for the info, and keep us posted.

Later on, when the Rugby War was at its most bitter, there would be a tendency of rugby union authorities worldwide to paint Turnbull and Levy as a couple of lightweights without even a glimmer of the business connections or wherewithal necessary to get something of this magnitude up and running.

This was untrue. *Pour l'anecdote*, it is worth noting that in her book, *The Bid*, on Rod McGeoch's role in the successful quest to stage the Sydney 2000 Olympics, the respected *Sydney Morning Herald* business writer, Glenda Korporaal, gives considerable credit to a previous Levy/Turnbull joint effort, when together with David Gonski they were the principals of what became known as the "Turnbull Group". The group, through working its worldwide contacts, helped deliver up to Sydney some crucial advantages in the endless quest for on-side Olympic delegates.

(A not unworthy achievement, given that Sydney was to beat Beijing by the margin of one hungry, skinny vote.)

And while Michael Hill had been aware for the past 25 years of what Turnbull was able to achieve through a combination of contacts and persistence, and had come to respect Levy's abilities also, even he was impressed at 3pm on Wednesday, May 10, when they were ushered into the Fifth Avenue New York apartment of Dr Samuel Pisar.

The elegantly dressed man who opened the door looked familiar, and for good reason. Only two days before, on the television, during the 50th Anniversary celebration of the end of the Second World War in Europe, Hill had seen American President Bill Clinton warmly laud Sam Pisar. Now here was Pisar in the flesh.

Pisar, the founding partner of a law firm with offices in both New York and Paris, was a survivor of the Holocaust who had risen to a position of pre-eminence in the world of international law. He had been an adviser to both John F. Kennedy and Valery Giscard D'Estaing, was currently counsel for the International Olympic Committee and a special adviser to its President, Juan Antonio Samaranch.

Michael Hill knew all, or most of these things. What he didn't know was the man's *presence*.

"It was amazing," Hill says now. "I suppose part of it was the feeling that this guy had gone through Dachau and Auschwitz, and here he was in these amazing circumstances, but there was something else also. I thought he was one of the most impressive men I'd met in my life."

For almost an hour, Pisar spoke to the Australians about their project. He was a man who not only knew the international sporting landscape, but also *loved* it, and he gave them advice that they keenly listened to about specific people they should talk to, institutions they should consult, traps they should be wary of . . . and so forth.

Turnbull and Hill came away with a long list of contacts, a whole new range of ideas, and a commitment from Pisar that both he and his partners in Paris would be available to them for advice and logistical support throughout their campaign.

But enough, already. While the initial plan had been for the trio to spend a full two weeks in the USA, Levy was already convinced.

"I felt that there was clearly enough interest there, that if we returned with the product we could create an auction between the [television interests]," Levy says.

So ...

"I've seen enough," Levy said to his companions at the conclusion of just three days in the USA. "Ross, take me to London."

So this was the famous London Ritz. Michael Hill looked around. It looked good, sort of like he'd imagined, only ... ritzier. The trio had flown in that morning, and Hill and Turnbull were now having breakfast in the magnificently regal Ritz restaurant while reading the British newspapers.

All of the broadsheets and tabloids alike were still chock-a-block with the enormous brouhaha that had been created by a comment the English rugby captain Will Carling had made on a British television program the week before.

"What gets me and a lot of players now is the hypocrisy of the situation," Carling had said as the cameras rolled. "Why are we not just honest and say there is a lot of money in the game?

"If the game is run properly, as a professional game, you do not need 57 old farts running rugby."

Well they never! Carling had been immediately dropped from the captaincy for his troubles, causing the controversy to enormously escalate. But other of Carling's comments, and the response to them, also give a feel for the temper of the times.

"There seems to be an awful lot of things the Union now does to make money out of the sport," Carling said, "but there is still this feeling that the players should not make any money out of it.

"Everyone seems to do very well out of rugby union except the players. It has become more than a fun game. You do not have a World Cup for fun and recreation."

The English Rugby Football Union Secretary Dudley Wood had said in reply: "We believe we are running a sport as a recreation for players to play in their spare time. I think money is a corrosive influence."

This enormous gap between the attitudes of the players and those of the officials, Turnbull says, was absolutely typical of what he discovered around the world.

"It was just extraordinary," he says now, "how everybody I talked to agreed that the players really disliked the officials, and that the officials simply didn't understand what the players were on about."

While in the case of Carling he had at least been reinstated as captain after a public outcry demanded it, the bottom line was that it was an extremely useful environment for the WRC trio to be operating in, given the specifics of their endeavour.

And what an environment it was, incidentally, particularly in this hotel.

Hill, not feeling particularly hungry, had just ordered an orange juice, when he noticed that the price was seven English pounds!

"Jeez!" he exclaimed.

"Just shut your eyes," Turnbull replied quietly, "and drink it."

Hill drank it.

They had a full day ahead of them, talking to British coaches, officials, ex-players and one or two agents.

"I wanted to talk to people from the English establishment," says Levy, "because I wanted to see what these blokes would think of the whole concept of professionalism. If they thought it would work, then I was going to feel a lot more confident about our chances of success, and the possibility that the Unions too might embrace the concept."

What was clearly important in something like this was to have a bit of "front". In Levy's words, "We had to make sure it looked like we had the bucks, as Packer wasn't yet behind us."

As ever, Ross Turnbull had the answer. Always a man of many contacts — wouldn't you know it but he also knew the doorman at the Ritz! A bit of a chat with him turned up the fact that no less than that hotel's famous Trafalgar Suite could be hired at an hourly rate.

Straight in they went. Into the magnificent Trafalgar Suite, with its imposing and beautiful high ceilings, ornate antique furniture all around, and a panoramic view onto Green Park opposite. One of the footmen had told Ross that the Packers and the Rothschilds had had a private dinner party there the week before and no one was the least surprised. It looked *exactly* like the kind of place where billionaires would meet when away from their own mansions.

It was perfect for their purposes.

One after the other, notable British rugby identities, all of whom had been organised in the previous two days, were ushered by a classically attired footman into the suite's luxurious web to come and hear about the "interesting business proposal" that Ross had promised them.

A bit of chit-chat, and then they got to it. There would be three "conferences" of ten teams each, the Australians explained, running concurrently and producing world champions at both provincial and international levels every year.

Between them all they would play 352 top-class games a year, producing 704 hours of quality television. Each team would have 30 players and five support staff, making 35 in all for each franchise, meaning WRC would be requiring 1,050 people in all. Personnel who would be extremely well-rewarded, they didn't mind saying.

For the most part, the people they talked to were initially sceptical. Levy remembers that the usual reaction was along the lines of "What is the International Rugby Board going to say about this!?!" and, more pertinently, "Who is going to write the very big cheques needed to get this all started?"

Good question. Common question. A question that simply *wouldn't* go away. As this impressively opulent WRC presentation at the Ritz was in reality built on only a few hundred pounds, was it not also a superb allegory for the whole WRC concept? As in, big front, but no moolah actually backing it?

Levy rejects this notion outright.

"We felt we had the money, or at least we would have the money if we could get it up. That was what that whole trip was about, to see if such a business concept for rugby was worth something in the international market-place. We didn't have the physical money, no, but the further we went, the surer we became that the *concept* was clearly very valuable."

The way he tells it, these gentlemen of British rugby came to believe it was, too.

After they'd been given the spiel, each visitor was handed one of the WRC brochures — replete with all the crucial financial figures — to study at home that night and hopefully come back for a meeting the following day.

It was amazing what a change 24 hours consideration could do to a man's attitude, Levy reports.

"At first they looked at us like we were from Mars," he recounts. "They thought we were mad, they kept saying 'How could you touch amateurism?' and 'It'll never get through the IRB.'

"But 24 hours later they were just stunned at what we'd come up with," says Levy. "The difference in their attitude after they'd read it was just extraordinary. The enthusiasm, the keenness, just blew me away. They saw it as the best way forward for rugby union into the 21st century."

Levy acknowledges at least one note of reserve, though.

"They were still concerned that we didn't interfere with players during the lead-up to the World Cup," he says, "or the World Cup itself. But as soon as the Cup was finished, they said they would be ready to go."

On their second day in London, the trio lunched in the Ritz dining room — all mahogany and lace and hovering people in white ready to land — with three of the principal rugby personages they'd been wooing, all of them leading coaches in Britain.

One of these, a famously successful Five Nations coach and beyond, was a particularly noted expert on the science of the rugby union scrum, and Geoff Levy just couldn't help himself. It was just too good an opportunity to miss. To the particular amusement of Michael Hill, the South African-born lawyer unburdened himself of a long-held theory he'd had about the source of the force of the famous Argentinian scrum and told the coach his theories exactly on what the best way to counter it was.

"See, if the props position themselves like *this*," Levy said, conscripting the salt and pepper shakers as the rugby forwards in question, "I reckon that ... "

And he was away. The famous British coach listened amusedly, while he ate. When the meal was over, the six men were walking out of the Ritz dining room, Hill in the middle, when suddenly all around him, his luncheon companions were peeling off to the left and right, for all the world like bombers in formation who had suddenly seen a Messerschmitt up ahead.

What the ... ?

Hill did the obvious and looked up ahead himself, only to see Alan Jones, the former Wallaby coach and now Sydney radio broadcaster, standing in the foyer with his back to them, talking to the English fly-half Rob Andrew.

Not a single one of Hill's companions cared to be seen by Jones, or Rob Andrew, to explain just what had brought such disparate rugby people together. But now that he was alone there seemed no harm to Hill in continuing on regardless.

A pleasant conversation ensued, with Jones relating that he'd come over to London to do a week-long broadcast on the 50th anniversary of the ending of the War, and asking his some-time acquaintance Hill how it was he had the pleasure of running into him here. The latter replied that he had come here to tidy up an enormous property deal that his mate Ross Turnbull had just put through.

The caravan moved on. On a quick trip to Paris, they met at a restaurant called Chez Pierre with the man who would become their agent in France, Eric Blondeau, together with one of Sam Pisar's American partners based in the French capital, Bob Simpson.

Blondeau, an accomplished 38-year-old businessman and rugby enthusiast from the famous French town of Cognac, had come recommended to Turnbull by Bob Dwyer.

"Bob is a good friend of mine," Blondeau recounts, "and he contacted me in late April to tell me that someone would call me regarding a project of a worldwide professional rugby competition. He recommended it to me and that made me take it seriously, because I knew someone like Bob would not back it unless he really believed in it."

For his part, Blondeau really was a good choice for the project, as apart from his undoubted business nous, he was intimately acquainted with both the French and international rugby scene, and had already done an enormous amount of work on it since Turnbull had first contacted him two weeks previously.

Simpson, for his part, was 52 years old and smooth as silk — "an immaculately turned out man-about-town" is how Hill describes him. And he was an equally accomplished lawyer, with an extensive background in both international sport and business. One of his previous clients had been Robert Maxwell, the famed British financier and newspaper proprietor who had come to a rather sad end.

On this evening, both Simpson and Blondeau expressed great

enthusiasm for the whole concept. As a matter of fact, Blondeau had come prepared with a list of the best 120 players in France — which he'd culled from reading the newspapers assiduously and quietly consulting his rugby contacts. Ninety of those players were to be spread around the three professional teams planned for that country — most likely in Paris, Grenoble and Toulouse — and the other 30 would go into the pool of "floating players" to be available as reinforcements for weaker teams around the world.

The mood at the table was very up-beat and optimistic. Bob Simpson remembers being quite taken with the Australians.

"I thought they were quite an impressive team," he recalls, "with each one complementing the others. Turnbull seemed like the gregarious salesman of the concept, Hill was the objective lawyer who stood a step back and examined things coolly, while Levy was the financial and legal brain trying to make it all fit together.

"Levy was *very* keen, though. I remember him saying to me, 'Do you realise, Bob, that this could go on my tombstone, that *I* professionalised rugby?'"

There was, however, at least one awkward moment between Simpson and his table companions. At one point the American suggested that his good friend Jean-Pierre Rives, the famous former French captain, would be an ideal person to get involved. Blondeau and Turnbull exchanged looks.

Blondeau had already had long conversations with Turnbull on this subject, and was adamant that Rives should have no part.

"I thought Rives was an excellent captain," Blondeau says now, "but I did not think he was much of a businessman for something like this. I thought he might be good as a kind of PR person, but certainly not to run the show … "

Turnbull said that the involvement or otherwise of Rives could be worked out down the line and they left it at that. They agreed to meet shortly with Blondeau in South Africa during the World Cup, while Simpson would mind the WRC fort in Paris. Blondeau also confirmed that he would make direct contact with the French captain, Philippe Saint-Andre, to tell him of what was in the wind.

The work of the trip was essentially done, and the three Australians were ready to return home.

At a meeting before they left, the travelling troupe reviewed just exactly what they had achieved.

"We definitely thought, this is on," Turnbull recalls, "that this could really work."

For all that, there was still not a total commitment to going ahead. In Hill's mind "the odds of it working were down to one in four", while for Levy, "I was getting more and more convinced that it could work, but still wasn't ready to make the final big leap into going all out after it."

Then again, Levy did spend a lot of time in the Boeing 747 on the way home thinking about the enormous billboard that dominated the streetscape opposite the Ritz, promoting Nike sports shoes.

The Nike advertising slogan, in three-metre high letters, **JUST DO IT,** seemed more than a little apposite for the occasion.

When Levy landed back at Sydney Airport on the afternoon of May 15, he preceded by just a few hours the departure of the Wallabies, on their way to South Africa for the World Cup.

It was a curious circumstance that the South African Airways flight taking the Wallabies to the World Cup, also bore the team presumed to be their greatest rivals to take home the William Webb Ellis trophy — the All Blacks. The two teams sat side by side up the front of the plane with a bare minimum of restrained chit-chat and a maximum of getting as much sleep as possible on the trip west. A fierce five-week campaign awaited.

Somewhere over the Indian Ocean, in high darkness, the ARU President, Phil Harry, decided to make his move.

As all around him Wallabies and All Blacks were sleeping or

resting quietly, he homed in on where the three key All Black officials on the trip were sitting, softly talking.

Up the front of the business section, with their charges just behind, the All Blacks coach Laurie Mains, team manager Colin Meads, and the World Cup manager Brian Lochore listened intently as he spoke.

"Look," Harry told them in hushed but passionate tones, "I'm a bit sketchy on the details, but I think you should know that Ross Turnbull has got some crazy plans to hijack international rugby for his own commercial ends, make a circus out of it. That means of course that the All Blacks and the Wallabies are going to be prime targets. We all should watch out for him."

Harry had made a similar speech to the Wallabies the day before in their training camp, advising them not to talk to Turnbull, and they had listened with some interest to know what it might all be about.

The New Zealand officials, though, listened from a different perspective, obviously concerned at the possible ramifications.

The plane droned on through the night. Westward ho.

"Now remember," Ian Frykberg briefed his companions, as they made their way to Sam Chisholm's apartment in exclusive inner London, opposite a particularly well-manicured green park, "don't waste Chisholm's time, don't say anything obvious and keep whatever points you've got to make *concise*. He's always bloody busy, and he likes to get to the point."

It was 11 o'clock on the morning of May 16, and a bevy of leading southern hemisphere rugby union officials, in Dick McGruther, David Moffett, Richie Guy and Rob Fisher, was about to meet the head of News Corporation's international television empire for the first time.

It was to be Chisholm's first look at the Perfect Rugby Product, which had been worked out over the previous weeks, and a chance for the officials to determine exactly what level of interest News Corporation really had.

Frykberg was there, as the agent of the three Unions, to sell the product and, just as importantly, as a guide through the labyrinthine ways of his old friend and colleague, Sam Chisholm. The two had worked together at Australia's Channel Nine, where Frykberg had had a sterling career through the '80s as an executive producer.

Chisholm had gone to BSkyB at the turn of the decade, and Frykberg had followed him a short time afterwards, as head of the News and Sport division — and though that hadn't worked out, it had not affected their friendly relationship.

In the business of selling the PRP to News Corporation, Frykberg's personal knowledge of Chisholm was going to be important. When dealing with Murdoch's main man, there were any number of land-mines, dead-ends and pits of verbal quicksand that could set you back if you didn't know where they were. And Frykberg was one of the very few people who had a map.

So the door to Chisholm's apartment opened. Standing there was Bruce McWilliam, Chisholm's ever-present lawyer, and, just behind him, Chisholm himself — a rather neatly compact sort of man, impeccably groomed and, for the moment, graciousness itself.

The apartment was spacious, stylish, filled with natural light from the large windows, and furnished, in the words of Rob Fisher, "with the kind of furniture I'd love to be able to afford myself".

Chisholm — a charismatic chainsaw of a man — remained the perfectly polite host right up until it came time to get down to tintacks, which was, by all accounts, only a few minutes after the rugby officials entered the apartment.

The meeting was begun with a presentation by Richie Guy about why they had come to see Chisholm, and just what it was they had to offer. When the host stood up and rather peremptorily announced his "rules of engagement". They went something like this:

He, Chisholm, was to be News Corporation's sole point of

contact on this deal, while his lawyer here, Bruce McWilliam, would see everyone through if there were questions of a legal nature.

He would need them to lay out the entire program, just what exactly it was that they were selling, and then they could work towards putting a value on it.

He wanted, as he was sure they wanted, to get this whole thing wrapped up before the conclusion of the World Cup. Time was of the essence, and it was important to have the deal locked up before all of the Test players might be tempted to charge off in a dozen different directions, without knowing there would be a lot of money in it for them if they stayed put.

He wasn't going to deal with any committee on this, but from their side of things would accept talking to only one person, just maybe two at most.

Everyone had to keep STRICTEST confidentiality on this or the whole thing was off. If he read a single line about it in the newspapers, then forget it, and he meant *forget* it. This was a deal between News Corporation and the three national Unions and he didn't want anyone else knowing about it.

If none of this was to anyone's liking, that was fine, because if we at News Corporation don't spend the money with you we're quite happy to spend it with someone else.

He preferred to deal with Ian Frykberg from CSI, whom he knew and trusted and who, in any case, as the Chief Executive of CSI had the rights to broker all international television deals concerning the three Unions.

All clear? Everyone understood?

Crystal clear, Sam.

A general discussion then ensued about the rugby model they wanted to sell, which Chisholm seemed to approve of, as near as they could reckon.

There was some talk also from the visitors about the fact that some of the Unions already had commercial arrangements in place with other broadcasters, and whether or not these arrangements might affect their dealings with News Corporation.

Chisholm didn't want to hear it. It was for the Unions to work out, he said, what it was that they were free to sell and what they weren't. Once they'd done that, he said, they could come back to him, and he would tell them what he was prepared to pay.

Fine. One minor hiccup, though. One of those present ignored Frykberg's previous warning, and opined that rugby really could be a very valuable product if it was packaged properly, whereupon Chisholm cut him stone dead with a withering, "Thank you for that penetrating glimpse into the obvious."

No one made any further pleasantries about the attractions of rugby. The meeting finished about an hour after it had begun, with Chisholm suddenly all bonhomie again.

"That was a pretty good meeting, wasn't it?" he asked nobody in particular. "I behaved myself, didn't I?"

But of course, Sam.

"Well, I will tell you what," Rob Fisher remembers Chisholm saying as they went out the door, "there is no such thing in our organisation as 'good cop, bad cop'. There is only 'bad cop and *worse* cop', and this is as good as it is going to get."

Everyone laughed.

"He was right, of course," says Fisher now, wryly, "but we liked him a lot."

There had been no talk at this early stage of anything so gauche as *money*, but that would be broached in due course.

Outside on the pavement there was discussion about where to go from here. The scheme at that stage was for most of the delegates to return whence they came, home to their various countries, including Richie Guy's plans to return to New Zealand.

It was at this moment that David Moffett spoke up. A generally quiet man, with an extremely self-effacing manner, Moffett could be surprisingly forceful when he chose and he was of the strong opinion that if everyone simply scattered to the four winds on the steel wings of different aeroplanes, the whole process would stall.

Surely it would be better if Richie Guy accompanied him to South Africa immediately, where they could meet with Louis Luyt and ARU Chairman Leo Williams, to try and nut something out to keep the whole process moving.

Richie Guy initially demurred, maintaining he had to get back to his farm-work in New Zealand, but at last agreed. It was a heroic effort from him. Suffering equally from chronic jet lag and gout, he actually "looked like death" in the words of one of the participants. But he also had a singularly strong sense of duty — which in this case was to make sure this deal went through. Soonest. The following morning, first thing, Richie Guy and David Moffett were at Heathrow, ready to fly to Cape Town.

A phone call. To Geoff Levy at his office in Sydney's MLC Centre. Did Levy know that there was a rumour going around that some officials from the ARU had flown off to London to see Sam Chisholm and talk about some new competition they wanted to sell News Corporation?

No, Levy didn't know it, but he was certainly very interested to hear it. Well, well, well, perhaps things were moving on the establishment front as well.

The magnificent Newlands Stadium in Cape Town also houses the headquarters of the South African Rugby Football Union. That institution was emerging from some very lean times. During the long period of international sanctions against South Africa there had been practically no need for a national body of rugby to exist — as there was simply no other nation willing to play them.

Now, though, things were changing. South Africa was back in the fold, their national Union again had enormous amounts of money flowing into its coffers — with a national team once again in the international marketplace — and a brand new Chief Executive Officer in Edward Griffiths to boot.

Even newer headquarters were being built all around, as the World Cup was about to get under way. It was in these emerging headquarters, on May 19, that Griffiths and Louis Luyt hosted a meeting attended by various of their colleagues from Australia and New Zealand, including Bruce Hayman, Leo Williams, Richie Guy, and David Moffett. They were there to discuss just what was the best way to go about dealing with News Corporation from this point on.

David Moffett still has a copy of the agenda from that meeting. The second-last item down reads:

Other threats? (Ross Turnbull)

The short answer, in the mood of the meeting, was reportedly along the lines of "not on your nelly he's a threat, and even if he is it doesn't matter".

Or something like that. Turnbull, at least in the minds of these people, was not someone to take seriously when it came to business manoeuvres within the rugby world. The reason? Essentially because Turnbull's difficult period in rugby administration in the mid-eighties, where he would be largely blamed for the financial fiasco that had resulted from the plan to turn Sydney's modest Concord Oval into a great rugby stadium.

The NSW Rugby Union had gone into debt to the tune of $A20 million in building it, and even though Turnbull had loaned the Union a million dollars of his own money to see the NSWRU out of the muck, it had not saved his reputation when it came to rugby administration.

That reputation was well known to the men from New Zealand and South Africa as well, so Moffett's item on the agenda about the "Turnbull threat" actually made little impact.

"The attitude of the people around the table," says Moffett, "was, even if he is out there, where is he going to get his money from?"

"Our intelligence at the time was that Packer was simply not interested in rugby, and we could never understand why he would be interested in it other than perhaps just to give Rupert one in the eye. As far as Ross goes we didn't spend a great deal of time discussing it."

The rest of the meeting was extremely fruitful. These good burghers of rugby decided they would form a company with two directors provided from each of the national Unions, and that its Chairman would be Dr Louis Luyt, while David Moffett would be the Chief Executive.

Luyt was the obvious appointee as Chairman because he was acknowledged to be a very tough negotiator — he obviously hadn't built his mountainous fortune in South Africa on any lack of business nous — while Moffett was an equally obvious choice as CEO because he had driven much of the discussion to that point and had the added advantage of being one of the few people around who could get on with the extremely domineering Dr Luyt.

The newly-formed board of SANZAR (South Africa New Zealand Australia Rugby) slightly modified the time frames of when the games would be played, and moved towards the conclusion that it should be a 12-team competition instead of 16. So, all present and accounted for. They now, finally, had the Perfect Rugby Product; they had a vehicle which could run it and distribute the profits to the Rugby Unions; they had basic agreement on how it would all mesh together.

As a matter of fact, they were in exactly the same position as WRC at that moment. The only thing both sides lacked was someone to write that mother of all big cheques they needed.

Back in his office at Ernst & Young, Turnbull had gone over all his figures again with selected personnel from the international accounting firm, testing them against what they had learned overseas, and, for his money, they still stacked up as well as before, maybe even better. According to his calculations — backed by Ernst & Young accountants, though they operated on assumptions he'd given to them — the net return that investors in WRC would have after three years would be 21.78 per cent and after six years would be an unbelievable 61.00 per cent. And that, he exulted, was not even counting the income from selling the pay-television rights!

With such huge profits available (contingent upon actually getting the whole thing up and running), WRC would not only be able to pay players beyond their wildest dreams, but they'd also have a lot of money to pay their chief revolutionaries in each country — in the form of "success fees" for the major recruiters and organisers.

This notion of "success fees", as in money that would only be paid once the job had been done, was to be a crucial factor in getting the whole thing done *quickly*.

He picked up the phone once more, always the blessed phone, called Michael Hill in Newcastle and got him to tweak the numbers in the contracts he was working on a bit higher still.

Chapter four

Manoeuvres on the veldt

It was in an elegant outdoor cafe of a refined Cape Town hotel, in the tense few days before the still incumbent world champion Wallabies would play in the opening match of the World Cup against South Africa at Newlands Stadium.

At one table of the cafe sat Bob Dwyer and the Australian captain Michael Lynagh, signing the occasional autograph for people who recognised them, but really just wanting to talk together. Privately.

"As captain and coach," Lynagh recounts, "I thought we should sit down and assess where we thought we were going. We were talking about the team and then the question of my retirement came up. I said, 'I am thinking very much about retiring after the World Cup, and ... '"

"And I thought," Dwyer recounts separately, "'Noddy' had been pretty much an amateur servant of the game at international level for 12 years, and maybe there was going to be a decent dollar in the game next year, and here he is going to announce his retirement.

"And so I said to him, 'Mate, okay, thanks for telling me. It wouldn't have mattered if you hadn't told me but you know that business that Phil Harry was talking to the team about … ?'"

It began to come out, as Dwyer set out the bare bones of WRC, describing it, he says, as "an international professional rugby circuit".

He stressed that it was all extremely confidential, but continued on.

"I said [to him]," Dwyer recalls, "'one of the principals, Geoff Levy, had spoken to me about the thing and … I said I don't have any idea really on the financial viability of this, however, to my knowledge, Levy is well respected in Australian business circles.

"'I haven't had any dealings with him but as far as I know about him around the tracks he is [well regarded], so maybe it is not a good time to announce your retirement just yet … '"

"And I thought," Lynagh remembers, "'What a strange time to be telling me about this!'"

Dwyer asked Lynagh whether he thought the other players would be interested in the whole concept.

Lynagh replied, as he remembers: "I would like to wait until after the World Cup. This is our object now, let's do this, [win the Cup], and *then* get on to that."

After more discussion, Lynagh says, "We both agreed that there were a couple of guys in the team under pressure from Super League. We should at least let them know what was around and that rugby would be getting money … that there was going to be an alternative for them to Super League."

Lynagh did go and talk, shortly afterwards, to three players: Jason Little, Tim Horan and Damian Smith. The Wallaby captain had something to show them, too — the WRC brochure that Bob Dwyer had given him at the conclusion of their meeting.

"I thought it was interesting enough," recalls Horan now, "but, like the others, I didn't want anything to distract me from what we were in South Africa to do in the first place."

News of the World Rugby Corporation was starting to seep out elsewhere, too.

An article in the Sydney newspaper, the *Sun-Herald* on May 14, by journalist Peter Kogoy, headlined PLAN TO PROFESSIONALISE RUGBY, established that Ross Turnbull, "planted the seed for a professional world rugby circus at an international convention of cable and satellite pay-television executives in Dallas, Texas, early last week."

To Kogoy must go the credit for breaking at least the bare beginnings of the whole story and he followed it up with another article in the *Sun-Herald* the following Sunday.

The Sydney journalist detailed a rough outline of Ross Turnbull's plans for a professional rugby circus, linked his name to David Lord, and confirmed that the former Wallaby prop had already been to America trying to market the concept.

(This "rugby circus" phrase, incidentally, had already been decided on by the Australian Rugby Union as the most appropriate way of deriding the whole concept, whenever the subject of Ross Turnbull came up. Already the propaganda war *within* the Rugby War had begun …)

In South Africa, the Wallaby second-rower, Rod McCall, read Kogoy's article in the team-room of the Australians' hotel in Cape Town, where faxes of all the rugby articles from home were gathered.

"It seemed odd to me, something like that out of the blue," this lanky and laconic Queenslander says now, "but I didn't really think a lot about it at the time."

However, a telephone call came through to McCall in his hotel room a few days after that. It was from his former Wallaby team-mate, Jeff Miller, who seemed initially to be ringing up to have a bit of a chat. After the usual pleasantries — "How's it going?", "Is Bob working you blokes hard?" and so forth — Miller finally got to the point.

"Rod, there's a few things happening back here," he said.

"They're trying to set up an international rebel rugby competition, and it's going to work like this ... "

McCall listened intently, for the most part without speaking, but was initially very sceptical. "I just couldn't see how it could work," he says. "But, of course, I was interested to know more ... "

The reason Miller was calling McCall was to determine if his own instincts were right — that it would be crazy and damaging to the Wallabies' chances of winning the World Cup to make any approaches to the whole team right now, in the middle of it.

McCall confirmed it was the very last thing to trouble the players with. "Out of the question," he said flatly.

Jeff Miller made up his mind. A few days before, he had been asked to go with Ross Turnbull and Mike Hill on their coming trip to South Africa to begin to talk with the Australian players. He had prevaricated, but after talking to McCall, now decided firmly against it.

"Firstly," he says, "I wasn't committed to the project, and secondly, my talk with Rod confirmed that it wasn't an appropriate time to be speaking to the players. Plus there was *still* no sign of the Unions being approached to become involved. From then on I refused to do anything unless they went to the establishment as such and spoke to them."

And that was that. Jeff Miller was out.

He was an old man, an extremely ill man, and he was in St Vincent's hospital in Sydney. Of this 73-year-old man's former robustness and vitality, there was little left. In the 1940s in South Africa, Julius Levy had spent a full month in the detention barracks for knocking down with a single blow an army officer who had called him "a dirty Jew"; what remained of that man was essentially only the will and still very strong personality.

Sitting, watching his father's life ebb away, Geoff Levy's thoughts were a maelstrom of childhood memories, grief and — as much as he tried to push it away — the pressing matter of the WRC (and whether or not they were going to push ahead with it). Despite the gravity of his personal situation, the younger man simply couldn't contain his enthusiasm for the project, nor the fact that he still had some lingering doubts about whether he really could accomplish something so extraordinary as the effective takeover of such an international game.

And as he had always done with his father, whenever he had anything whatsoever on his mind, he talked to him about it. "I said to him 'Dad, you know this thing could really happen. It could really work.'" Geoff Levy recalls. "'Nothing is sure, I'd have to take off a lot of time, take some risks, but our trip really showed us that it really might go.'"

It was at this point that Levy Snr made what was effectively a death-bed speech that, in his son's memory, infused him with the will to expel his doubts and go ahead with the project. Painfully propping himself up on one elbow, the old man said:

"Geoff, all your life you've been talking about rugby and how it could be organised better. So … rugby … it's not a big deal, it's not life and death, but you always talk about it, so *go for it*, do this thing.

"You know I'm lying here and I'm thinking, 'I've done some great things in my life — the best things are you and your brother — but if you can turn around and say you changed something in the world, that's something. That is a lot.' So if you really think you can change rugby for the better … *do it*."

Levy Jnr, not surprisingly, decided then and there to do it. By the time of his father's funeral a few days later, he was fully committed to giving every ounce of his energy to the project.

Ross Turnbull came to the funeral, and though it was out of the question for Levy to accompany him and Hill to the World Cup for this next trip — in the "Shiva" of the Orthodox Jewish religion, mourners must not shave or leave the home for seven days — they discussed briefly just what the goals of this trip were.

"We knew we had great television interest," Levy says. "We felt we'd have no trouble getting backers if we could prove that it could work, but what we needed to be able to demonstrate was that we could also get the players, which would mean delivering the product.

"The World Cup trip was to work out just how easy or otherwise that would be."

An interesting man is Ian Frykberg. An enormously physically imposing fellow — read *big* — he's a former rugby union prop from the Western Suburbs club in Sydney, who in his professional life had been a print journalist of such note that he wrote the lead story on the front page of *The Sydney Morning Herald* on November 12, 1975, the day after Australian Prime Minister Gough Whitlam had been dismissed by the Governor-General, Sir John Kerr.

From there he had had a brief stint as editor of *The Bulletin* magazine, then moved into television, and on to his present incarnation as the Chief Executive of CSI. It was in this role that he would never be more than spitting distance from the pivotal point of the action throughout the Rugby War.

Unfortunately, at this moment, that pivotal point was something known in the trade as "number-crunching" — working out exactly what price could be asked from News Corporation for the rugby model, which would annually generate over 750 hours of hopefully absorbing television in three nations.

In a hotel room in Cape Town, Frykberg and one of his associates from CSI, Jim Fitzmaurice, worked from sun-up to sun-down and on into the night, trying to calculate the figure to the nearest lazy 10 million or so.

"It was a very intense time," recalls Fitzmaurice, "but also very exciting. We both had a very strong belief in the product, and felt that what we needed to show was how rugby was right on the edge of becoming a dominant world sport, if only it was marketed and packaged in the right way. We were trying to put numbers against not only what the product was worth now, in various markets around the world, but what it *would* be worth when everything was done properly."

These numbers, mind, were not easy to elucidate — trudging through the drifting sands of dry data to get to financial fountains of information that could near knock you over if you didn't know how to handle them. But they kept going.

"Hello? Room service? Send up another couple of hamburgers please, pronto."

What the product was worth at the end of the day was *precisely* what Sam Chisholm was prepared to pay for it. The process the two men were engaged in was designed to work out just how far Chisholm would be pushed. They'd also have to come up with data to demonstrate that the package really was worth what they were asking.

At least they were able to take one break when the opening game of the World Cup took place at Newlands stadium — when the Springboks beat the Wallabies in a magnificently action-packed match — but that was it. It was a quick look at the real world outside, a reminder that the rugby spectacle really could be splendid and televisually valuable when all the conditions were right. And then straight back to it ...

It had taken a while but the job was done. Over an intense three-day period, Michael Hill had worked in his Newcastle office to get together a standard contract, with which WRC would be able to begin signing the world's best rugby players.

His starting point was the standard contract of the New South Wales Rugby League, which he spliced together with — ironically enough — the new Super League contract.

"If ever there is a compromise between the Australian Rugby League and Super League," Hill jokes, "I'd like to think I started it off first with my WRC contracts."

To ensure that the contracts were kosher, and would stand up to the most searching legal attack, if ever it came to it, Hill passed them by Roger Gyles QC, one of Australia's most eminent lawyers.

"The issue was of more than ordinary interest," Mr Gyles recalls, "as by then I was acting for News [Corporation] in the Super League litigation. I considered the document with a barrister, Mr David Hammerschlag, who, as it happens, was a good friend of Geoff Levy. We developed some suggestions which, in our view, improved and strengthened the draft contract which had been produced, and we met Mr Hill on the afternoon of Thursday, May 25, with the re-drafted contract which, in our view, was suitable for the purposes of the client."

In short, while there would be criticism later on as to the legal enforceability of the WRC contract, it really did have expertly sharpened legal teeth, and Michael Hill had Roger Gyles QC's backing to say so.

The contracts themselves were very cleverly constructed. They had to be organised in such a way that WRC could get players to sign up on the promise of big dollars, even though the organisation's net worth was — dot three, subtract two, carry one — about *zero*.

With this in mind, Hill, on Levy's advice, framed the contract so that it was would only become operative when one of two conditions had been met. Either:

1. *The company has funds available to it in excess of $US100 million by November 22, 1995;* or

2. *The company has executed contracts with commercial enterprises such as TV rights, sponsorship and other commitments to the competition, sufficient for the company to meet its contractual obligations, with a certificate from Ernst & Young accountants affirming this to be so.*

There would be many permutations of this standard contract as it was fitted and framed to be operable within the many legal systems around the world that it would be used in. But the basics remained the same.

November 22 had been chosen because it was the date when the All Blacks would be home from playing their last Test of the year, against France, just as England and South Africa would also have played their last Test of the year, at Twickenham. It was the veritable end of the international rugby season for 1995. But to the contracts …

"What it was about," Hill says, "was saying to the players, if you give us your signatures on these contracts, you will be giving us time to organise to get this competition up. It was the chicken and the egg, and we explained to the players very clearly that we had to have the signatures *first*, in order to get the backers to back us."

One of the keys to getting the players was, of course, the number of dollars offered, and these were in fact huge. There were to be five basic tiers of payment.

The top tier would be called, appropriately enough, the "Jonah Lomu" tier and as a matter of fact the awesome New Zealand winger would be the only one on it. "We felt he was worth $US1.5 million for three years," says Hill. "And that's what we offered him."

After that it was a little more standardised, with the key players of the leading eight rugby nations being offered $US825,000 for a total of three years playing, all the World Cup Squad players from those same eight nations on $US725,000, and two tiers beneath that of $US300,000 and $US200,000.

Not bad dosh, by any measure. So long as someone was actually prepared to sign the cheque for $US100 million to make it happen.

Out of a clear blue sky, Ross Turnbull and Michael Hill landed in South Africa on the morning of May 28, 1995. Just before landing, the captain of the plane went through the usual formalities of welcoming them to the country, thanked them for flying with South African Airways, and then said: "You have just completed the safest part of your journey. A violent crime is committed every minute of the day in Johannesburg. So be careful … and enjoy your stay."

Riiiiight. The captain wasn't kidding, though. That very night, outside the first-class hotel where the new arrivals had checked in, a security guard was shot dead. Such were the times.

True to form, Ross Turnbull checked into the biggest, most opulent hotel in all of Johannesburg — the Sandton Sun, located right in the middle of the gold city's new business nerve centre. That this was also the hotel all the rugby officials from around the world were using as their base — meaning Turnbull and Hill would necessarily be running across people all the time whose Unions they were trying to take over — was not deemed a problem by Turnbull. Far from it, in fact.

"I made a point," Turnbull recalls, "of staying there, *because* all the members of the International Board and so forth were staying there. I had no interest in hiding, or lurking around corners. I was going to be out there openly, doing what I was doing, and if they wanted to talk to me and I wanted to talk to them, then that was fine. But I wasn't going to be hiding. We had nothing to be ashamed of."

"It's like this, Rob," Ian Frykberg was saying to Rob Fisher at the offices at Ellis Park stadium in Johannesburg, where yet another meeting was taking place. "If we get a 10-year contract with News Corporation we can ask, and receive, about 25 per cent more per year than if we get just a five-year deal."

It was a persuasive argument, and particularly potent at a time when, back in Australasia, the Super League battle was continuing unabated. The fees being offered to those few League players still not committed to one cause or the other were continuing to rise, making rugby union players even more attractive options than previously — and the consequent need of the Unions to come up with cash to hold their own players was ever more pressing.

Richie Guy, for one, was not happy with rugby committing itself for as long as that, but when the difference between the two figures per year was spelled out to him, he too came to believe.

"The fast-moving developments in telecommunications made it difficult to predict exactly what the rights would be worth in 10 years," the NZRFU Chairman acknowledges, "but clearly the figures being talked about were enough to make us think it was worth that long a commitment."

From Sam Chisholm's side of things in London, he maintains he simply wasn't interested in a period of less than 10 years.

"We wouldn't have accepted less," he says now flatly. "We didn't have to; there are plenty of other things to spend the money on. I mean we haven't got an unlimited amount of money, but we took a judgement that rugby was a sport that had potential, and we wanted to be with them for a long time if they wanted to be with us for a long time. If not … fine."

The men of the French rugby team were not *heureux*, not *heureux* at all. Up on the Pienaar River (no relation to the Springbok captain), their training camp in these early days of the World Cup was way, waaaaay out there in *Deliverance* country, about two hours north of Pretoria through hard country, rough enough to grate cheese on.

On that hot May day, Turnbull, Hill and Eric Blondeau — whom they'd joined up with in Johannesburg — made their way out there in a rented van, driven by an engaging black South African who seemed never to have left the confines of Johannesburg before. On occasion, these rugby entrepreneurs were as lost as all get out, despairing about whether they could even find their way back to Jo'burg, let alone get to the French encampment in the jungle, but finally they made it through the wilds and down a dusty road to the camp, where the team in question was just sitting down to lunch.

In a long discussion in the van on the way up, Blondeau had recommended that the best way to handle negotiations with both players and coaches generally was to steer away from the complexities of contract fees, and simply state the net total of money that would accrue to them over the three years that they would be engaged by WRC. Sweet as a nut, good idea, let's do it that way.

Turnbull and Hill stayed on the margins of the group, sitting at another table. Then, near the conclusion of the lunch, Blondeau brought over French captain Philippe Saint-Andre, centre Franck Mesnel and coach Pierre Berbizier.

It was a surreal scene, with many French journalists also nearby, casting the occasional curious glance at the visitors, as did some members of the team. If anyone asked, or came near, the plan was to maintain that the visitors were preparing a book on the World Cup. As an added precaution, they all spoke softly.

But to the point …

Berbizier didn't seem to like it much at all. As he is a taciturn character at the best of times, it was always going to be a little hard to tell with Pierre, but he certainly didn't seem to be jumping through hoops about this whole idea of a professional world rugby competition.

And the French captain, Philippe Saint-Andre? As a matter of fact, he spoke English like a Spanish cow — to use the French expression — so was not able to communicate directly his feelings on the whole thing, but with Blondeau doing the translations, it was obvious he really did like the idea. As did Franck Mesnel, who, back in Paris, was a very successful businessman in his own right.

These two undertook to pass the word to the team that something called the WRC was out there, organising, and they'd be in touch. But they did not want, and they were *very* clear on this, for there to be any further contact between WRC and the French team. They would take it from here, they said, and handle the whole thing on an "inside" basis.

Hill and Turnbull left in the company of Blondeau a couple of hours after arriving, a little surprised in spite of themselves at how easily it had all gone. Their belief that if the players could just hear what their concept was all about they would readily embrace it was proving correct.

On the way home, Hill couldn't get out of his head a comment that their driver Joseph had made when they'd briefly walked together down by the river after lunch. Hill had asked this like-able and rather happy-go-lucky fellow just how he thought the "new" South Africa was going, and the driver had suddenly become serious.

"Our country started with the gun," he said sadly, "and it will finish with the gun."

No, Hill wasn't totally sure what he meant either, but he thought about it all the way back to Johannesburg.

Frykberg had the figure. He and Jim Fitzmaurice had kept on going, through late nights that had all too soon turned into early mornings, but they'd got there, confident that they not only had the right number, but that they could demonstrate how it really was worth as much as they claimed. For 10 years worth of television rights, they would be asking News Corporation for … *well over* half a billion American dollars.

For the record, while this figure did in fact look like an extra-ordinary amount of money for rugby paupers, it wasn't actually "out of the ballpark" when judged against other transactions Murdoch's organisation had made in recent years.

In 1992, Murdoch had paid a reported $US450 million for the rights to televise the English Premier League soccer in Britain over five years. There had been much informed criticism at the time that Murdoch had paid way too much for it, but it had, in fact, proved well worth it.

Only months after the deal had taken effect, the number of subscribers to the fledgling BSkyB had taken off. It was the single televisual product Murdoch had that had persuaded hundreds of thousands of Britons to take the final plunge into pay-television. Suddenly, the whole thing had turned into a profitable venture.

At the time he got the Premier League, BSkyB possessed only 100,000 subscribers, but this figure had quickly broken through the one million mark, and in 1995 had gone to four million.

A similar process was under way in the USA. In December 1993, Murdoch's Fox Corporation had committed themselves to paying $US2.8 billion over four years for the rights to the National Football Conference — and the early returns had indicated that that, too, was going to be well worth it.

Here, the company of the three Rugby Unions, SANZAR, was offering a product which had a guaranteed major interest in important burgeoning pay-television markets for the Murdoch empire. Though at that time Murdoch had no pay-television outlets in either New Zealand or South Africa, and his Foxtel network in Australia was yet to be launched, the money would be recouped by selling the rights back to outlets already established in those countries. Later on, the rights might return to Murdoch's own newly-opened outlets.

A final factor was that top-of-the-table clashes between say, New Zealand and South Africa, would have very keen audiences in many of Murdoch's northern hemisphere markets.

Turnbull, dead ahead. Phil Harry saw him in the breakfast room at the Port Elizabeth Holiday Inn tucking into a plate of bacon and eggs, in the company of Michael Hill and one of Bob Dwyer's support personnel, Barry Ross, and immediately decided to take action.

It was May 31, just seven hours before the Wallabies were due to play their second Test of the Cup, against Canada. "We knew Turnbull was around," Harry says. "We didn't like it, and we *definitely* didn't want him talking to the Wallabies, particularly not in the middle of something like the World Cup. I decided to approach him then and there."

In terms of the exchange that followed, Harry maintains he was fairly controlled, though Michael Hill, who witnessed it all reasonably dispassionately, opines that, "Phil Harry gave me the impression that he'd thought about it all night, like, 'If I see that Turnbull, I'm *really going to give it to him*.'"

Turnbull remained seated, while Harry stood above him and, after a curt observance of the basic form of greeting, said, "Ross, I don't want you going near any of our players with your scheme."

Turnbull, by Harry's account, simply point blank denied it. "There *is* no scheme, Phil, I don't know what you're talking about."

"Well, if there's no scheme, you won't need to approach the players then, will you?"

"Look Phil, I've been hired as a consultant by a group looking at a different set-up for rugby, and I've signed a confidentiality clause, so I really can't talk to you about it."

"I *don't* want you talking to our players."

"You are aware, Phil, that I have played for Australia. I understand what is required to prepare for a Test match."

"I'm aware of that … I'm telling you, DON'T GO AND TALK TO OUR PLAYERS."

"Don't threaten me, Phil."

"I'm not threatening you, Ross, I'm just telling you."

With which Harry walked off to get his muesli — when he suddenly sensed a presence at his elbow. It was Turnbull. He was unhappy. Very unhappy. And not a little hurt, to boot.

"You shouldn't talk to me like that in front of people you don't know," Turnbull said.

"I'll talk to you any way I damn well please," Harry remembers the conversation continuing. "And I do know who those other people are anyway, so what's the problem with me talking like that in front of them?"

"Well, if you don't know that, you'll never know anything," Turnbull replied with some exasperation. With which he then turned on his heel and walked off.

Mark one down for posterity. And the first instance of open aggression between the two emerging camps. There would prove to be plenty more where that came from.

Whatever Phil Harry's admonitions of the morning, it certainly didn't stop Turnbull and Hill meeting with the Wallaby captain, Michael Lynagh, that night. Australia had had a difficult win against Canada only hours before, and after the Wallabies' Happy Hour — where he'd had a long chat with Bob Dwyer about just where the team was situated — Lynagh had come to Turnbull's room.

(Lynagh might actually have been the second important visitor from the Australian camp to Turnbull's room during their stay there. A leaked WRC report has it that Bob Dwyer himself had gone there the previous evening, where the subject of possible coaches for Australian franchises had been discussed. Among potential appointments were Alec Evans for Brisbane, Wayne Smith for Melbourne and John Connolly for Perth.)

On this evening, Michael Lynagh, Hill remembers, "was fascinated, if we could get it up. He said he'd play in Italy, but he wouldn't recruit in Italy. He said, 'I'm a guest there and I wouldn't feel that I should be doing that, but if you can get it up, I'll play there.' He also was interested in maybe playing in New York. His fiancée might want to go to university in New York."

The Australian captain confirmed to them that at Bob Dwyer's behest, he had told Jason Little and Tim Horan of the basics of the WRC scheme. Both of those players, he reported, had wanted to know, not unreasonably, who could be behind such a scheme and, most importantly, who could actually write the cheques when it came right down to it. As a matter of fact, Lynagh was a little curious on that subject himself. However, the issue of the moment, from the point of view of the older men, was whether an approach should be made to the team as a whole.

As Michael Hill recalls, "We didn't really tell [Lynagh] enough about it for him to know details, just enough to be able to say 'fellas, there's something else that is going to come along after the World Cup, so hang on'."

Michael Lynagh remembers the conversation going much the same way, though on the subject of whether the team as a whole would be interested, adds this:

"I said, 'Yes, they would be interested in hearing your ideas, but I, as captain of the team, don't want them to be talking about this as a team. I don't want them to be approached as a team before the World Cup is over.'"

At least, from the point of view of WRC, the crucial thing was that formal contact had been made. WRC had now opened lines of communication with the elite rugby communities of France, England, Australia and South Africa — as well as at least preliminary contacts with a host of other countries. There remained one obvious omission, in that New Zealand to this point had been left out of the whole picture.

It was time to put that right. Late that night, from the privacy of his room, Turnbull put a call through to the Land of the Long White Cloud. This first contact was with John Hart, something of a rugby impresario. Apart from having been an extremely successful coach at the provincial level with the famed Auckland side of the 1980s, Hart also came replete with communication skills and a renowned business brain.

He had already got a preliminary phone call on the subject of WRC from Bob Dwyer the previous evening, and now that Turnbull went into far greater detail he listened carefully.

"I was interested," the New Zealander says now, "because I realised that with the Super League threat something had to [be done]. Unless rugby did something to face the issue of profession-alism then it ran the risk of being raped in terms of its players."

Turnbull told him that WRC was already "well advanced" in its plans, and what he really wanted to know was whether Hart would be interested in being their main man on the ground from the New Zealand end of things?

The short answer was, "maybe".

"My main concern right from the start," Hart says, "was that whatever was done had to be done with the input of the rugby authorities and I guess the concern I had right through with the WRC approach was the fact that they were wanting to tie up the players, but they weren't wanting to address the issue of dealing with the Unions which I thought was pretty fundamental."

(Ross Turnbull, for the record, maintains there was never any question that the Unions had to be involved in the whole WRC infrastructure. "It was absolutely imperative," he says unequivocally, "and we made that clear to Hart.")

In the then and there, though, Hart agreed he would stay in touch, and come to a meeting in Sydney in a couple of weeks.

The Australian expression is "busier than a one-legged man in a bum-kicking competition". In the late days of May and early days of June, David Moffett was just that — endlessly trying to maintain peace between Louis Luyt and his Australian counterpart, Leo Williams.

The two notably headstrong Chairmen simply did not get along, did not mind expressing it, and on two occasions simply refused to have anything more to do with the other. It was part of David Moffett's role to get them back together and talking again. Just how did Moffett accomplish it?

"I'd speak to Louis to find out what the problem was," he recalls. "He'd tell me, and I'd call Leo to see if we couldn't sort something out. Then I'd call Louis back and we'd go from there. Mostly my role was to get consensus between them about just exactly how we were going to present the final rugby product to Chisholm, even when the communication between them wasn't great."

Finally, though, it was all over. Agreement had been reached between all three Unions on all the fine points, and now Moffett found himself on yet another whirlwind trip to London. This time he was in the company of Louis Luyt, and they were going to see Sam Chisholm to present him with both the refined version of the Perfect Rugby Product and, more particularly, the price they were asking. The two were met by Ian Frykberg in London.

At Chisholm's offices at BSkyB — rather well-appointed, Moffett thought — they cut to the chase quickly. Moffett opened his briefcase, and took out the document containing their proposal. He handed it to Chisholm and waited, watching carefully to see just how he would react. Chisholm skimmed the first few pages, his eyes moving restlessly over the words, obviously looking for something until *Bingo!* He found it. There was the final price they were asking, at the bottom of the fifth page.

$US650,000,000.

With an air of mock theatricality, Chisholm gripped his chest and grimaced fiercely, feigning a heart attack.

"This is going to kill me," he said with a long and hearty laugh, before abruptly continuing:

"And we're not paying that much."

Dr Luyt, an extremely practised business negotiator, said that was absolutely fine with him, and appeared unconcerned. It wasn't as if News Corporation were the only media company in the world. He left with David Moffett back to Heathrow shortly afterwards.

That night, at a nearby favourite local watering hole, the Gloucester Hotel, Frykberg and Chisholm went at it.

Chisholm told Frykberg that he wasn't paying $US650 million, not now, not ever, and the CSI man shouldn't even waste his time thinking it was a possibility. Frykberg replied that if Chisholm didn't pay it, then SANZAR would be forced to take the deal elsewhere, perhaps to a consortium of different television outfits. Chisholm said that was fine with him.

"I said to him," Chisholm recalls, "that at the end of the day, prices are determined by what people are prepared to pay for them. Nobody knew what I was prepared to pay at that stage."

For the moment the two agreed to disagree, and see if they couldn't find some common ground in later discussions.

It was an odd kind of meeting, in early June, and once again it was in that most popular of all sites when one is engaged in serious business in South Africa — the Sandton Sun Hotel in Johannesburg. A kind of vertical Las Vegas without the gambling, it is all glitz and shiny surfaces, a maze of restaurants and bars, escalators and lifts, gaudy tackiness and all-you-can-eat luxury.

On this particular afternoon, Louis Luyt, Richie Guy and David Moffett were returning from a long lunch, and were just going into the bar for a cleanser when *hulloa!* they practically knocked over none other than Ross Turnbull and Michael Hill. Turnbull, in a manner straight out of *Advanced Ebullience For The Absolutely Unstoppable*, stuck out his hand and said robustly, "Hello Louis, how are you going?"

Luyt, seemingly caught between anger and surprise, managed a rather thin, "Just here for the rugby are you?" And left it at that.

Didn't say another word. Turnbull left it as long as he could to see if Dr Luyt would continue with the conversation, but came up dry. Finally Turnbull returned with, "Okay, see you later," and moved on.

Luyt, Moffett feels, did not take Turnbull seriously at that time because, "He simply believed his players would never sign with someone like him. Luyt wasn't really concerned about Turnbull, because he was convinced that firstly, Turnbull was a man of no substance, and secondly, that Packer wasn't behind it in reality."

Dr Luyt, for the record, offers another reason for his initial nonplussedness.

"I just didn't recognise him," he says. "He was greyer, older, and his hair was thinner than when I last met him [in the mid-eighties]."

Fair's fair. Ross Turnbull would make Dr Luyt a little older and greyer himself before the Rugby War would be over.

Turnbull and Hill kept moving around South Africa. It had been said of the rugby league scouts that were swarming all over the country, that with such a concentration of talented international footballing flesh all in the one country, for them it was "like shooting fish in a barrel".

So too for the men of the World Rugby Corporation. Scattered around the country was pretty much all the playing talent, coaching and administrative expertise that they needed, and while the World Cup proceeded apace around them, they simply moved from town to town, making contact after contact.

In those few days, the two Australians had long conversations with everyone from Canadian coach Ian Birtwell, through Bryan Williams of Western Samoa and Jack Clark who coached the American Eagles, to Alec Evans — the Australian who was coaching Wales.

Evans was particularly keen that something like this come along to save the day in Wales, recounting to the duo how desperate the situation was there, how league scouts were everywhere, and how they still lacked a national sponsor for the Test side.

(True. That very month, a marketing firm in London called Alan Pascoe Associates had finished their approach to 500 prospective companies doing business in Wales, in their search for a national sponsor and come back with ... *nothing*. Not a single company was interested.)

"What I was particularly impressed with in their brochure," says Evans, "was how concerned they were with juniors and supporting the grass-roots level of the game. It all looked like a very good concept to me."

Apart from promising to keep in touch with them on their project, Evans suggested to them that if they wanted someone to liaise with British players, then the injured Wallaby, Troy Coker, would be an excellent choice.

Coker. A Wallaby since 1987, he had had to pull out of the

Australian World Cup Squad early in the campaign because of a recurring hamstring injury. But his contacts within the international playing ranks were excellent, as he'd lived and played in England for a long part of his nine-year international career.

Coker was contacted while still with the Wallabies, met with Hill and Turnbull, and flew to Britain shortly afterwards, to lay some groundwork over there.

Delighted. Delighted. Delighted. Back in Australia, Geoff Levy was following closely the progress of Turnbull and Hill through South Africa. In very long and involved daily telephone conversations, he would soak up what had happened in the past 24 hours, and give his own ideas about how they should proceed in the next 24.

Neither Levy nor Ross Turnbull minded a bit of a chat, when it came right down to it, and Michael Hill remembers them, "Going at it for hours, talking over how it was going."

The bottom line was that it was going extremely well. Partly that was because the people they were dealing with seemed to believe in the concept, but it also didn't hurt any that a lot of them were being placed on hefty success fees.

"[Most of our agents]," says Levy, "were engaged on a 'success basis' which said that if it happened then we would have the product and we would go and sell it and we would have the money. So, in other words, 'success' was delivery of a certain number of players or World Cup squads by a particular date, and payment then only if the whole competition occurred.

"We never made any payments up front. We had to [use], therefore, people who could put up their own expenses if necessary. As soon as we could bring in sufficient financial backing, at least all their expenses and everything would be paid, but there was never going to be anything other than [payment] on a success basis."

This business plan of attack would work, clearly, a charm. Very occasionally, people who were approached would refuse the offer of the success fee. Most didn't.

And why would they? Take, as an example, how it worked in one of the Five Nations countries. The coach of this particular team was offered, and accepted, a \$US300,000 recruitment success fee to get his players signed up, and a contract of \$US175,000 a year thereafter for coaching the side. The captain of the side was offered exactly the same terms as his coach — albeit that the second part of the payment was for playing — and he accepted just as quickly.

It was not the men of WRC's concern whether or not the people they offered this money to would in turn tell the players they were recruiting the kind of success fee they were on. The concept of a success fee was an entirely accepted business notion, and though at the end of the day that might not sit well in the middle of rugby's culture of one-in-all-in, that was not their affair.

Clearly, with such financial rewards on offer, if only the thing got up, it was a very very hard proposition to refuse. Lest the situation be misunderstood, though, the captain above who accepted the sign-on fee was an exception.

"Mostly," says Levy, "players didn't need to be offered success fees, because they believed in the concept already, and because the salaries that they were being offered over three years was already motivation enough."

Or at least so it proved in South Africa, with Turnbull and Hill continuing to move around and make contacts, leave behind contracts, and report constantly back to Levy. At this stage, though, reports of what was happening in South Africa did not go straight from Levy to the Packer organisation, the former maintains.

"I did not want to approach them again until I could prove that we had at least the players of the top eight countries of the World Cup signed up," Levy says. "We had to be able have something *tangible*, to be able to say 'here's the product' so as to then get the backing."

So this was Harry Viljoen. In person. At a breakfast meeting at the Sandton Sun, Turnbull and Hill made personal contact with the man Bob Dwyer had told them could very well be useful for their purposes in South Africa.

Viljoen was a notable South African rugby personality who had a background as a successful coach with both Transvaal and Natal, and was also in passing a millionaire businessman who had made his fortune in the insurance industry.

In terms of his relationship with the key Springboks that WRC would be going after, Turnbull was particularly impressed that Viljoen was credited with both "discovering" the Springbok winger James Small, and also taking a punt in 1991 on making Francois Pienaar captain of the Transvaal side despite the claims of more senior players. (He'd been heavily backed in this decision by Dr Luyt.)

At this meeting the mood was bright, cheerful and optimistic. Turnbull reported to Viljoen the enormous progress that had been made to this point, and Viljoen expressed appropriate excitement that things should be falling into place so quickly.

At one point, Turnbull, though he was not hopeful, wondered out loud about the possibility of meeting the charismatic Springbok captain, Pienaar. Viljoen, to Turnbull's surprise, said that shouldn't be too much of a problem and would make contact to check out his availability. Perhaps Francois could come over to meet them in a few days time, on an afternoon, after the Springboks had finished their training.

Viljoen was as good as his word.

On the Wednesday afternoon of June 7, at around three o'clock, there was a knock on the door of Turnbull's room. When he opened it, there stood Viljoen with not only his lawyer and close friend Jennis Scholtz, but just over his right shoulder … a smiling Francois Pienaar himself.

Turnbull was impressed.

"He had a magnificent sort of physical presence when he came into the room," he recalls, "with his multi-coloured South African hat, his Springbok gear and obvious athletic prowess ... he just looked *fantastic*."

The two shook hands, with Turnbull also being impressed by the Springbok captain's firm grip and clear-eyed gaze. Michael Hill, also in the room at this time, remembers equally powerful first impressions.

"He just *looked* like a strong leader," he says now, "like somebody you could absolutely count on."

And so they talked. With Pienaar sitting on the chair beside the desk, Turnbull for the next hour or so paced the room and set out the WRC agenda. His busy left arm once again carved out in the sweetly air-conditioned atmosphere a whole rugby empire that was just waiting to be formed, once players the ilk of Pienaar and his Springboks gave the say-so.

Pienaar was enthusiastic from the beginning, the way the Australians remember it, occasionally breaking in with quick comments like "This is fantastic", "I can't believe it", and "Great!", as Turnbull continued to speak.

"But he didn't even have to say those things, for us to know that he was keen," says Turnbull. "I mean, you could just see it in his expression and his body language as I talked. He was *in*."

Turnbull still had one significant qualm though. Both he and Michael Hill had the impression that of all the national Union administrations they were attempting to out-manoeuvre, it was the South Africans who had been the most assiduous in finding their way around the amateur regulations to ensure that their players were well-recompensed monetarily. Both Turnbull and Hill were expecting that it would be the Springboks who would be most reluctant to go against the desires of their officials.

With that in mind, Turnbull gently broached the subject of how Pienaar thought the South African Rugby Football Union might react to the whole WRC concept and if they were dead-set against it, how he thought his fellow Springboks might cope with …

Pshaw!

Pienaar, in both Hill and Turnbull's memory, was entirely dismissive of *whatever* the South African officials might think about the matter.

"He just made it absolutely clear," Turnbull says, "that he and his team had absolutely no time for their officials whatsoever."

The meeting broke up with Pienaar making a firm commitment there and then to approach his players on behalf of the WRC, and said he would get back to them with the answer, which he was sure would be positive.

After more warm handshakes, and even a little back-slapping at this early stage, the door clicked shut as Pienaar, Viljoen and Scholtz took their leave.

"That," said Ross Turnbull firmly as he turned back from the door to face Michael Hill, "is one of the better men I've ever met in my life. I feel privileged to have been in that bloke's presence."

Hill did not disagree.

There remained one more important meeting before returning home to Australia. A report of it was written by Turnbull and Hill, as part of the process of keeping their investors and prospective investors back home informed. It went like this:

On the afternoon of Thursday, June 8, a meeting was held between Ross Turnbull, Michael Hill, Harry Viljoen and Keith Parkinson, the chairman of the Natal Rugby Union. Harry had given Keith some indication of the project and Keith was anxious to learn more in general and how he could participate with his Union in particular. Ross Turnbull repeated to [Parkinson] a statement [Turnbull] had previously given to Leo Williams that [Turnbull] was under a confidentiality contract and that when he had completed his plan he would be only too happy to speak to the appropriate people in South Africa. After Keith Parkinson left, Harry Viljoen signed a contract. Additional clauses put in the contract [make an] undertaking to Harry that we would engage the services of Francois Pinaar [sic] on a success fee basis.

Turnbull and Hill returned to Australia the following day, to make assessments of just where they were up to, what they had achieved, where they wanted to go to … and make ready for their next trip.

Michael Lynagh could feel the wind of the ball as it *whooshed* past his desperately outstretched fingers. The ball had been launched as a drop-goal from the boot of his opposing fly-half, Rob Andrew, in the final minute of the England versus Australia quarter-final on June 11 in Cape Town. The score stood at 22-all, as the ball sailed forth.

The Australian captain turned to watch its course. If it went through, then England would have won the game, and the Wallabies would be facing an ignominious exit from a Cup that only a little over a fortnight before they had been favourites to win. If it missed, the Australians were at least heading for extra-time and a chance to go on to victory.

It went through. Australia had lost and would be heading home. Coming off the field, crushingly disappointed, Michael Lynagh felt even then that his mooted retirement was now, at least in his mind, definite.

"I decided that I'd just had enough of international rugby, and there were plenty of other things to do," he says now. "I'd loved it, it had been fantastic for me, but I'd just had enough."

It was a fateful decision, even if it would take a few weeks for him to express it. Lynagh's retirement from the Wallabies would mean that the long-time Wallaby hooker Phil Kearns would soon be installed as captain — taking over the reins at the precise instant when the national team would hit far and away the most turbulent period of its history.

Two days after their elimination, the Wallabies headed home to

Australia. At that stage, a few of the players knew some sparse details of what WRC was planning, but they were essentially still only rumours.

And the coming Murdoch deal? Nary a whisper.

Question: What do you call people who hang around with footballers?

Answer: *Backs!*

Geoff Levy likes the joke. It's the sort of riddle rugby players delight in telling each other, touching as it does on an age-old theme of the game that while the backs are the glory boys with all their fancy footwork and la-de-da manoeuvres, it is the forwards who do the hard yakka and are the real workers.

And though Levy himself during his rugby career had alternated between the forwards and the backs, he was firmly persuaded that generally, character and moral resolve were more likely to be found among the lads up-front with their cauliflower ears and broken noses, than among the fellows of the backs who still had discernible parts in their hair even late in the game.

"It was my experience," Levy says, "that if there was a really tough stoush on, then it was the forwards you could count on to stand and fight, while the backs would run everywhere. This was obviously going to be a fight, a big fight, and wherever we had the choice I preferred to work with people who were forwards."

Ross Turnbull, for his part, had a predilection for working with team "leaders": players who, although they may not be captain or vice-captain, or even among the better players, were still the ones that the other players followed. Andy Haden, the most renowned All Black forward of his era, had been one of the leaders of his day, just the sort of man Levy and Turnbull wanted to work with.

A sometimes controversial figure, Haden knew the international rugby landscape backwards blindfolded at midnight, and yet was

The three men who fought long and hard for the World Rugby Corporation, a concept they believed would take rugby union to the forefront of international sport.

Left: *Geoff Levy, a rugby fanatic who saw in his favourite sport a means by which Kerry Packer could successfully counter Rupert Murdoch's attempts to control rugby league in Australia.*

Above left: *The ex-Australian Test prop (and a former leading rugby official), Ross Turnbull, a passionate and relentless individual who developed Levy's original idea further than even Levy could have imagined.*

Above right: *Turnbull's long-time business associate, Michael Hill, who joined Levy and Turnbull as they set about establishing the feasibility of their vision for the game.*

Above: *Simon Poidevin (centre, with Australian players Willie Ofahengaue, left, and Tim Gavin), a legendary flanker for NSW and Australia through the 1980s and early '90s, and a key figure in the move to involve News Corporation in the funding of professional rugby union.*

Right: *David Moffett, Executive Director of the NSWRU throughout 1995. In addition to his duties in Australia, Moffett was appointed Chief Executive of South Africa, New Zealand and Australia Rugby (SANZAR), when that body was formed in May 1995 to continue negotiations with News Corporation over backing for a competition involving the three countries.*

Right: *New Zealand-born Sam Chisholm, the head of Murdoch's global television empire outside the USA and the man who negotiated News Corporation's massive TV deal with SANZAR.*

Below: *Phil Harry (left), President of the Australian Rugby Union, with NSWRU Chairman and ARU Director Ian Ferrier.*

Two of the key figures in New Zealand rugby union's fight against WRC:
Above left: *Rob Fisher, Deputy Chairman of the New Zealand Rugby Union.*
Above right: *Former All Blacks flanker Jock Hobbs, whose persistence in pursuing current and potential members of the All Blacks squad was a critical factor in the NZRFU's ultimately successful battle to keep their team intact.*

Below: *The chairmen of the three major southern hemisphere Rugby Unions, Leo Williams (Australia, left), Dr Louis Luyt (South Africa, centre) and Richie Guy (New Zealand), at the June 23, 1995, press conference where the deal between SANZAR and News Corporation was announced. South Africa's memorable extra-time victory over the All Blacks in the World Cup Final was just 24 hours away.*

Above: *Laurie Mains, coach of the All Blacks between 1992 and 1995.*

Left: *Mains' successor as New Zealand coach, John Hart. WRC's first contact with a major New Zealand rugby figure had been with Hart, in late May, 1995. However, by the end of the World Cup a month later Hart had curtailed his involvement with the rebels.*

Right: *Controversial New Zealand prop Richard Loe, battling Australia's Phil Kearns during a Bledisloe Cup Test. Loe stunned Ross Turnbull at their first meeting by getting up and jogging on the spot. "Mate, I don't want to miss out on this for anything," said Loe, on hearing details of WRC's intentions. "I've already started my training!"*

Below: *Winger Eric Rush, who first learned of the WRC proposal during the World Cup in South Africa, and later, because he is a practising solicitor, played an important role in the contractual negotiations between the All Blacks and the WRC.*

*Forwards Rod McCall
(above) and Troy Coker
(left), the Wallabies
who acted as primary
negotiators between the
Australian team and
WRC.*

Right: *New Zealand captain Sean Fitzpatrick (centre), with winger Jonah Lomu (left), prop Craig Dowd (right) and the Bledisloe Cup, after the All Blacks defeated Australia in Sydney on July 29, to sweep the 1995 series.*

Below: *Wallaby hooker and captain Phil Kearns leaves the Sydney office of Ian Ferrier on August 1, after an often tense discussion with Ferrier and Phil Harry about the impasse at which they found themselves.*

outside the loop of the reigning administration. It was always going to be a great advantage that he was entirely unintimidated by the thought of being unpopular with rugby officials. Levy couldn't have asked for better if he'd called Central Casting, and was extremely happy that John Hart had brought Haden along to this meeting at his offices in Sydney's MLC Centre.

And Turnbull? He too — now just returned with Michael Hill from South Africa — was delighted that Andy Haden be brought into the picture. It had been a propitious twist of fate, as a matter of fact, that had put both Haden and Turnbull together on a train stuck in a snowstorm in Wales in the northern winter of 1980.

At that time Turnbull was one of the most influential of the Australian administrators in the world of international rugby politics, moving towards becoming a member of the International Rugby Board, while the gigantic second-rower Haden had just played for the All Blacks in a Test against Wales.

The train was taking them back to London from Cardiff, and the snow stopped them long enough for them to do some serious talking.

The subject? Strangely enough it was on the possibilities of professional rugby. Haden, long an advocate of rugby turning professional, remembers being impressed that, "At last here was somebody who was not only listening to what I had to say, but also *agreeing* with much of it."

Hart's presence at the meeting was delicate. He was one of the directors of the Auckland Rugby Union, and as such was somewhat putting himself out on a limb by holding talks with a crowd that was clearly a rebel organisation. But after a long conversation with the Chairman of the Auckland Rugby Union, Reuben O'Neill — who thought it at least a good idea to know more of what this crowd were on about — Hart had come.

Both Haden and Hart seemed to become increasingly enthusiastic about the project as they learned more details. As Michael Hill recalls, "There was no discussion whatsoever about whether or not the whole project could succeed. We all were taking that for granted."

Haden, particularly, reported an enormous dissatisfaction at provincial level with the NZRFU, portraying them as staid and conservative and not going anywhere. With that in mind, he was dead keen to get the provincial Unions involved in WRC, saying that even if the national Union wouldn't touch it, they would.

There was further discussion between all present along the lines of whether New Zealand should field four or six teams in the WRC competition, once it was up and running.

At the conclusion of the meeting Levy was of the firm impression that "they were with us", which, in Haden's case at least, is acknowledged as totally correct.

"I thought it was a terrific concept," Haden says flatly. "It was exactly what was needed, that when rugby went professional it needed to go on one time frame, one uniformity of pay scale, one competition. It shouldn't end up like boxing, for example, WBC, WBA, IBF and all that bullshit that goes on with them. I came away very impressed and agreed to be their agent in New Zealand. We had a loose arrangement that if it got up, I would have a job with them somewhere down the track."

Hart, on the other hand says he was more circumspect.

"I thought it *was* a great idea," he admits, "but on the proviso that the Unions had to be involved. Without them, I felt it simply wouldn't work."

Back in South Africa, the World Cup continued apace. On Sunday, June 18, England played New Zealand in a semi-final that would live long in the memory of everyone privileged enough to be there — a game of rugby for the ages.

It wasn't just that New Zealand had triumphed, 45–29, using a kind of dynamic, inventive, *spectacular* rugby rarely witnessed, it was the performance of a young man on the New Zealand wing by the name of Jonah Lomu. A freight-train in ballet shoes from first to last, Lomu had touched the ball seven times in the game, and scored four tries for his efforts, including a particularly staggering one in the first 30 seconds of play.

It created an instant *world* superstar — perhaps rugby's first — out of Lomu. The praise for him afterwards was universal, up to and including from the two unfortunate English players who had borne the brunt and grunt of his relentless attack.

Watching the game in London, Sam Chisholm was delighted.

Given that the South Africans had beaten France the day before, it now set up a South Africa versus New Zealand final for the World Cup — a good result for Chisholm, in that he was getting very close to committing an enormous amount of his corporation's money to 10 years of a competition which boasted those two very teams.

Someone else was pleased. Chisholm was still trying to come down from the fantastic game when he took a phone call from the man he refers to as "the boss" — Rupert Murdoch.

Mr Murdoch was also delighted. *Really* delighted.

"Absolutely amazing," is the phrase Chisholm remembers the Chairman of News Corporation saying, as he realised, perhaps for the first time, just how enthralling rugby could be when it was played at its spectacular best.

"It's the most electrifying thing I have ever seen," Chisholm says he replied. "And that was when Rupert said, 'This is amazing, we've got to have that guy ... '"

As it turned out, Rupert Murdoch was not Robinson Crusoe in wanting to have Lomu for his competition, but anyway ...

Turnbull and Hill were making ready to head back to South Africa to see the final on June 24, and "complete the process of signing up players and coaches". One of their tasks was to finish a report to more prospective investors in the scheme, where they gave a very up-beat view of how things stood.

"We believe the following," they wrote:

1. *The first two trips undertaken were highly successful.*
2. *The interest shown by all people, be they players, coaches, administrators, bankers or entrepreneurs, with whom the proposal was discussed was of unanimous excitement. This underpins our belief in the project.*
3. *The attitudes indicated by those associated directly and indirectly with the traditional authorities has been highly encouraging. This leads to the current belief that a long-term arrangement with the traditional rugby authorities, national and provincial, is probable.*

Not that they didn't think the Unions couldn't stand a little encouragement on that front. It was around this time, Geoff Levy says, that the men of WRC gave particular focus to the concept of signing up a "critical mass" of players in each country.

"Basically," Levy says, "what we wanted was to work out how many elite players formed the backbone of each country — how many we would need to sign before the different Unions would simply have no choice but to come on board with us.

"Our plan always was to get the World Cup Squad people first, on the basis that if they were interested and they were the cream of their country, obviously the next lot would follow ...

"In terms of the overall critical mass, though, we decided we had to get 150 Englishmen, 60 Welshmen, 150 New Zealanders, 150 South Africans and so on. We needed to get lists together of who were the best players in each country, up to the number we needed."

High in the Sydney offices of Ernst & Young, three of Australia's best-known coaches were gathered on the afternoon of June 21.

Bob Dwyer, Alec Evans and Bob Templeton sat around a table, jotting down various names. A couple of hours before, they had been briefed by Ross Turnbull in his office about just where WRC was up to, and shortly afterwards been hosted to a lunch in one of the Ernst

& Young private dining rooms by Ken Rennie — the partner of the firm who had been most involved in providing the accounting support necessary for the WRC venture to this point.

"It was a good lunch," as Rennie recalls, "and I remember talking a lot with Bob Dwyer about the whys and wherefores of Australia's loss to England in the World Cup."

They'd been joined a little late at the lunch by Geoff Levy, and from that point there had been only one topic of conversation that counted — the plans of the World Rugby Corporation.

Now it was time, though. At the lunch's conclusion, Ross Turnbull had asked the three Australian coaches to draw up a preliminary list of players in Australia who might be valuable to the cause, and they'd retired to this room to do just that.

As Templeton recalls it, "We had the meeting and then they just sort of said, write names down and see what players would be available. That was the whole scheme as far as I was concerned. Just to write down and say how are we going to get these squads [totalling] 120-odd players. Because there were four teams of 30 — one based in Melbourne, one in Perth, and one [each] in Sydney and Brisbane. It was finding out who could play centre and the availability [of various positions] … It got very thin towards the end, if you can imagine."

Templeton's presence there, particularly, is a measure of how seductive the WRC concept was at this point, at least to those who had been exposed to it and given time to think about it. Templeton, long considered the grand old man of Australian rugby — and a Traditionalist with a capital 'T' — had come to the meeting reluctantly, but felt there was simply no other option for Australian rugby than to throw in their lot with WRC.

"At that time we knew absolutely nothing about any Murdoch deal," Templeton recalls, "but what I did know was that the Wallabies would be absolutely decimated by players going to Super League if someone didn't come up with some money for them."

"The WRC fellows also wanted me to act as a recruiter for the Wallabies, in return for an enormous fee. I refused that, but did agree that I would at least pass on the message to the Queensland Wallabies about the basic concept of WRC, so they'd at least think twice before going to Super League."

Alec Evans, ditto. As the then coach of Wales — easily the most "raped" country in all the world by the rugby league bandidos — he knew better than most that if rugby didn't get some big-time money flowing into it quick smart, then rugby at the elite level would be reduced to being a Mickey Mouse affair.

Of his own involvement on that particular day, he remembers that, "There was a lot of talk about me coaching in one of the franchises in Australia, but at that stage I felt my commitment was very much to Wales."

He remembers being asked to compile the list too, but felt that, "For myself, after three-and-a-half years out of the country I didn't know enough about the players to do something like that properly, and I went in to Ross Turnbull and told him. Even the other two, with all their knowledge of Australian rugby, only really knew about the elite level of the game, so it was a very unsatisfactory exercise."

Bob Dwyer acknowledges that such a meeting took place, but vehemently denies taking part in the drawing up of any lists.

"My positioning at this time concerning WRC was that I continued to support their concept, while in no way forming an opinion about the financial viability of the project," he says. "I thought that it was in the best interests of the survival of the game, and of the continued presence of our players in the game.

"However, at all times I presented the view that the concept should run under the control of the ARU."

Chapter five

Murdoch moves in

It was agreed. Even as the World Cup continued all around, with the final only four days away, Louis Luyt flew from Johannesburg to London to meet with Sam Chisholm. It had only been a little over five weeks since he'd first been there to open negotiations with the head of News Corporation's television operations, but in that time the principal rugby union authorities had traversed an enormous distance.

From a standing start, where rugby in the southern hemisphere had no firm product to sell and no agreement between the three principal southern Unions on how to sell it, and who to sell it to, they had now moved to the point where the deal was practically done.

Luyt had turned up at Chisholm's apartment on the morning of June 20 with his 27-year-old son, Louis Jnr, explaining to the assembled company of News Corporation executives, and Ian Frykberg who was there for the occasion, "I brought him along to show him how you men operate, how business is done at the very top level."

Funny he should say that. For the way News Corporation does

business on such things is surprising. A business and legal neophyte would have thought that for such a massive deal, involving such enormous sums of money in exchange for such a momentous allocation of rights over 10 years, that the relevant document would have been drawn up by a battalion of lawyers on one side, and minutely examined by a whole army of roving legal beagles — *hunt, doggy! hunt!* — on the other.

In this instance at least, this was not the way it transpired. When Luyt arrived that morning, there was, as a matter of fact, no document in existence! Instead, it was to be drawn up by Bruce McWilliam on a portable computer perched on Chisholm's dining room table and progressively printed out on a portable printer set up on the same.

This was not, mind, last-minute modifications of an existing draft. "We started fresh," says McWilliam simply. "We mostly do it like that."

The reason?

"I think in everything we do," the lawyer says, "a quick deal is a good deal. If you need to go a long time, all you do is start negotiations rolling and they go and get other bids from other people. There is no point in giving someone an open bid because all they will do is take it away and ring up all the other broadcasters and show them. You've got to just go in and say, 'look, this is the money, it is only there for a certain amount of time, do you want to take it or not?'"

So it went. The document that would be at the base of guiding rugby in the southern hemisphere for at least the next 10 years, formed up beneath his fingertips.

As each page came off the printer, Luyt would read it over carefully, making the odd request for a change here and there. Some were granted, some were declined. And so the document was drawn up over the next hour or so.

Entitled a "Heads of Agreement" — as in the broad-brush strokes of the deal which would later have its detail filled in — the emerging document gave News Corporation wide powers.

Over who exactly? Well, as a matter of fact, Dr Luyt was going to be signing on behalf of an organisation not yet in formal existence. The opening line of the document read:

Dr LOUIS LUYT signing on behalf of a new entity to be formed by the organising bodies for rugby union in the countries of Australia, New Zealand and South Africa (SANZAR).

Among other points of interest from the document were the following clauses:

1. *News agrees to acquire from SANZAR exclusive worldwide television, radio and video (in all forms whether now known or hereafter devised) rights for all international and representative matches played in the originating countries ... excluding (only for the years stated) National Provincial Cup [sic] (New Zealand) for 1996 and Currie Cup (South Africa) for 1996.*

2. *SANZAR shall use its best endeavours to assist News in the creation of a Five Nations and Tri-Nations champions tournament and to obtaining worldwide television rights thereto ...*

3. *Without limiting the generality of the foregoing it is a fundamental condition of this agreement that ... Each member must use its best endeavours to contract all players and must not allow any players to breach his contract with that member.*

Clause 4 said that News Corporation could on-sell the rights to whomsoever they pleased, and then it was time for The Big One — Clause 5.

In the period since Frykberg had first put forward the $US650 million figure, he and Chisholm had agreed to lop $US100 million off the original asking price. Now, as a sweetener, and after a little of the usual haggling, Chisholm had agreed to up the ante by another lazy $US5 million — to bring the contract size to $US555 million — "so long as you sign today".

Luyt was agreeable. So Clause 5 read:

5. *In consideration of the rights hereby granted, News shall pay to SANZAR or as SANZAR may otherwise direct in writing the sum of FIVE HUNDRED AND FIFTY-FIVE MILLION UNITED STATES DOLLARS ($US555,000,000), payable four equal instalments payable* [sic] *on the 7th of January, April, July and October in each of the following years.*

> 1996: $32 million
> 1997: $43 million
> 1998: $46 million
> 1999: $48 million
> 2000: $52 million
> 2001: $57 million
> 2002: $61 million
> 2003: $66 million
> 2004: $72 million
> 2005: $78 million

This incremental method of payment, incidentally, was an effective counter to one of the frequent criticisms that would later be levelled against the deal: that it made absolutely no allowance for inflation. However, it is admittedly difficult to know just what $US78 million will be worth in 2005.

Clause 7, also invested a lot of power in the television overlords.

7. *SANZAR shall:*
Ensure that all matches are convened and scheduled to maximise the value of television rights. Without limiting the generality of the foregoing, News shall have the right of veto over schedulings and match timings although such right shall not be exercised unreasonably or capriciously.

Just what "unreasonably or capriciously" meant was not defined. Clause 8 would become important later in the Rugby War, when the issue was whether or not the Unions were legally obliged to get their players signed quickly.

> 8. *This constitutes a legally binding agreement. The parties must work together in good faith to execute such further documents and to do all other things as may reasonably be required to give full effect hereto.*

Clause 9 said that SANZAR acknowledged the right of News Corporation to use injunctions against them when appropriate, and Clause 10 affirmed that both parties were required to keep the terms of the agreement confidential.

Finally, Clause 11 also seemed more than passing generous towards News Corporation.

> 11. *For the next five seasons after the Term* [as in at the conclusion of the 10 years], *SANZAR shall negotiate with News in good faith in an endeavour to agree the terms for News obtaining similar rights as set out in this agreement and in any event shall not grant such rights (or rights included in such rights) to any other party (which offer shall be on bona fide commercial terms capable of acceptance by News and shall remain open for not less than seven days).*

A five-year option no less, which if taken up would bind rugby with News Corporation right through until 2011. With the document now ready, but still unsigned, Luyt and his son went off to lunch with Frykberg at the nearby Carlton Grill Room.

Sam Chisholm had a call to make. To Rupert Murdoch at his Los Angeles headquarters.

Luyt and Frykberg, both men of healthy appetites, were tucking into the main course, of massive ribs, when Frykberg's mobile rang.

It was Chisholm.

"The boss has given the 'okay'," he said. "Get back here now, and let's sign it."

Luyt was not happy about leaving the ribs half eaten, as Frykberg recalls, and enquired if the signing couldn't at least wait just a little while until they'd finished their meal. Frykberg, truth be told, wasn't too thrilled himself, but insisted they head back to Chisholm's apartment immediately.

So the job was done. Louis Luyt initialled every page of the five-page document, with his signature on the final page and dated it 20/6/95. Sam Chisholm counter-signed, and that was that.

Oddly enough, there was no hoopla, no fanfare, no air-punches from either side. A simple shake of the hand all round. A broad smile from Luyt with a reflection to his son — "You see how business is done at this level? Straight talking, and give your word." — and then the two departed with the men of News Corporation's best wishes for a safe trip.

Oh. And one more thing.

"Make sure you get all your guys signed up soon," Chisholm says he said just before the door closed. "You've got to get those players signed immediately."

Luyt and his son headed for Heathrow airport. The three most powerful national Unions of the southern hemisphere were now formally and legally committed to the project, just as News Corporation was committed to them, and all was set for the announcement to be made in three days time, on the day before the World Cup final. Back at Chisholm's apartment, Bruce McWilliam and his boss were also busy …

What, precisely, were they up to?

"We'd moved on to the next deal, in another sport," McWilliam recalls.

If there was to be a low point of the World Cup, it was surely this. In Pretoria, on the afternoon of Thursday, June 22, England played France on Loftus Versfeld in the consolation final for third and fourth places, a game of such overwhelming lacklustre-ness it would make a brown dog weep.

Neither side seemed particularly interested in winning, in running the ball, in expending much effort at all — but it must be said that England were more than merely passing dreadful. Dropped ball succeeded dropped ball, passes went awry, tackles were missed, simple manoeuvres botched, inadequacy abounded.

They were so bad, sooooooooooooooo bad, that mid-way through the second half, it was announced that back in Britain, the Prime Minister John Major had resigned. It was the only decent thing to do under the circumstances, even if the PM did steadfastly maintain later that it had actually been part of a political ploy to consolidate his leadership against the advances of the Minister for Wales, John Redwood, and had nothing to do with the performance of the English rugby team.

It was shortly after this announcement in the press-box, and shortly before England finally lost the game, that the Chief Executive Officer of the South African Rugby Football Union, Edward Griffiths, moved among the journalists, handing out an announcement that there would be a very important press conference held the following day back at the Ellis Park Headquarters in Johannesburg.

"What's it about?" one Australian journalist enquired.

"Something that is going to be very good for rugby," Griffiths replied with a rather odd kind of Mona Lisa smile.

And so to the announcement. If it wasn't quite rugby's version of the Magna Carta, it was at the very least an enormously significant and historical unveiling of something completely and utterly new on earth.

On the very eve of the biggest rugby event in history to that point, the Chairmen of the three biggest national Rugby Unions of the southern hemisphere had summoned the world's rugby press to the prestigious trophy room at the Ellis Park stadium to make an announcement.

Ahem. That announcement was that Rupert Murdoch's News Corporation had bought the television rights for the next 10 years to a triangular series, both at a national and provincial level, between New Zealand, South Africa and Australia. And the amount he would paying for these rights would be ... $US555 million!

The imposing figure of Ian Frykberg hovered a little nervously at the back of the conference, monitoring closely just how the world's press would react to the unveiling of his plan. The answer? Essentially, stupefaction. For close on an hour, reporters fired question after question at the collective Chairmen, looking for more information even as they were trying to work out the ramifications of such an enormous amount of money coming into what was still, in most parts of the world, a nominally amateur code.

Louis Luyt point blank denied that the announcement was a unilateral declaration that amateurism was finished, saying po-faced that the money would be going to "rugby development". But he may as well have saved his breath. It was obvious to all and sundry that such a massive amount of money was not going to be spent on buying new goal-posts around the world.

Speaking of which, most journalists there were staggered at the sheer size of the numbers involved. As were others ...

Simon Poidevin was thrilled when he heard. He took a call from Ian Frykberg while on a jaunt with his fiancée, Robin, at the Sun City resort, a couple of hours out of Johannesburg. As Robin recalls it, "Simon put the phone down, hugged me, and was very, very pleased. He said rugby's really going the right way, and he was really proud that he had had something to do with it."

It was proof of the secrecy in which the whole deal had been carried out that Poidevin should only learn of the figure right at the death, and other people involved were in exactly the same position.

Rob Fisher had only found out himself the night before the announcement, after a phone call from Richie Guy. Ian Ferrier from Australia found out at roughly the same time.

Both men were overjoyed at the announcement of this much money flowing into rugby's coffers, most particularly when judged against what all the national Rugby Unions had been getting. In Australia, for example, the rights to the Australian Rugby Union's television output for 1991 — the very year they won the World Cup — were sold for $A200,000. Now, only five years later, for the 1996 season, Australia's share of the Murdoch proceeds would be around $A11 million. "I thought it was an extraordinary figure at the time, and I still do," says Ian Ferrier, the ARU's main money man.

One other figure bears Ferrier out. For the 1995 season, the sum total of what Australia, New Zealand and South Africa had received for their television rights was $US5.7 million. In 1996, that total would rise to $US32 million — close to a six-times increase.

Hey, the deal had *something* going for it.

One would have thought that for the movers and shakers of the World Rugby Corporation, the bleeding obvious beckoned — this was THE END.

With Rupert Murdoch putting that amount of money towards it, and with the three principal national Unions 100 per cent behind it, surely it was obvious that the whole WRC vision lay lost and bleeding behind Ayers Rock?

No chance, the way Turnbull and Levy tell it.

On the morning in question, Ross Turnbull was in the office section of Harry Viljoen's enormous compound, feeling pretty good about the way everything was going. He and Michael Hill had flown back to the Republic the day before with a duffel bag full of contracts; they'd already made further positive contact with Pienaar, plus other key rugby people in town for the final. As always with Ross, it was all systems go.

It was then that Viljoen's fax machine started rolling out the news, line by line. Turnbull tore it off, read it, didn't blanch.

"I thought, mmmmm, that's interesting," Turnbull recalls, "but when I thought about it, $US555 million might sound like a lot, but by the time you've taken out all the various commissions and divided it three ways, it wasn't that much. I thought it was stupid that those national Unions had sold themselves to Murdoch for such a long period of time and effectively put a salary cap on the code until well into the next century.

"But it made no difference to us. We had all the people we needed to make contact with, and our teams were in place in a highly organised fashion. They might have had the Unions, but I felt sure that we were going to have the players. For me it was full steam ahead, regardless."

Michael Hill's observation stands: "Ross's greatest talent is his ability to plough on regardless."

Back in Australia, Levy was of a similar up-beat view to Turnbull, to the point that he maintains to this day that far from hindering their plan, the Murdoch announcement actually aided them enormously.

"To begin with," Levy says, "it highlighted the fact that rugby really was the sort of valuable commodity that could command those sorts of figures. Up to that point I think some of the people we were talking to just couldn't see how rugby could ever be worth *that* much, and believed we were living in a kind of fantasy-land.

"The Murdoch thing showed WRC's vision was not a fantasy, but their deal still had a lot of weaknesses which left us with a lot of room to manoeuvre."

That much was inarguable. Not only did the Murdoch plan ignore 80 per cent of the rugby world — making sure that those left out of the largesse were more keen than ever to sign up with a commercial organisation (*any* commercial organisation, so long as it had money and they wouldn't be left behind), but it still left the players entirely free to sign with whomsoever they damn well pleased.

"None of the Unions ever asked the players what they thought," Levy says. "The players simply woke up one morning to find that their services had been sold to Rupert Murdoch without so much as a query as to whether or not the players were happy about it.

"I think that worked greatly in our favour, as a lot of the players resented it."

And nor was there any doubting that the rugby establishment worldwide still had simply no idea that a threat existed to their age-old order.

In England, for example, Dennis Easby, the Rugby Football Union President who had taken perhaps most umbrage at being described by Will Carling as "an old fart", seemed to miss the point entirely. On the first occasion that a rumour of the massive Murdoch deal had broken free of Sam Chisholm's still fierce desire for secrecy, Easby had gone on the BBC *Super Sport* program to give his view of the news out of South Africa.

Far from acknowledging that *the times they had a'chang-ed*, that the elite players in his neck of the woods in particular would be exceedingly vulnerable to *any* entrepreneur with money if the whole Murdoch deal got up, he chose to take issue with the whole idea of such a deal in the first place:

"There's no way Mr Murdoch must be allowed to take over rugby union," he said. "If the southern hemisphere countries decide to go pro, that's their business. But I cannot see any other country, including England, agreeing to follow them.

"We'll not sell our souls to Murdoch," he said. "By August, hopefully, the International Board will have worked out a way in which our players can be properly recompensed and we'll stand by that. We want the top players to be fairly treated — and they will be. But I cannot see any way the game will go pro. The southern hemisphere is obviously attracted by the money Murdoch will offer. But if they use that cash just to pay players, they'll be making a grave mistake."

Dennis Easby's attitude was not one-out, but typical of the prevailing attitude of many administrators in the northern hemisphere. Their attitude was admirable in the sense that it was undoubtedly born of a genuine love of *the game for the game's sake* — the very same view that had powered rugby through the last century and a quarter of its glorious history — but the bottom line is that it was clearly out of touch with the attitude of the players.

The generation actually out there on the field providing the entertainment had continually expressed a desire to be better recompensed, and had just as continually been rebuffed. More often than not, with great venom. A few seasons earlier, when that fine Scottish captain and man, David Sole, had politely indicated to his Union that perhaps his players could be a tad better monetarily rewarded for their efforts, he was described by one of the Scottish Rugby Union delegates as "a cancer at the heart of Scottish rugby".

Such was the environment that Turnbull would be working in internationally, when he decided to press on. He would be doing it, though, without the services of some of the people who had been backing him, at least tentatively, to that point. John Hart had flown to South Africa to see the All Blacks in the semi-final and the final. On the flight back from South Africa on Sunday — after New Zealand had lost the World Cup final 15–12 the day before to the Springboks — he had mentally composed a long letter to Turnbull which he did in fact send two days later.

He wasn't sure if Turnbull was going to go on with it, he wrote, but if he was, Hart had to advise him that he was now "out":

I have decided, that with the SANZAR agreement currently in place, your approach could lead to a bidding war unless you have the support of the major Unions …

This would bring significant disruption to the game and its various

*relationships and, as you know, my first allegiances have always been
to the players of the game …*

*I respectfully therefore advise that I do not wish to advance our
discussion any further …*

With best wishes, etc …

In Australia, Bob Templeton took a similar stance. He had not
slept well the previous few nights, wondering whether or not he
should be getting at all involved with something that at least in the
first instance was going to be acting contrary to the interests of both
the ARU and his beloved Queensland Rugby Union. However, the
announcement of the Murdoch deal made it clear to him what
action he should take.

"I was terribly concerned it was going to rip the game apart and
for that reason I didn't want to be in it."

So …

At a Sunday morning meeting of most of the Queensland-based
Wallabies at the home of Wallaby centre Tim Horan, Templeton
honoured his commitment to Levy and Turnbull by telling the
Queensland players the bare basics of what WRC was all about, but
then added this rider.

"Men," he said, in his inimitably Churchillian manner, "I think
I've got to make clear my position on this. I'm a life member of both
the QRU and the ARU and so I'm not going to have anything
further to do with it.

"You fellows will do what you want of course, but if I were you I
wouldn't sign with any bastard until you've at least seen what the
ARU has got to offer you. Now that they've signed with Murdoch,
they're at last going to have the money to give you what you blokes
deserve."

He left it at that.

Chapter six
Signing 'em up

It was arranged. By an unfortunate quirk of airline schedules, the dispirited All Blacks had had to remain in Johannesburg for three days after the World Cup final, while their officials had flown on home.

Hearing that the New Zealanders would be twiddling their thumbs at their Johannesburg hotel until the Tuesday night, and that they were *sans* officials, Ross Turnbull knew there would never be a better moment to launch. Their "in" to the All Blacks was via Michael Hill, who had met the All Black winger, Eric Rush, a few years previously — when Hill had been Deputy Chairman of the Newcastle Knights rugby league club. On that occasion, Hill had been trying to recruit the New Zealand centre Frank Bunce for the Knights, and Rush had come along for the ride to a few of the ultimately unfruitful meetings.

Hill called Rush, to tell him that he had "an interesting business proposition" to put to him and a few All Blacks and …

And they arrived that very afternoon at Harry Viljoen's house. This was not the first time the All Blacks had got wind of the whole

WRC concept, as rumours by this time were swirling, but it was the first official contact. Rush was accompanied by four of the other All Blacks, including one of the most senior of the team-members, front-rower Richard Loe.

Into the Viljoen lounge room went the All Blacks, out came the well-practised spiel from Turnbull. Up went the level of interest from the All Blacks, down went the beers that their host had so thoughtfully provided. Turnbull felt he was doing well, by the fascinated expressions on the All Blacks' faces, but really received confirmation when suddenly Richard Loe jumped to his feet and began running on the spot.

"What are you doing?" Turnbull asked, a little nonplussed at this unusual behaviour, right when he was building to the climax of his presentation.

"Mate, I don't want to miss out on this for anything," Loe replied. "I've already started my training!" The meeting broke up shortly afterwards, with the All Blacks at that meeting promising to pass on the gist of what had been said to some of the senior members of the team.

(In fact, they would have something of an informal team meeting that very night, with all those who had been present at Viljoen's house passing on to the others the detail of what they had learned.)

The following day, senior All Black flanker Mike Brewer and All Black captain Sean Fitzpatrick went around to Harry Viljoen's house for lunch. In the words of Michael Hill, "These two were obviously the team leaders and acted like it, though they were both clearly still a bit flat from the loss against South Africa."

Turnbull covered the same ground as the day before, and the two All Blacks responded. They were, by the accounts of both Turnbull and Hill, particularly keen on a couple of aspects. What they seemed to like most was that under the WRC proposal the players were going to be involved in the running of the show — as both felt that they and their team-mates had been quite ignored in the current set-up. Each expressed annoyance about the Murdoch deal announced three days previously, feeling that their services had been sold without even the courtesy of someone consulting them.

How well did the whole thing go in the end?

"Well enough," Hill reports, "that at the end of lunch, Brewer took 30 contracts away with him."

In the American Civil War there was a military convention that generals in the field should never lower themselves to the grubby business of taking direct potshots at each other. So too in the Rugby War, at least in these early stages. That night, after the successful meeting with the two senior All Blacks, it turned out that Turnbull was dining in the same Sandton Sun restaurant as ARU President Phil Harry.

These two Australians abroad, long-time acquaintances, saw each other but made no acknowledgment — neither a nod of the head, nor even a glare. They simply continued their meals with their separate parties. While Phil Harry could hear nothing of what was being discussed at Turnbull's table, he could at least see that things were upbeat. Clearly, Turnbull did not have the demeanour of a man who had put three months of his life into something only to have been left dead in the ditch by the Murdoch announcement.

"It was obvious that Ross was still out there, still going," Harry says now.

Turnbull was that.

As was his ever-widening band of agents around the world. Back in Australia, it was Geoff Levy who had taken charge of the recruitment drive. On a morning in Sydney shortly after the World Cup final, Levy and David Shein met with Rod McCall and Troy Coker at the Comtech offices near Sydney Airport. David Shein, with his brother John, had by this time come on board as personal investors in WRC, which was why their premises would become something of a nerve centre, though the Comtech company they ran was not involved on a financial level.

And while Coker at this stage had already been advancing WRC's cause for about three weeks, this was a meeting to determine if McCall wanted to be involved as well. Geoff Levy was in command of the meeting:

Levy: "Rod, we know you are very close to [Queensland coach] John Connolly. You have to understand you can't talk to him about what we're going to tell you. Is that a problem?"

McCall: "Yes, that's a problem."

Levy: "Well we can't go further, then."

From that initial impasse, the meeting nevertheless moved to the point where Levy agreed that he would actually tell McCall everything for this one meeting, and that McCall would sign a confidentiality agreement. Levy then gave his spiel, while he, Shein and Coker all watched McCall intently to see how he was reacting to it.

McCall gave nothing away and at its conclusion simply said he wanted to think about it, but added a little unnecessarily, "If I tell you I'm not in, I'm not in."

For three days after that, Levy was in constant contact with McCall, realising that the Wallaby forward was crucial to the concept's success. He was one of the rugby team "leaders" that Turnbull had been talking about.

At one point, Levy remembered the way it had worked with Pienaar and offered McCall a massive success fee if he ended up delivering a lot of the signatures required.

McCall, by Levy's account, was shocked. There was a long pause on the other end of the line, and then McCall came back and said to Levy quite coldly, "Listen, if I do this, it will be because I think it's the best thing for rugby and not because of any success fee."

Not that he was Mother Teresa for all that. Another factor,

as McCall acknowledges, was that if it did get up and running he would be getting the same salary as other key players, in the vicinity of $US250,000 for the first year. Not bad dosh.

It took a while, but McCall eventually decided to go with it.

"I'm in," he told Levy.

It was early in the afternoon of June 26, 1995. At Orly International Airport in the outskirts of Paris, Eric Blondeau had organised a private room for the returning French team to file into. They had completed the long flight from South Africa a short time previously, and were suitably jet-lagged-bedraggled at the conclusion of their six-week campaign — in which they'd been narrowly knocked out by the Springboks in the semi-finals.

Waiting for them in the room was Blondeau, international lawyer Bob Simpson, a whiteboard and a briefcase full of contracts. Blondeau took the floor, explained the concept in detail, and did the best he could while many of the French players talked quietly among themselves. Some, actually, talked not so quietly, and had plainly switched off.

It was the great French centre, Philippe Sella, who got the meeting back on track. According to French journalist Richard Escot, who chronicled the meeting, Sella suddenly took the floor himself and told his team-mates to shut up. For once they had someone telling them something interesting, he said, and the least they could do was listen.

Not that Sella was totally convinced himself of the concept, but he did want to know all he could about it.

In his words: "It was like a ball rolling in your own in-goal. Before knowing if I should ground it for the 22m drop or run it myself, I have to analyse the situation, look where the opposition is and see how my own team-mates are placed. There it was the same. I wanted to listen and I wanted to absolutely understand what they were proposing to us.

"I think it's an attitude that all the players should have had."

Which maybe they didn't, but when it came time for handing out the contracts they were certainly attentive. The contracts, or "Letters of Intent" to be more specific, had been specially modified by Bob Simpson so as to be still binding under French law. (A curiosity of the situation in France was that it was actually illegal for players to sign contracts that would result in them being paid money for playing rugby, when that sport was still nominally amateur.)

Simpson and Blondeau retired to an adjacent room and then saw the French players one by one, and gave each of them his contract. The players took them away, to show their own lawyers, with the agreement that once they were satisfied they would post the contracts to Eric Blondeau at his Cognac office.

Blondeau, for one, was very happy with the way things had gone, recalling now, "When they saw the contracts they were quite like kids in front of a Christmas tree. They were very, very excited and I felt they really believed in us."

Ross Turnbull, too, when he heard that the French had all taken contracts and were already showing signs that they would sign, was delighted, and says of the French now, "They were far and away the most professional of all the groups we dealt with, straight down the line from the very beginning and never any problems."

In Western Samoa, the contracts were at this time already very close to being signed, sealed and delivered. Requiring only 16 players to establish a stranglehold on elite rugby on the island, this was always going to be one of the easiest of WRC's tasks around the world.

In fact, the required "critical mass" had been reached shortly after the Western Samoans had returned home after the World Cup — powered in large part by the fact that that island nation had of course been left entirely out of the Murdoch deal.

Bryan Williams, the former All Black winger who was installed as the technical director of the Western Samoan Rugby Union, had particularly felt that without WRC shoring up the financial walls around his players, the team would be entirely overrun by league scouts. It was he who had signed up the players.

The agenda of the WRC was being advanced, all over the world ...

On Saturday, July 1, at around 10 o'clock in the morning, 10 or so of the Brisbane-based Wallabies who had been in the World Cup Squad sat around the living room of Brisbane solicitor Eddie Kann, and went over the contracts that Rod McCall had with him.

By this time the players in the room were already very well informed about the essence of the WRC proposal, having been able to quiz Geoff Levy extensively a couple of days previously via a "video conference" — a whiz-bang bit of video technology atop ordinary television sets at the Comtech offices in both Sydney and Brisbane.

No one had been allowed into the room without first signing a confidentiality agreement, but no one deemed that a problem. All concur that the mood of this video conference was very positive, and it was from this launching pad that the players were now ready to look at, and possibly sign, actual contracts.

McCall had organised this meeting at Kann's home as a preliminary surveying of the legal ground that the Wallabies would be embarking on with WRC. While some of the players wanted to contact their own lawyers and get advice on it, others seemed happy with it from the beginning — two players going so far as to ask, then and there, for a pen to sign!

It was exciting, it was radical, it was lucrative, it was *new*.

And, while it seemed clear to all that the Unions would be invited to take part once things had become more advanced, there was equally no doubt that everyone understood that secrecy was the supreme concern of the moment.

That feeling was illustrated by a small incident that occurred upon leaving the meeting, when Jason Little found himself in a car with three of his team-mates. Suddenly, up ahead, they saw Leo Williams, the Chairman of the ARU, who also lived in Brisbane, driving his car in the next lane. Instinctively, all players bar the driver hit the deck.

"There was no law against us being together," Little says with a laugh now, "but it just seemed like the right thing to do."

Whatever. As early as the following night, McCall and Troy Coker would be out and about in Brisbane, getting signatures. What this entailed, for the most part, was a phone call, asking could they come and see the player to talk to him about the contract. And they went from there. They had three signatures on contracts already by that Sunday night, and others who seemed in basic agreement but wanted to show their solicitors first.

One of the methods of persuasion used, and it was a potent one, was that their signatures still did not lock them absolutely into the WRC. "We told the players we would not hand them over to the WRC crowd until there were enough players Australia-wide to guarantee it," McCall recalls. That figure would be put at 60 players, signed and sealed, before they would be delivered.

It was also made clear, McCall claims — and it is backed up by what happened on at least one occasion — that if the players changed their minds at any time and wanted their contracts back before they had been lodged with WRC, McCall would give the contracts to them no questions asked.

There was haggling, of course. Some of the players wanted more money, some wanted longer contracts, some refused to deal with Coker and McCall and instead insisted they deal with Levy directly.

"For about a week," Geoff Levy says, "it seemed like I was talking to lawyers from Brisbane all the time. Each of them wanted to go over every clause of the contract individually, but if that's what it took to help the signed contracts keep flowing, then that was okay."

The Palace of the Lost City rises out of the South African wilderness like a modern medieval kingdom transplanted onto the veldt by some cosmic mistake. It is part of the Sun City resort — the Republic's answer to Las Vegas, with 24-hour gambling, and hot and cold running luxury all put together on a stunning palatial scale.

It certainly wasn't to everyone's taste, but seeing its lights up ahead in the darkness, the CEO of the South African Rugby Football Union, Edward Griffiths, was tiredly pleased. It had been a long trip from Cape Town by "trains, planes, and automobiles", as the saying goes, but at least he could now relax. Griffiths had come to talk about contracts with the Springboks, who'd been offered a few days up there with their wives courtesy of SARFU, to thank them all for their wonderful efforts during the just-finished World Cup.

The general plan was to begin a few leisurely negotiations the following morning, to try and work out just what kind of contract the Boks would be happy with.

Right away, though, almost from the moment he'd parked his car and made his way into the hotel's reception area, he could sense something was wrong. A Springbok whom he knew particularly well and liked a lot seemed reluctant to look him in the eye as they shook hands. Another did the same. Presently, after a little bit of chatting with a few of them, some kind of garbled story came out.

Something about "WRC", "signing session", "Ross Turnbull …", he couldn't get it straight. He went to bed that night a little worried, if not alarmed.

The morning, and there was Francois himself, sitting across the table from Griffiths. The CEO did not take long to broach the subject, albeit gently. Had something happened last night? he asked the Springbok captain, something about signing contracts with another organisation?

"They are just rumours," Pienaar replied, and declined to discuss it further. What he did want to say was that the team did not want to enter into any negotiations with SARFU right then and there.

Griffiths, as understated a man as they come — with nary an italic or exclamation mark ever sighted in his general conversation — did not expostulate with Pienaar on the spot, and even now speaks about it rather emotionlessly.

"I thought something had happened," he says, "but I still didn't think it was anything urgent. I simply didn't think Ross Turnbull would have the capability to do something like this."

That morning, even while Griffiths was in the same hotel, one of the South African players who had not signed with WRC the previous evening, went to Francois Pienaar's room to sign up. Not that the documents Pienaar was asking his fellow players to sign were presented as iron-clad "contracts" as such. In the words of one of the Springboks who put his signature on the paper, "Francois simply said to us that by signing this we were giving WRC an option on our services, but that we weren't yet committed, that we could get the contracts back from him any time we wanted before they were lodged."

Which, again, was true enough. One of the players, the famous winger Chester Williams, would later change his mind and get his contract back, to reportedly have it cut to shreds.

Secrecy throughout the whole exercise was, of course, paramount. When, early in the piece, it had come to Turnbull's ears that Jean-Pierre Rives had been spouting his mouth off to journalists at the French Tennis Open that he was going to be the new boss of the French part of a professional rugby circus that was being set up, Turnbull had got Bob Simpson on the phone immediately.

"Tell Rives to shut his mouth," Turnbull had told him, and the American-born lawyer had promised he would do just that.

McCall and Coker were going great guns up in Queensland, getting the contracts signed and in the first instance storing them in the bottom drawer of a filing cabinet that McCall had in his home office.

To the south, in New South Wales, there was still precious little happening in the way of contracts. Levy in consultation with McCall decided that Phil Kearns — the man who would shortly be taking over the reins of the Wallabies as captain — would be right for the job in conjunction with his front-row partner Ewen McKenzie.

They were forwards, they were team leaders, they were perfect. Geoff Levy personally got them signed up first, and then cut them loose.

Kearns has acknowledged that a success fee was a part of the package he was offered, though he says it was not enormous and was not significant in his motivation to get involved.

"There was an amount of money if it all went through," he told journalist Peter Jenkins. "But it was minimal, was only mentioned once, and was not brought up again. For all the shit that went on, and the hassles, they would have to offer me 10 times the amount for me to do it all over again. But I can certainly say from my point of view the money was not the issue.

"I'd agreed to speak to players and tell them about the idea. But I wasn't working for [WRC]. I just thought it was a good idea and wanted to pursue it."

He did just that, in the company of McKenzie. The two NSW players began to do the job in much the same fashion as McCall and Coker had to the north, having secret meetings after training, meetings with players in the Comtech offices, taking phone calls, making phone calls, gradually collecting up the contracts.

On his way to and from these recruitment meetings, Kearns would drive daily through the suburb of Glebe, right past Shearer's Hotel in Bay Street. Enter a nice touch of historical symmetry to the whole exercise. For it was in that hotel, some 86 years previously, that a similar saga had been under way.

On that occasion, in that hotel, an entrepreneur by the name of James Joynton Smith had launched what would be known ever afterwards as The Great Wallaby Raid — the signing for rugby league of 14 Wallabies who'd returned just six months earlier from a victorious British tour.

Then, as now, the principle was the same — getting financial rewards for your skills. Then, as now, the relationship between the players and their administrators was vexed. On the subject of the ARU and his loyalty or otherwise to them, Kearns says this:

"My first loyalty was to the players and what was the best for them, and *after* that the ARU. But as far as individuals of the ARU go, we reasoned that as they were mostly businessmen, they'd also see the good business sense in it."

Ross Turnbull was busy. Very busy. Flying in over the white cliffs of Dover under the cover of darkness with Michael Hill, the two had no sooner arrived back at the London Ritz than they'd set up a very private little shop in the Trafalgar Suite and were open for business.

Among the first of their callers was the English fly-half, Rob Andrew, the English captain, Will Carling and Carling's agent, John Holmes, plus a well-known British rugby coach. Alas, from the beginning, something just did not "click" in terms of the chemistry in the room. The cocky Englishman, Holmes, and the knockabout Australian, Michael Hill, particularly, were never destined to hit it off. When Turnbull was doing the introductions, he introduced Hill to the others as someone who had done some of the legal work on Kerry Packer's World Series Cricket.

Holmes broke in immediately to say he had been involved as an agent back then himself, and had strongly advised his players to have nothing at all to do with it. Hill couldn't contain himself.

"Well *that* was a master stroke," he observed dryly.

That exchange proved to be a high point of the whole afternoon tea, at least insofar as John Holmes and Michael Hill were concerned.

While Andrew seemed quite positive about the concept from the beginning, and Carling initially kept his peace, Holmes' theme throughout was that the WRC scheme couldn't possibly get up.

"ITV hasn't got the money," Hill remembers him saying, "the BBC won't deal with you; Murdoch will be against you everywhere you turn, and the Rugby Football Union will always be against it. You just won't get it up."

Turnbull held his fire then, but not now.

"I think you could say he was aggressively against it," Turnbull says. "I thought he had other objectives outside of what we were discussing. Other people we dealt with — rugby people — could see the benefit of what we were doing for the game. Holmes didn't fit into that category at all.

"He was strictly business, and what you've got to understand is that both Carling and Holmes were very happy with the status quo even if it was being run by 'old farts'. They were both making a lot of money out of the fact that he was captain under the current regime. Carling probably thought it was not in his or Holmes' best interest to disturb that arrangement."

When the meeting broke up, Turnbull thought he had advanced his cause with Rob Andrew and the British rugby coach, but mentally put down both Holmes and Carling as lost causes. This feeling was exacerbated some 20 minutes later when he and Michael Hill went outside for some fresh air on this beautiful midsummer's day to see the Englishmen still standing on Piccadilly, which runs past the Ritz.

Holmes was clearly upset about something, and though he had stopped gesticulating by the time Hill and Turnbull had come into earshot, the way he looked at them as they passed seemed to make it clear that he was even then moving to torpedo their plans.

The story that came to Turnbull's ears later, rightly or wrongly, was that it was Holmes' intention to get a copy of a WRC contract, so as to pass it on to the Rugby Football Union to see, firstly, if they would match the money being offered by WRC and secondly, to forewarn them that there was a lion prowling in the woods.

Whatever the truth of that story, what *was* sure was that it would be the last time that Turnbull would have any contact with either Carling or Holmes in the whole affair. Thereafter, in Turnbull's perception at least, was born "the Carling Factor".

"What I mean by that," he says, "is that there was a sentiment in English rugby which was anti-WRC and I think slowed us down on making as much headway as we otherwise would have there."

Holmes, for one, is happy to acknowledge that he was against it.

"I thought the whole thing was Mickey Mouse from the beginning," he says, "and not a serious business venture. They had no television interest firmly lined up, and were just taking a punt that that would come later. It was *not* the way that that sort of business is done."

The reception for the returning World Cup finalists at New Zealand's parliament had concluded. But the All Blacks had two stops to make before reaching Wellington Airport, from where the elite of New Zealand rugby would soon be scattered again to the four winds. It was the afternoon of July 5.

The first stop was to the NZRFU's office in downtown Wellington, where Richie Guy made the first concrete offer to the All Blacks. Their share of the Murdoch money spoils, he said, was to be a guarantee of a minimum of $NZ150,000 a year for three years, with individuals possibly able to negotiate higher than that.

In response, the All Blacks were underwhelmed, with one All Black later noting privately, "You didn't have to be much of a mathematician to realise that we weren't going to be getting anywhere near as much as we were making for the Union."

Sean Fitzpatrick concurs, describing the whole thing now as "a bit of a laugh".

What Guy had been offering them was as little as a fifth of what WRC was offering to one player, and around a third of what most of the rest of them were being offered. That was presuming, of course, that WRC would actually come good with the money.

The All Blacks were *so* underwhelmed by the numbers, that during a brief break in proceedings — after coach Laurie Mains asked the CEO of the Union, George Verry, if the team could have a bit of time to consider things — the New Zealand team simply upped and left.

Onto the bus boys, and let's go. Richie Guy looked out the window of his office to see the bus disappearing down the street. Though aggrieved, he was not actually staggered.

"I felt they just weren't listening to me," he says now. "All the time I was speaking to them, I felt they weren't there with me. One of the things I think they were most sour about was that at that stage we said they'd only be paid if they played, whereas they wanted a guarantee that they'd be paid whatever happened."

In the bus, the All Blacks had one more stop to make. The manager of the nondescript little motel adjacent to Wellington Airport couldn't contain his wonder. Not only had the famous Andy Haden just booked his conference room for a couple of hours, but before his eyes the most famous sportsmen in all of New Zealand, the All Blacks *themselves*, were filing into his motel.

"What's this all about?" he asked Haden.

"Just a little awards ceremony for the boys," Haden replied, before disappearing behind the double doors.

At the front of the room a table had been set up, behind which sat Geoff Levy in the middle, Derek Dallow of the Auckland law firm Davenports on the left, and a seat on the right for Haden. Beneath the table, beside Dallow's legs, was a briefcase filled with 26 contracts, based on the original draft that had been given to him by Michael Hill, which he had drawn up over the previous week. Davenports was the Auckland law firm that Eric Rush worked for, hence their connection with the All Black side.

If things went well, the men of the World Rugby Corporation didn't think it beyond the bounds of possibility that they might be able to sign the boys up there and then. Levy stood up a little nervously, looking out upon some of the All Black officials, including Laurie Mains, and 25 tired, dejected All Blacks, still dressed in their formal black jackets from the parliamentary reception.

And there was one other All Black there too, up the back on the left, with headphones on, no blazer, and what looked to be a baseball cap on backwards. This, of course, was Jonah Lomu, and if he wanted to sit there like that, one out, that appeared to be fine with everyone.

So Levy took a deep breath and began. He set out the basic concept and saw a slight quickening of interest, and then got to the money part and felt that the interest increased somewhat.

"When Jonah Lomu lifted off one headphone after about five minutes, I thought I was getting somewhere, and when he lifted both of them off after 10 minutes and really started listening, I thought I had them," Levy recalls.

Then came the questions. To Levy's mind, the hardest of these came from Eric Rush. He was the only lawyer in the side, and asked a lot of probing questions about the way the WRC would be structured worldwide. But there was also an aggressive line of questioning from Laurie Mains, because, according to Levy, "he didn't like us at all".

"Laurie thought this was disgusting," Levy recalls. "But suddenly, as I continued talking, I saw this twinkle in his eye as he realised what we were trying to achieve. One of the things we promised them, and we emphasised this all around the world, was, 'if you don't want it, if the players don't want it, then it will never happen, but if you do want it, it will'."

The All Blacks declined to sign contracts on the spot, but rather formed a three-man committee — comprising Mike Brewer, Sean Fitzpatrick and Eric Rush — which would be the point of liaison between the All Blacks and the World Rugby Corporation for further negotiations.

No firm commitment had been made by the New Zealanders at

this stage, but their clear approach was that they would either be all for it, or all against it. They were a *team*, and they would move as a team or stay as a team, and that was that.

As Levy was winding the meeting up, he couldn't help but notice one particularly intense, and notoriously *tough* All Black sitting — appropriately enough, on the left of the front row — right before him and watching with quite an aggressive look topping his bristling moustache.

"He was looking at me like I thought he was going to come and strangle me," Levy recalls, "and he was sitting next to Zinzan Brooke — quite a formidable guy — and then when I finish and they start to file out, he comes right up to the table, leans over right at me and says, 'Where do I sign?'"

"What do you want to sign?" Levy replied.

"The thing everyone else signed," the enormous All Black returned.

"That was the confidentiality agreement and you've already signed one … "

"Well, I want to sign it *again* … "

Levy took a mental note that, whatever happened, wherever this road might lead, there was one All Black heart that beat true for his concept.

There remained one other All Black whom Levy particularly wanted to talk to before they all disappeared back onto the bus. That was All Black Lomu — the most famous, most lethal, most marketable rugby player on the planet at the time — the one man who guaranteed credibility to any rugby competition. He was, perhaps rugby's first true international star. Own Jonah, and rule the world.

They made a curious pair, these two, talking in the foyer of the modest hotel — the smallish and bespectacled South African-born lawyer and the gargantuan Tongan-born rugby player — and the other All Blacks brushing past had a bit of a laugh just to see them together.

"Jonah," Levy was saying, "you've got to understand how important this is for you to sign and be with the World Rugby Corporation. You've got to understand where this can lead for you. You could have your image up on the billboard at New York's Times Square!"

Lomu nodded, but made no commitments whatsoever.

Oh God. Sitting in a cafe in Cape Town, just around the corner from Newlands Stadium, Michael O'Connor was sure that his worst fears had been confirmed. The Australian Rugby League recruiters had beaten him to it.

Back home in Australia, the fight for control of rugby league had continued unabated, and O'Connor had come to South Africa on the extremely delicate mission of snaring Springboks for the rebel league competition. It was delicate because he was a Murdoch man attempting to snare players from one Murdoch competition (SANZAR) to go to another Murdoch competition (Super League).

But O'Connor, a dual union/league international who was now trying his hand as a Super League executive, thought it simply had to be done. The word was that the ARL was also going to be in South Africa looking around for players, and O'Connor and other Super League officials felt they simply couldn't risk being done over by the ARL in this crucial arena.

Now, though, these two Springboks he was negotiating with — Tiaan Strauss and Tinus Linee — together with another leading South African player, Christian Stewart, seemed suddenly to have gone cold on the whole idea of signing with Super League. Strauss and Stewart kept talking in Afrikaans about something that was obviously sensitive, while Linee kept pressing Strauss to tell O'Connor about "the other option".

O'Connor twigged immediately. The "other option" was obviously a reference to the Australian Rugby League, and O'Connor knew he was probably too late. Dammit!

But wait. After more muffled conversations in Afrikaans, the leader of the trio, Tiaan Strauss, decided to come clean and tell O'Connor at least something of what they were referring to.

"Look, we do have another option," O'Connor remembers Strauss saying at last to him in English. "It involves a rebel group, a rebel organisation with a backer, a big backer who has associations with cable television, buying players and then selling them back to the provincial Unions."

O'Connor was relieved on one count, but suddenly alarmed on another. It was terrific that at least the ARL wasn't the recruiter in question, but quite distressing what the implications of this rebel group's coup were for Murdoch's SANZAR deal if it got up. O'Connor pressed for more details. They were not forthcoming.

The following day, however, O'Connor had partial confirmation of Strauss' story. The recruiter met with one of the Springbok World Cup Squad members in whom Super League was particularly interested. This player, living in extremely modest circumstances that quite shocked O'Connor to see, offered his regrets, but said that he too had signed with "another organisation" that had offered him an enormous amount of money.

This other organisation was a rugby union one, he said, but it certainly wasn't SANZAR. The main thing is, this organisation was offering very big money indeed — much bigger than O'Connor could offer for Super League, so he really didn't want to do business with him.

(This, at least, was a moment for the rugby gods in heaven above. Here, perhaps for the first time, was a rugby union player refusing to negotiate with a rugby league recruiter because the league man simply couldn't afford him!)

With more chatting though, a lot of the details came out. Ross Turnbull was mounting this scheme and he'd intimated that the whole thing was being backed by Kerry Packer.

Please do go on.

Pretty much all the Springboks had signed, the player said. It was being organised by Francois Pienaar, who held the contracts for the rebel organisation — and some 130 *other* South African provincial players had also signed.

That night, O'Connor got the head of Super League, John Ribot, on the line.

"So what's happening over there?" Ribot asked. "Have you signed any players? Has the ARL been signing players up, too?"

"Mate, don't worry about the ARL over here," O'Connor began, "there is something much bigger than that happening … "

Waaaaaay to the north, the work of WRC was continuing apace. Throwing out the spiel, hauling in some very big rugby fishies along the way …

From London, Turnbull and Hill had travelled to Paris to meet Eric Blondeau and Bob Simpson again, before heading to Edinburgh, where they had a very quick meeting with the great Scottish full-back Gavin Hastings, who had recently retired.

They all had lunch in a hotel near the airport, Hastings confirmed his interest, and the caravan moved on to Wales to see the Welsh captain, Mike Hall, whom they'd previously met in Johannesburg during the World Cup.

Everywhere it was the same thing.

"What the players wanted, uniformly," Turnbull says, "was a fair return for playing, to be a part of a top-line international competition, and to have a say in the running of the game. WRC gave them all those things."

Then to Ireland to see Brendan Mullin, the recently retired Irish centre. Though Hill and Turnbull both liked Mullin, he clearly wasn't what you'd call their kind of bloke.

In the words of Michael Hill, Mullin was an "establishment bloke. Not helpful to us. Very protective of the Irish.

"But a lovely fellow," recalls Hill quite warmly. "There was no discussion about success fees or anything with Brendan. It was just us asking, 'Do you think Irish players would be interested in this?' and him saying, 'Yes, of course they would be, but it's a big step and we don't want to fracture Irish rugby. Let's wait and see what the International Rugby Board decides at their meeting in August.'"

He eventually agreed to put Hill and Turnbull in touch with a solicitor friend of his, Seamus Connolly, to go over the draft contract, and perhaps he might also have a bit of a discussion with the boys to see what they thought ...

Leo Williams, Chairman of the ARU, had the floor and was setting out the figures to some of the Queensland Wallabies — $A110,000 a year as a base payment, and then another $A110,000 on top of that if they played all the Tests.

The Wallabies listened, for the most part silent, watching, waiting, but like their brethren across the Tasman they certainly weren't doing air-punches. Finally, Rod McCall, always the boldest of the senior Wallabies, put his hand up to speak.

"Leo, I've got a bit of a problem with that formula. You might think that's a lot, but I don't think some of these players are going to stick around for 220 grand."

Williams would have none of it, quickly returning fire, as McCall remembers it: "When you're Chairman, Rod, you can do it the way you like."

Dan Crowley, another of the senior Wallabies, then joined in. A tough undercover policeman in the Queensland Police Force, he was not a man to be cowed easily and so ... he waded in.

"What if we get injured, Leo, what happens to our match payments after that? What do we get of the second 110 grand?"

"Then you'll get nothing," replied Williams.

All up, it was not perhaps a performance best tailored to get the Chairman into the diplomatic service, but in saying all this Williams was totally in tune with the thinking of his own rugby generation.

His rugby attitudes were formed at a time when the honour and glory of wearing the jersey was not only enough, but there were literally thousands of players out there who would have been prepared to cut off their index fingers for the life-long pleasure of having worn that same jersey in battle even once.

He stood there, too, as the head of one of the three most progressive national Unions in the world, which had done more to advance the cause of remunerating the players than any other Union bar New Zealand and possibly South Africa. It was not surprising that he should have been a little nonplussed at the seeming lack of gratitude of the players.

The problem, of course, was that the young men he was speaking to had already moved way beyond that line of thinking, and had made the colossal leap to the point where payment for playing was not a privilege, so much as a *right*.

Some of the assembled players there were sifting their way through as many as *five* offers — from the ARU, the WRC, Super League, the Australian Rugby League, and one or other of the many countries of the northern hemisphere that were prepared to pay truly enormous sums for talented, high-profile, rugby union players.

In England, the WRC agenda was inching forward. Will Carling, at this point, was definitely "out", but he had been replaced in the scheme by that famously pugnacious English hooker, Brian Moore, who was far more Ross Turnbull's kind of bloke.

"I liked him a lot," says Turnbull, "and thought he would be very helpful in accomplishing what we needed."

The "Carling Factor" wouldn't quit, though. According to Carling's agent, John Holmes, "Will had talked to most of the younger players in the team and been told by them that what they most wanted to do was to play for England, that they didn't want to risk all that for WRC. Some of them told him that they were feeling railroaded by Moore and Andrew, and he'd told them just to have nothing to do with WRC but instead work on getting the English union authorities to the table to give the team a good deal."

Moore and Andrew went ahead anyway, at least making some headway in the early stages in getting some of the older players signed up.

It was a two-page fax, coming into Andy Haden's home office in Auckland. It was from Laurie Mains, and it began:

Andy, these players are seeded in order of our assessment of them. I would see it necessary to get some input from senior players to fill the number. We are required to dig a bit deeper than New Zealand selectors would normally go ...

What followed was a list of players in New Zealand, from the "next tier" beneath the All Black level. The required quota in New Zealand was 150, and Laurie Mains' list of 70 or so players was his contribution towards getting the numbers up.

Andy Haden got busy. What was clearly necessary in this exercise was to establish a rough kind of network around the country with "agents" in each major city, together with someone else to get out and about with contracts and a spiel to sell the concept to the provincial players.

What motivated Mains to send the list?

"The request first came from Eric Rush," he recalls. "Sean Fitzpatrick and Eric Rush spoke to me about a list of players that Andy Haden was putting together and I said to them that 'really that list of players should come from people who *know* the players'.

"So Eric and Sean and I discussed it, and ... the result of that was the list being sent. It was to ensure that the right players, with an even spread around the country, were going to be included."

Eric Blondeau was rolling around France. Moving from village to city to village again, he was making contact with players in every rugby stronghold and signing up the players he needed to get his "critical mass". His original list of 120 players had been modified somewhat, as the internationals he already had on contract gave their opinion on a suitable five to six players from their own clubs that would be good for WRC. But the bottom line remained — his briefcase was filling with signed contracts, just as his mailbox had been in those early days of July.

Even now, Blondeau is still staggered at how easily everything had gone for him in the whole exercise.

"*J'ai trouvé* the whole thing extremely exciting," he says, "and just unbelievable how strong the rugby network was. It was like the underground during the war. I mean, most of these players had never met me before, never heard of me, and yet because the internationals that I'd already talked to had told them that I was 'okay', they trusted me. I gave them the contracts, talked to them about it, and then moved on to the next place to do the same. But the power of the rugby network was *extraordinaire*. Once you were locked into it, all things were possible."

By the time Blondeau had returned to Cognac, the first of the signed contracts from these provincial players had already come in.

He also had nearly all of the French World Cup Squad signed up by this time, with the notable exceptions of Philippe Sella and Adbelatif Benazzi. Sella was still unsure whether or not he was going to sign, and Benazzi had gone to Australia on a brief playing stint with Sydney's Warringah club.

The plan was for Benazzi to sign the contract when he was ready, and then hand it directly to the men of WRC in Sydney. So maybe Blondeau didn't have absolutely *everyone* that counted in French rugby on his books, but he had just about everyone else.

The bottom line? Ross Turnbull's "vision" of three months previously, worked out in his Bellevue Hill study, was actually starting to fill up with players — *flesh and blood!* — committing themselves to backing it, so long as the money came through.

So long as the money came through …

Some of the Australian boys were worried. In both Queensland and New South Wales the signed contracts had flowed freely — and there had been absolutely no breach of security back to the Union or the press — but a few second and even third thoughts were starting to set in.

Was this really a go-er? Was there actually backing? Would they be pilloried for betrayal? As one player recalls, "I signed it at the time basically because all the other guys were and I didn't want to be left behind. But then I kept wondering if I was committing myself to something that was obviously a bloody risky proposition, while cutting myself out of the Murdoch money, which was obviously solid."

In his office on the 23rd floor of the MLC Centre — now the virtual WRC command post — Geoff Levy could see that while things had gone better than they could have dreamed in terms of getting the Australian players to sign contracts, it wouldn't hurt to have a little bit of a pump-up session with all the lads together, to calm a few of the jitters.

This was where the resources of one of Kerry Packer's companies, Publishing and Broadcasting Limited, came in very useful. While Packer's organisation was yet to formally commit to the project, they *had* of late been closely monitoring how the signed contracts were coming in, and were happy to help out in such an effort.

With that in mind, two of their leading sports commentators, the former Australian cricket captain, Ian Chappell, and former English cricket captain Tony Greig, were called in to explain to the players just how it had been when World Series Cricket had been formed right under the guns of the establishment.

Chappell had previously had long conversations with Rod McCall about the whys and wherefores of launching something like this, and McCall for starters was a great admirer of the Chappell viewpoint.

The pump-up session went wonderfully well. The Queensland

and New South Wales players all gathered together in the Comtech offices in Sydney and Brisbane for the video conference — while Greig and Chappell in Sydney talked the players through it and answered their questions.

"What can we expect," one player asked, "when WRC launches?"

Chappell gave it to him straight, in the memory of the participants.

"For a while it'll be tough on all of you, as the media gets stuck into you," he said, "and a lot of your just retired team-mates who have missed out will criticise you for having sold out. But eventually it will all come back together and the nastiness will be forgotten.

"You'll have to go through some pain, sure, but the game will emerge a lot stronger because you have had the courage to stay with it, and keep everything secret till the time is right to unveil it. Just like it happened with us when we were setting up World Series Cricket ... "

It was a great speech, and the atmosphere in the studio that night was delicious. It was just like the Bob Dylan song said, "There was music in the cafes at night, and *revolution* in the air!"

Chapter seven

What the hell is going on?

Rupert Murdoch. Sitting right there. At the board-room table. Michael O'Connor was nervous. He'd been rather suddenly summoned by John Ribot to the meeting at News Corporation's Sydney headquarters at Holt Street. He was asked to tell the half-dozen bosses gathered there — including THE BOSS himself — what he knew about this Turnbull scheme he'd come across in South Africa — which clearly had the potential to scupper the deal with SANZAR.

O'Connor, sensing that with blokes like this he should be brief and very much to the point, got as far into the story as he could — 130 South Africans signed, Turnbull and Packer involved, Francois Pienaar organising it, players signed all over the world — before he was interrupted by Sam Chisholm.

Chisholm said he had recently been talking on the phone to Louis Luyt in South Africa, and Luyt had personally assured him that everything was fine. As a matter of fact, Chisholm recounted, he had even recently received a warm letter from Francois Pienaar congratulating him on the SANZAR deal. Chisholm even produced the letter there and then.

O'Connor couldn't help himself.

"Well, I believe Pienaar is a double agent!" he blurted out.

Chisholm stuck to his guns, that Luyt couldn't possibly not know what was happening in his own Union, and that Pienaar couldn't have written a letter like that if he'd signed with another organisation.

O'Connor backed down, way down.

"I didn't think it wise to go on with it," he says now, "because I think I was beginning to look like a fool."

Rupert Murdoch listened, for the most part silently, though he did comment briefly that it would be a very good idea to "keep a close eye on it".

The meeting moved on to other business, and O'Connor was ushered out the door.

In New Zealand, Jock Hobbs was only too pleased to help. The 35-year-old Wellington lawyer and former All Black captain — who had been the youngest ever appointee to the 19-member Council which controls the NZRFU — had been asked by Richie Guy to involve himself in some of the negotiations with the All Blacks. Guy said he couldn't quite pick it, but there seemed something a little odd about their attitude and he thought it might help to have someone younger and closer to the players like Jock Hobbs on board.

Hobbs had, after all, captained Sean Fitzpatrick on the latter's debut tour, in 1986, and they generally got on well.

So it was that Hobbs turned up at the Auckland Airport Travelodge on the morning of Sunday, July 9 — a little under a fortnight before the first of the two Bledisloe Cup Tests between Australia and New Zealand was to begin. Hobbs was joined in the nondescript little hotel conference room — its focal point a table with a white cloth and a bowl of mints at its centre — by other NZRFU negotiators in B.J. Lochore and Richie Guy.

B.J. Lochore, or "B.J." as he is known, had graced the All Blacks firstly as a fearsome forward, then had become a very successful captain of the side, and then later on been the 1987 World Cup-winning coach. He was deeply respected by the players and administrators alike. On the other side of the table, representing the players, were Sean Fitzpatrick, Ian Jones and Eric Rush.

(Interestingly enough, Laurie Mains sat up at the end of the table, appearing to be with neither one side nor the other. Colin Meads, the All Black manager, was also at the meeting.)

What the meeting was about, as far as the negotiators were concerned, was to try and come to some agreement about what the pride of New Zealand would accept in the way of payment for their services. At that time, the New Zealand administrators still had no idea whatsoever that the World Rugby Corporation was out there. All had been done under cover of darkness, with amazing success.

Sure, there was the odd rumour, the occasional sighting of Turnbull here and there around the world, a phone call or two from Australia to say the man was busy and they'd better be on their toes, but it seemed to them at that time that the game was all over.

The NZRFU had signed with Murdoch and that was that. It was very much a case of "Read it in the papers!" as the old sporting expression goes.

Actually, not quite ...

It became apparent very early in the meeting, through the attitude evinced by the players, that the All Blacks were still a long way away from being in the mood to sign any contracts binding them to their national Union.

In oddly formal terms — "speaking with deliberate caution", as Jock Hobbs describes it — the three current All Blacks told the All Black elders that the deal being offered by the NZRFU wasn't good enough, and as a matter of fact they really didn't want to talk about it — *at least* not for another three weeks, when the Bledisloe Cup would be over.

It was an awkward moment. They were all All Blacks in that room, past and present, all legends of the game that's woven deep into the fabric of New Zealand's soul. And yet the gulf between the two sides was an enormous one.

The older generation had played at a time when the principal physical reward of playing for the All Blacks was a solid gold guarantee that you'd have stitches inserted around your eyebrows and, perhaps, one or two teeth knocked out, as in Test after Test you bled for your country.

The younger generation, on the other hand, while just as honoured to wear the famous jersey, were part of the Jordan Generation of sportsmen around the world: not necessarily avaricious or greedy, but simply wanting a fair share of the wealth that they knew they were creating. Just as Michael Jordan had done, with such enormous success.

And, for the first time in rugby history, this group of players was sitting down opposite their administrators, with what seemed like a genuine *alternative* before them. No longer did they simply have to accept whatever conditions their national Union was prepared to grant them.

The WRC proposal was seen among the All Blacks of that time as the best chance they had of staying together, and not being pulled apart by the raid of Super League. The money that Richie Guy had been talking about to this point (around $NZ150,000 a year), was clearly not going to be enough to stop them leaving. No fewer than eight of the All Black World Cup Squad were ready at that time to go to Super League.

In sporting terms, this would have been an enormous pity. For while it is a part of the rugby round that as the seasons come and go sides will undergo a constant process of change, every now and then special teams emerge and there was no doubt from anyone that the 1995 vintage of All Blacks was one of those.

At their best in South Africa they had been beyond "devastating", and in the semi-final against England, particularly, they had seemed to move the possibilities of the rugby game into a new dimension. It was natural that their desire to stay together through whatever means was strong, though what rested as a moot point was whether it was worth staying together if they risked no longer wearing the All Black jersey.

The meeting broke up with the understanding that they would meet again in three weeks so as to formally open serious negotiations.

It was the middle of July, and the figures were good. Back at Wentworth Associates, Geoff Levy was daily examining just how many contracts from around the world had been signed.

The best news was that South Africa and Australia were substantially done, with most of their World Cup Squads having signed up. However, these contracts had not yet been officially "lodged". In both these countries the agreement was that a certain number of World Cup and provincial players had to be signed to WRC before the contracts would be formally handed from the various recruiters to the organisation proper, and consequently have *real* legal force.

The case in New Zealand was similar, if more legally technical. There, the signed All Black contracts were being held *in escrow*, sitting in a safe at Davenports law firm in Auckland. Each of these contracts still required the formal signature of each player on what was effectively a "release form", to enable them to become legally binding and in the possession of the World Rugby Corporation.

Also looking good were Wales, France, Scotland and Western Samoa, where the vast majority of players had legally committed themselves to WRC with very little trouble indeed.

Sure, there remained some significant problems with both Ireland and England, but Levy felt they too would soon fall to the logic of WRC.

Hayman Island lies just off the east coast of Australia, in an area known as the Whitsundays. An oasis of luxury in the middle of the impossibly blue Pacific Ocean — with hot and cold running amenities as far as you can hit a golf ball — it is a location of choice for international conferences and rich tourists alike.

On a weekend in mid-July, the worldwide empire of News Corporation gathered for a conference there.

When Rupert Murdoch summons, people come, and this particular conference boasted such luminaries as the British Opposition leader, Tony Blair — the man touted as that country's next Prime Minister — as well as the incumbent Australian Prime Minister, Paul Keating.

They mixed with heavyweight News Corporation executives from all over the world, including, of course, Sam Chisholm. Chisholm, in the words of one conference delegate, was, "in fantastic form that weekend.

"He was as happy and relaxed as I'd seen him for a long time, right at the top of his considerable game."

And perhaps with good reason. He'd just concluded an enormous ground-breaking deal with one of the biggest sports in the world, he was back in his own Australasian neighbourhood, unchallenged as the most powerful television executive on the planet, the sun was shining, the sea blue, and the reports he had to make to the conference overwhelmingly positive.

A particularly dark cloud was gathering, though — one that was about to rain on his festive parade. On the Saturday night when Chisholm returned to his room, a fax awaited him from Ian Frykberg.

It was a two-page letter detailing a rough outline of WRC, with Frykberg's estimate of where Turnbull was up to — quite advanced

— and it included a copy of a WRC contract that had been leaked to Frykberg from one of the Western Samoan players.

Concerned, if still not quite alarmed, Chisholm showed the letter to the ever-present Bruce McWilliam and asked him his lawyerly opinion. McWilliam read it and replied that as far as he could see, no one would be crazy enough to sign such a vaguely worded document.

Chisholm was not so sure. While the News Corporation conference continued around him, he began to do what he would be doing a ridiculous amount of in the coming weeks — working the phones, ringing contacts in various parts of the world to try and elucidate just what exactly the state of play was.

No progress with signing the Springboks to SARFU. The situation had worsened on all counts. Edward Griffiths had simply been unable to make any headway in getting the World Champions to show any interest whatsoever in having serious negotiations with the national rugby body — but that wasn't the worst of it. The relationship between the players and the administrators had generally become very strained …

On the Monday immediately after most of the Springboks had signed up with WRC at Sun City, the Transvaal-based Springboks had walked out of a Transvaal training session in a serious dispute over their remunerative packages, *or lack thereof*, with the Transvaal Rugby Union. Their catchcry had been, "a professional return for a professional commitment".

According to Johannesburg's *Sunday Times*, "They asked for net monthly remuneration of R15,000 for six months for July to December …

"[The players] also requested that negotiation should begin for the establishment of a medical aid scheme, a pension fund and a fund for the payment of disability benefits."

Unheard of! *Rugby* players having the wherewithal to say they simply weren't going to cop it any more, that if they were going to be instrumental in creating all this wealth, then they bloody well wanted their fair share.

And the attitude of Dr Louis Luyt, who was also the President of the Transvaal Rugby Union? Not happy.

When the players had failed to turn up by the required time on Wednesday afternoon, he had succinctly indicated his own implacable stance on the subject when approached by a radio journalist, and asked a question about the "Springboks" concerned.

Dr Luyt corrected him: "You mean the 'ex-Boks'."

Boom. Boom.

Dr Luyt wasn't kidding, and but for the intervention of Edward Griffiths and Springbok coach Kitch Christie a major sacking of the World Champions of only two weeks previously might well have occurred. Griffiths and Christie managed to come up with a kind of compromise — whereby the Transvaal Springboks would agree to say they were sorry, and Dr Luyt would agree to indeed remunerate them better.

There was still no realisation that Ross Turnbull or this so-called World Rugby Corporation might be the story behind the story, giving the players this unprecedented steel to stand up to the formidable Dr Luyt.

Nothing Edward Griffiths saw or heard during that time persuaded him that it was worth forestalling a trip to Scotland to attend the British Open golf championship, and he flew out a few days later.

Clearly, the situation *vis-à-vis* the All Blacks was increasingly tense, and needed to be resolved quickly. News Corporation took action on its own account. In New Zealand, Richie Guy received a fax from Ken Cowley in Sydney, offering the backing necessary which would enable Guy to guarantee the All Blacks an annual $NZ300,000 a man for three years if they signed *immediately*.

A follow-up phone call to Guy established that this offer would only remain open for 24 hours.

Guy got Sean Fitzpatrick on the phone immediately, telling him of the offer, pointing out that the All Blacks could hardly hope for better than have every man-jack of them guaranteed as millionaires on this one deal alone. Fitzpatrick said he would consult with the players and get back to him …

He did just that. The answer was, "No."

"I just couldn't believe it," says Guy, "and still can't."

For his part, Fitzpatrick cites the episode as an example of how the All Blacks were committed to the WRC concepts for reasons other than simply the financial bottom line.

"We could have quite easily," he says, "if it was [just] a money thing, signed with the New Zealand Rugby Union when they offered us 'x' amount of dollars to sign there and then — no strings attached.

"And maybe in hindsight it would have been a better thing to have done — if it was a dollar issue — but it wasn't, and … I am proud of what we did as a team.

"It wasn't just a money thing."

A brief meeting back in Sydney, just a week before the first of the Bledisloe Cup Tests. Bruce Hayman, the then Chief Executive Officer of the ARU, was asked by Phil Kearns to forestall all negotiations with the team about the Murdoch money, and to make it known to the press the same — that the team not only didn't want to have negotiations, they didn't want to be bothered with questions about them until after the Bledisloe Cup was over and done with.

Hayman readily agreed, then and there, and while in ARU circles there would be some discussion about Kearns' request that the players be left alone, there was no particular consternation.

In the words of Phil Harry, "It was, after all, a rugby sort of decision, 'Hey, let's not talk about this stuff for a couple of weeks, let's beat the All Blacks, and when that's over, let's fix it up.'"

The other factor, of course, was that the threat of Ross Turnbull still wasn't being taken seriously, as Harry acknowledges.

"We had no idea, at that stage, just how far advanced Turnbull was," the ARU President concedes now.

The man in question was actually back in London at that time. Hill had gone on home to tie down the legal end of things in the southern hemisphere, to work the phones, fill the faxes, and make sure that the flow of signed contracts pledged to the World Rugby Corporation kept on coming.

Turnbull was working the British patch, and was trying particularly hard to help Brian Moore and Rob Andrew get the English team signed up.

Turnbull and Moore got on particularly well. Both were lawyers by profession, and both had similar rugby outlooks: Turnbull had been christened "Mad Dog" in his day, just as Moore was known as "Pit-Bull" now. At one point in one of the phone conversations between Turnbull and Moore, the Australian mentioned that he had just come back from a lunch with Simon Le Bon and his supermodel wife Yasmin.

"*Really?*" the English hooker exclaimed. "I've always wanted to meet them … "

"Oh well, why don't you come to dinner with us tomorrow night at the Grill Room at the Savoy?" Turnbull replied.

And so it went. Brian Moore had a good time. Ross Turnbull had a good time. Even Simon and Yasmin Le Bon seemed to enjoy themselves.

Back in Australia, Geoff Levy was delighted to read in Turnbull's daily fax a report of the dinner with the man from Duran Duran.

"We were looking for the Rod Stewart of rugby," he says, "some high profile person who could help make the game more glamorous by their business association, the same way Stewart had with soccer. We thought Simon Le Bon might be that man."

It was late, very late, on the evening after the All Blacks had comprehensively beaten the Wallabies at Eden Park, Auckland, in the First Test of the Bledisloe Cup Series. The dishes from the after-match formal dinner in the Carlton Hotel had long ago been cleared away, and the rugby identities had formed up into little knots all over the room — like you do — drinking and talking.

In one corner of the room, a little after midnight, NZRFU Deputy Chairman Rob Fisher could be seen talking to the All Black breakaway, Mike Brewer. That morning, at a meeting of the NZRFU Council, Fisher had been appointed to the negotiating team with Jock Hobbs and B.J. Lochore, after it had been decided that Richie Guy should take a step back from the whole thing.

Now, Fisher was stumped. Really stumped, as he recalls it …

"I think I said, 'Well Mike, geez, *what* do we have to do to get you guys to sign contracts?'"

After all, what was wrong with Murdoch's money? Wasn't $NZ150,000 a year a pretty good reward for your efforts?

The way Fisher tells it, Brewer could hold it in no longer. After all, he was the same All Black flanker who, when Louis Luyt had been so undiplomatic as to make remarks at the World Cup dinner after the final that South Africa would likely have won the previous two Cups, too — if they hadn't been barred by sanctions — had fronted Luyt then and there to tell him what he thought.

And though he was a lot less aggressive in this instance, he now took a similar approach with Fisher. No, he told Fisher, $150,000 bloody well wasn't a lot of money, especially not when you judge it against the amount of money the All Blacks make for the Union.

And if the NZRFU didn't wake up to themselves, they just might find that the All Blacks will have flown the coop, to join up with "another organisation". It was then that some of the general details of the whole WRC set-up started to emerge.

Before his eyes, Fisher began to get just the barest glimpse of an organisation that had already signed up the world's best players, while all the national Unions had been, figuratively, slumbering peacefully.

Surely it can't be that far advanced. Could it, Mike?

"Fish," Brewer said, looking him right in the eye, "she's all over."

Fisher reeled.

"I was absolutely shattered, *absolutely shattered*," the administrator recalls. "I just couldn't comprehend that all this was happening so close to us, and yet we were so bloody ignorant about it."

The two kept talking. At one point Fisher interrupted Brewer to question why on earth the All Blacks wouldn't at least wait until the International Rugby Board meeting in Paris at the end of the next month, when it was thought they would make a lot of changes to the amateurism regulations — making it even easier for the elite rugby players around the world to earn big-time bucks *within the fold*.

Brewer slowly shook his head. Fisher simply didn't understand how far this thing had gone, how committed the leading international players around the world already were to it.

"Fish," he said, and Fisher remembers these exact chilling words, "I hope you enjoy the last meeting of the International Rugby Board."

Mediiiiiiiccc! Man down near Table Five!

They left it at that. Fisher was profoundly shocked at what he heard, saying now: "If I'd had a little bit too much to drink at the beginning of that chat, I finished it absolutely stone-cold sober."

But at least that night as his mind roamed restlessly, there was some thin comfort in that he'd really only heard this from one player. Brewer had been very circumspect about just who else in the team was actually involved, so there was no telling quite how widely the whole thing had spread into the rest of the side. Maybe, just maybe, Brewer had been exaggerating a bit.

That skinny hope was to die a quick but still *miserable* death the following morning when Fisher, in the company of Jock Hobbs and B.J. Lochore, held a brief meeting with the All Blacks at the

Poenamo Hotel on Auckland's North Shore, to tell them how they planned to proceed from here with negotiations on the Murdoch money.

Before the meeting had even begun, Sean Fitzpatrick asked Fisher on behalf of the team if it would be alright if "our lawyers" sat in.

Our lawyers. Suddenly a formal distance had been built up between the team and the administration. Trying to traverse that distance from this point on would indeed require dealing through those lawyers, Bernie Allen and Derek Dallow from Davenports.

The All Blacks listened to what Hobbs and Lochore had to say about the way they wanted to handle negotiations for the Murdoch money in what seemed like a rather stony silence. When they didn't even perk up upon Hobbs telling them that the NZRFU had decided to give them all $NZ10,000 for the previous day's Test, it was obvious that things were looking grim, but it was only after the players left that the really scary part came.

It was in the suddenly empty conference room that the trio of NZRFU negotiators sat down with the men from Davenports, to see just what the situation was.

As Brewer had been the night before, the lawyers were circumspect, but still revealing in their way. Without specifically confirming or denying the existence of anything called "The World Rugby Corporation" — instead calling them "another party" — they left none of Hobbs, Fisher or Lochore in any doubt that the situation was "quite advanced".

"You've got to understand," the NZRFU trio remember one of these lawyers saying, "that there are offers on the table that are very, very significant, and when players see these sort of figures being mentioned, detail matters less ... "

Though the lawyers did not divulge any figures at that time, the truth of the matter was that the very best of the All Blacks (after Jonah Lomu) would be looking at getting some $NZ500,000 a season, if WRC actually got up, while the establishment money was still locked in at around $NZ150,000 a season.

The NZRFU negotiators sensed they were a long way behind.

The way Jock Hobbs remembers it, "I said [to the lawyers], 'It sounds like we have a lot of work to do,' and they said, 'Well, you know … it's probably *very* late in the day.'"

Hello, New Zealand Rugby Football Union? This is your wake-up call.

Laurie Mains had not been sleeping well. In his Dunedin home, and then in the team hotel, he'd been endlessly tossing and turning, stopping only long enough to stare at the cracks in the ceiling, before returning to toss and turn the whole thing over in his mind some more.

"It was a very, very hard time," he acknowledges now. "One of the toughest times of my life."

He had first heard about WRC on the plane bringing the All Blacks home from South Africa, he says, and though he'd initially been dead-set against it, had at least listened to what his senior players had to say about it. They liked it a lot, and Mains had held his fire.

He acknowledges that one of the turning points in his commitment to the cause was the Geoff Levy presentation at the Wellington motel.

"Geoff Levy impressed me greatly," he says now, "as a man who had a great business sense, who had sympathy for rugby, and as someone who had the ability to actually make something like this work. To me he gave it credibility.

"There came a point when I could see that rugby was going to benefit out of it and I discussed it with Sean and two or three of the senior players and said, well if nothing else comes out of WRC it is going to put pressure on the New Zealand Union to create a better professional environment and better conditions for the players."

The other factor, and perhaps the most crucial of all, as far as Laurie Mains goes, was that the sort of money that WRC was talking was obviously enough to prevent his team being split asunder by rugby league raids, his worst fear of all.

"I would describe my own feelings on that as almost paranoia," he says, "because what I had seen was a crop of young players come along who were outstanding rugby players, able to play the game the way it should be played today and I was distraught at the thought that rugby was going to lose the people that made rugby such a great game."

So, around July 11, he had signed a preliminary commitment to the WRC cause. He could still get out of it if he wanted to, but it was a crucial first step.

"I did not want to be involved at a nuts-and-bolts level, at that stage," he says, "and I did not want to do any recruiting. I had been approached by a WRC agent in New Zealand to accept money to sign up players. I rejected that offer outright."

On the Sunday afternoon after 1995's first Bledisloe Cup Test, in Mains' room on the second floor of the Poenamo Hotel, the All Black coach had a long heart-to-heart with the All Black manager, Colin Meads.

"Colin and I were very close," Mains recounts, "and I had to tell Colin what was going on. I could not look the man in the eye. I mean Colin is as straight as a die and I just couldn't live with it a second longer, so I told him totally about my involvement.

"I didn't give him names of any players or anything like that but I told him exactly what I was doing, in confidence. I told him that I was bound by this confidentiality agreement and would he please respect it, but I couldn't look him in the eye without telling him. So I told him everything."

Meads listened silently, and thereafter kept his counsel, though, as Mains recalls …

"Colin thanked me for telling him my position and said, 'you have got to do what is best for you'."

Through much of the Rugby War in New Zealand, Meads' position would be difficult to discern, perhaps even for himself. In the words of one of the New Zealanders close to the action, "Colin was for the players, he was for the All Blacks, he was for Laurie, and he was definitely for the NZRFU."

Contradictory? Of course, but …

"That about sums it up," says Meads himself. "I found the whole thing very, very difficult."

He wasn't Robinson Crusoe either.

For the following two days in Wellington, Hobbs, Fisher, and the Chairman of the NZRFU Finance Committee, Richard Crawshaw, worked their way through data of how much money the Murdoch deal would actually bring in and how many players it would best be distributed among. In so doing they were able to come up with the figures to put on contracts that they were even then fine-tuning.

There would be four categories of contracts — Elite All Blacks, All Blacks, At Risk Players and Standard Contracts.

The money offered to Elite All Blacks at this time was $NZ250,000. The remainder of the All Black Squad would be on around $NZ200,000. A third category were At Risk Players — top fringe players likely to defect to league — who were also on $NZ200,000.

Finally, there were the Standard Contracts, which were essentially for the provincial players. They were offered $NZ50,000 if they played in all the Super 12 games, $NZ15,000 for all the National Provincial Championship games, and the balance of up to $NZ85,000 if they made it into the All Blacks. This made it a total gross payment of $NZ150,000 for new Test players who completed a full season.

At least, at the bare, hungry, sniffing minimum, the negotiators had something to show the lawyers from Davenports on Wednesday when they met them in their Auckland offices. Here, see, we too are well organised, with serious proposals to make, and this is what the contract looks like.

Oh yeah? Well this is what a list of the grievances of the All Blacks looks like, all eight of them, ranging from a desire for greater player representation at the decision-making level of the administration, to a warning that the contract terms detailed so far were simply not good enough.

At the conclusion of that meeting, nevertheless, Jock Hobbs and Rob Fisher were able to persuade the lawyers that it would be a good idea if they could come to Sydney the following day to talk to Sam Chisholm of News Corporation, who would be in town. He would be able to give them a clearer picture of where the Murdoch money stood in all this.

In agreeing to attend that meeting, the Davenports lawyers were operating on the assumption that the best way to advise their clients — essentially the All Blacks, though many of the players were receiving independent legal advice — was to have as much information as possible on just what offers were on the table, and the level of backing for each offer.

North of the Equator, news of what WRC was up to was just starting to reach the press. The famous French rugby newspaper, *Midi-Olympique*, had published an article on Monday, July 24, setting out the bare basics of the WRC scheme and reporting the disturbing fact that some of the internationals might already have signed. It was followed up the next day by *L'Equipe*, France's leading sports newspaper, which quoted Philippe Sella saying that while he had decided against going on with it, he was here to tell the readers that the whole thing was under way. He was not complimentary about the way the WRC men in France had gone about it.

"It seemed to me from the beginning," he said, "that the

organisation behind the concept was even more important than the contents of their contract. We wanted to have time to study it all with lawyers, to weigh up the different arguments. But the two emissaries from WRC wanted to go as quickly as possible, in order to be able to deal with the television stations and potential sponsors. That jumped right out at me."

Sella said that he had been offered 1.2 million francs (about $US250,000), just for one season, but that he wanted no part of it.

Others around the world did decide to be a part of it, though sometimes with extreme reluctance. Back in Sydney at around that time, the Wallaby fly-half who had replaced Michael Lynagh in the Test team, Scott Bowen, had just been on his way to go to training from the team hotel, when he was obliged to finally make a decision on whether or not he was going to sign with WRC.

Approached by recruiters, Bowen told the journalist Peter Jenkins that, "I was told I needed to sign now. If I didn't, they might start looking elsewhere.

"It was like: 'WRC don't want you on board unless you come now. You could lose the chance and you could be left playing in a Mickey Mouse competition if you're not part of it all.'

"I was pretty naive about the whole thing and was going with the flow," he said, looking back on it. "I signed because everyone else was. I think only Jason Little, Tim Gavin, and a couple of others hadn't put pen to paper … "

The stranglehold of WRC on the world's elite players was clearly tightening, and if the "establishment" side of the fight weren't yet fully aware of that, it was at least obvious that Sydney was the main theatre of operations for the skirmish at that time.

For it wasn't just Chisholm who was heading to Sydney Town at that time. Ian Frykberg had flown in a few days before. Louis Luyt had come from South Africa. Kevin Roberts had winged his way from Auckland, as had Richie Guy. Partly it was to see the second Test of the 1995 Bledisloe Cup Series, but in many ways the result of that game was now a matter of total indifference. There was a *far* bigger game going down, and everyone knew it.

The stakes on the SANZAR deal with Murdoch, and whether it lived or died, were suddenly and obviously enormous. Screamingly apparent was the fact that if the World Rugby Corporation really did get up and running, then the deal between News Corporation and the three southern Rugby Unions would be profoundly off.

It was Chisholm's opinion that, under the terms of the document that Dr Luyt had signed, he and his organisation would be free to walk away from it if the Unions did not secure their top players.

And something even worse beckoned. If the deal fell through because the players hadn't been signed, Sam Chisholm claims to have had legal opinions to the effect that not only might the Unions be legally *liable* for not having done so, but so also might be individual directors of those Unions whom, he claimed, had not followed through on their part of the deal.

Both were threats he gave free vent to in these trying days, and at least one of the Chairmen took the threat seriously enough that he sought legal advice as to whether or not he could be held liable.

But come, come, come, we're all men here. Would Chisholm have actually gone to the point of suing the Unions, possibly even the officials of those Unions?

"I never make a threat that I'm not prepared to carry out," Chisholm says flatly.

The national Unions, in Chisholm's mind, "had gone to sleep at the wheel" — and he certainly was not in the mood to hear any excuses that the players had simply declined to negotiate.

Not good enough.

His business success had been built on the notion that "assumption is the mother of all [stuff]-ups", and while *he'd* never assumed that the players were in the bag, he'd at least trusted that the Unions would heed his warning to get them signed quickly.

And now, clearly, they hadn't done it.

What to do then, from his own point of view?

"Well," he said, "we could have sat back and said, 'We've bought these rights and we want them delivered to us.' But we formed a judgement that they couldn't do it on their own and there was little point in me sitting on the side-lines, so I rolled my sleeves up and got into it."

And how.

Chisholm arrived in Sydney with a fair idea already of how generally serious the situation was, even if he still lacked for detail.

For days and nights, from his London headquarters, he had endlessly worked the wires, trying to ferret out what was going on. A man of many contacts, Murdoch's chief of world television operations usually had the ability to winkle information out of walnuts, but in this case it was initially proving hard to do.

Simon Poidevin was Chisholm's key man on the ground in the international rugby landscape, relaying reports on what seemed to be happening with the players, who it might be a good idea to call now, what the personalities of the various people he would be talking to were like, and suggesting how it would be best to handle them.

In terms of hard information, though, as in numbers of players signed up, even Poidevin was mystified at this early stage at "just how much the rot had set in", even in his own stamping ground of the current Wallaby team.

Rumours swirled; there was a lot of talk of "letters of intent", suggestions that maybe the whole lot of them had promised themselves over, but nothing actually solid.

Ross Turnbull's original premise — that the "Tour Secrets Act" would hold — was proving entirely true in the Australian case.

A breakthrough, if you could call it that, came at lunchtime on the Wednesday before the Second Bledisloe Cup Test, in Sydney. Poidevin and Ian Frykberg had arranged a midday meeting at the Japanese restaurant at the top of Sydney's ANA hotel, with the Lion Nathan chief, Kevin Roberts.

Poidevin and Frykberg had asked to speak with him, because they felt at last they might be able to get some hard information about just what the hell was really happening.

Roberts arrived late, and was the bearer of bad news.

"They've gone," he said simply. "Most of the All Blacks have signed, most of the Wallabies have signed, nearly all of the Springboks have signed too. They've gone."

Roberts was not whistling dixie. For the past few days, he too had been ringing around and talking face-to-face with the key players in the saga. His relationship with both Laurie Mains and Sean Fitzpatrick was particularly close, and he had fronted both of them — saying to them he wanted the truth, he wanted it *now*, and he wanted it totally. They were not to hold anything back. They didn't.

Both men told Roberts the essential details of the scheme, and how far advanced it was around the world. While Roberts had a great deal of sympathy for their stated goals — getting the All Blacks a fair shake for their skills, and keeping the team safe from the predatorial advances of Super League — he was equally frank with them in return.

"I said to them," he recalls, "'I understand what you're on about. But *nobody* is going to take the game away from New Zealand, and you are going to see incredible public antipathy if this is tried. I approve of the ends but I will not approve of the means and I don't think New Zealand will either.'"

In his lunch with Poidevin and Frykberg, Kevin Roberts did not recount any of the detail of his conversations with Mains and Fitzpatrick — or the many talks he'd had since with other leading players, including Eric Rush — but he did hammer away at the fact that the situation was extremely well advanced.

"I suppose what I was saying," Roberts says, "was, 'listen guys, don't think you have got a lot of time on your hands, don't think this is conceptual. Don't think that what you've got on the table at the moment is sufficient. You've got to *get serious*.'"

And his agenda in telling them?

"I wanted to see rugby reformed," Roberts says. "I was trying to get a better deal for the players and for rugby, but under the auspices of the Rugby Unions. I did not want this game taken away from the Unions."

After Roberts had made his points, the rest of the lunch went by in a daze of discussion about just what the ramifications of the signings were, whether the WRC crowd really would be able to come up with the $US100 million that they'd promised by November 22, and just what the best way to proceed from this point was.

Before dessert, Roberts had to leave to go to another meeting, leaving Frykberg and Poidevin to ponder alone. If there was to be a rock-bottom in the whole affair, at least in the minds of Frykberg and Poidevin, it was to be here and now. By Poidevin's count a full five minutes went by before either he or Frykberg spoke.

"We simply sat there, unable to speak, consumed by the misery of what Roberts had told us," he recalls.

"We were dumbstruck," Frykberg agrees.

It was done. On this very day, July 26, almost at that very hour, Kerry Packer's organisation PBL had at last, formally, come "on board". Though this Loan and Option agreement signed between Publishing and Broadcasting Limited and the World Rugby Corporation is likely never to see the light of day, its essence was that in return for an initial outlay of some $A4 million, PBL was given an option to acquire majority ownership of the World Rugby Corporation Pty Ltd. The deal was structured so that at various time intervals over the next few weeks, the Packer organisation could put in progressively greater amounts of money, and assert ever greater control. Or, they could pull out if things were not to their liking, with only the funds already committed gone ...

Whatever, in the first instance Levy, Turnbull & Co. now had the money they so desperately needed to keep going on the project, and they also had some much needed credibility in the ongoing struggle to demonstrate to players that they really did have some serious backing.

It was marvellous, incidentally, what just the mention of the Packer name could do at all levels of the saga ...

Few knew that better than Rod McCall, who was by this time moving through the second and third tiers of Australian rugby and signing them up also. (The brutes hadn't picked him in the Test Squad to play the New Zealanders, so he found himself regrettably free.)

"Guys would say to me at the beginning, 'What chance do you reckon there is that this can really come off?'" McCall says, "and I'd say, 'probably 70/30 against us'.

"But once I knew Kerry Packer was really in, I could say, 'Well, I know one thing for sure: *he's* not an idiot, and he's going to have to make a go of it and sell it worldwide and make his money. You know he's involved in it, so it *has* to be viable.'"

Specifically why Kerry Packer supported WRC to the tune of several million dollars at this time — the first financial commitment he'd made to the project — is a moot point. And it is likely to remain one, as he is not a man prone to divulging his motivations.

What is clear, though, is that this deal had inbuilt advantages for him. If the whole WRC concept worked, then he would have control of a first-rate televisual "product", in demand all over the world, and over a half share of a corporate money-making machine that could well prove the envy of the professional sporting world. And if it didn't work, well, then this famously heavy gambler was still no further in the hole than he would have been after a bad night at a Las Vegas casino.

But even if it didn't work quite to the extent that PBL wanted, it still was a significant pressure point to have on the Murdoch body corporate, to press down hard upon when other matters between the Murdoch and Packer camps were to be negotiated in a few weeks time.

The Murdoch crowd had $US555 million of their capital promised to this venture over the next 10 years. For the sake of a lazy few million dollars, Packer was able to sit at the table of the endless poker game that seems to be the business relationship between he and Murdoch, happy in the knowledge that he was holding one extremely troublesome joker that could irk his opponent more than somewhat.

The evening after the agreement had been signed, Geoff Levy was having a quiet dinner with his wife at the Hakoah Club in Bondi, on Sydney's eastern edge, when his mobile phone rang.

It was one of the Wallabies, who was extremely upset because he'd just been told that his job with his provincial Union was in jeopardy because of his presumed association with WRC. It took Levy some four phone calls, but he was fairly quickly able to secure this Wallaby a guaranteed job with one of his friends. He called the Wallaby to pass on the good news, and then the mobile rang again.

This was a rather more significant problem. It was WRC's lawyer in Johannesburg, Jennis Scholtz, and he was in the company of Francois Pienaar.

The lawyer told Levy that he had Pienaar here, and that the Springbok captain had confirmed that the contracts were signed and he was holding them for WRC.

"Have you got that on paper?" Levy asked.

"No," the lawyer replied, "but we've got Francois' word that he's holding the contracts as agent for us … "

"I don't *want* the guy's word because I can't show that to the backers!" Levy remembers exploding. "I want his commitment, *on paper*. I want you to get him to sign something which is proof positive that he's holding the contracts for us."

There was a pause on the other end of the line, as Levy remembers it. Then the voice returned.

"Listen, we can't ask him to do that. I think we just have to accept his word."

"Look, put him on!" Levy finally burst out.

A conversation then ensued between Geoff Levy and the Springbok captain, which included, in Levy's memory, the following interchange:

"Hello, *Meneer* Levy."

"Just call me Geoff," Levy replied. "Francois, how do you hold these contracts?"

"Geoff, there's no problem, I hold them as your agent. Don't worry, all the boys are going to do what I tell them," Levy remembers him replying.

"Francois, I have to have that in writing."

"Why do you need it in writing?"

"Because I've got backers and I have to prove to them that you hold them as agent, I have to have it in writing!" Levy continued a little more aggressively, starting to feel his gander rise again.

"What's the problem, what are you getting excited about? Look, I'll send it to you now, I'll fax it to you now, don't worry. Calm down. I'll send it to you now."

And Pienaar was as good as his word.

Ten minutes later a phone call from Jennis Scholtz confirmed that the fax had been sent, and the following morning when Levy arrived at work, it was there waiting for him on his desk. Beneath the letterhead of Scholtz and Botha lawyers, it read:

I the undersigned, FRANCOIS PIENAAR,

hereby confirm that I hold 28 agreements of the TWRC as furnished to attorneys Scholtz & Botha, in the same form as the agreements furnished to the said attorneys, which agreements have been entered into with 28 players of the S.A. World Cup Squad.

The agreement with Chester Williams has been destroyed, at his request.

I confirm that an amount of $US300,000.00 has been agreed by your Mssrs M Hill and R Turnbull for my services as agent in this regard.

I confirm that I will hand over the agreements as soon as the financial commitments, as per the TWRC agreement has been verified by the Ernst & Young auditing company.

Yours faithfully,

Francois Pienaar.

Levy was satisfied. He filed it in one of the now bulging WRC files, and got busy with more phone calls.

In London, the International Rugby Board hauled up its colours. They ignored the whole thing, and hoped it would go away.

"Look, we really are not commenting at this stage," their administrative officer, Hugh Penman was quoted as saying. "It's at a wait-and-see position but I doubt it's going to happen.

"[IRB] controls the game around the globe and we have a meeting in three weeks to discuss payments for players.

"The Packer proposal is a non-event for us. Wait for exciting news after our next meeting."

"It was pretty strong stuff," Jock Hobbs recalls. That Thursday he'd flown in from Auckland in the company of two Davenports lawyers, Bernie Allen and Christopher Morris, and they'd gone straight from the airport to Sam Chisholm's house in St Ives on Sydney's quietly green North Shore. At least it was mostly quiet ...

On that morning, according to Hobbs' notes of the meeting, Chisholm had launched at them along the lines of, "I have put up the money, made the commitment, was assured that the players would be there and now it is a *bloody mess* and I am very pissed off.

"My expectation was that all the players would sign and if it's not resolved I am going to send a battery of lawyers to New Zealand and will sue all and sundry and the whole thing will get bogged forever."

Hobbs and the Davenports lawyers listened, and left.

The plan at that stage was for the men from Davenports to make contact with their clients, and then come back and meet with Hobbs, Rob Fisher and Frykberg in the bar of Sydney's ANA Hotel at 2pm.

"Well then, Phil, why don't you come and talk to some of the News Corporation people?" Poidevin remembers asking Phil Kearns, that same Thursday lunchtime. The two had spoken at a Carbine Club rugby luncheon, and Poidevin was seeking, with something close to desperation, to have the Australian captain at least open lines of communication with the News Corporation side of things.

He still didn't know for sure if Kearns had signed with WRC or not, but strongly suspected he had. So why not at least come and talk to the Murdoch folk?

"I'll have to check with Fitzy," the Wallaby captain replied, referring to Sean Fitzpatrick. It was all Poidevin could do to keep himself from groaning out loud.

Time changes all things, all relationships. In 1989, a 22-year-old Phil Kearns had been plucked out of the Randwick Reserve Grade side to make his debut with the Wallabies. Against the All Blacks at Eden Park.

Before that game he had a long talk with Poidevin in the privacy of the Wallabies' hotel about what Test-match rugby involved, what was expected from the new boy, and how Poidevin had every confidence that Phil would acquit himself well against the highly-regarded All Black hooker Fitzpatrick.

So long as Kearns never let himself be intimidated, Poidevin told him, so long as he kept boring into Fitzpatrick in the scrum and belting him on suspicion in open play, Kearns would go well. It was a confidence that proved well placed, as Kearns had a strong debut in what would be the first of many torrid encounters between him and Fitzpatrick.

Throughout that particular Test, on the occasion of the scrum, Poidevin could occasionally hear snatches of Fitzpatrick insulting Kearns, telling him such things as, "What are you doing here?", "You're just a little boy" and "Why don't you go home to Mummy?"

Kearns had just taken it without making particular reply, concentrating on his own play, and Poidevin had been proud of how well he'd gone. And *now*, Kearns had to check with Fitzpatrick before meeting with some of the News Corporation people!?!?!

"I guess it was then that I really felt that we'd lost him," says Poidevin.

Kearns, for his part, remembers the conversation going substantially the same way, adding only that, "By this time, the whole thing was an international movement, and I thought in doing something like that it really would be a good idea to check with Fitzpatrick."

So where the hell were the lawyers from Davenports? At the appointed time, Hobbs, Fisher and Ian Frykberg had waited, and waited, and waited some more in the bar of the ANA — going through bowl after bowl of peanuts, as other clientele came and went — but there was still no sign of the lawyers as the hours ebbed away.

The three sat talking quietly, staying away from the alcoholic drinks so as to keep totally clear heads for the negotiations that they hoped were to come when the lawyers arrived. Finally, at 6pm, Fisher had had enough, and called the lawyers up at their hotel.

"Yes," he told the receptionist, "I'd like to speak to Mr Bernie Allen please."

The reply came back quickly from the hurried receptionist.

"Mr Allen's on the phone," she said before perhaps recognising Fisher's New Zealand accent. "Is that *you*, Mr Mains? Because I think he is trying to ring you at the moment in response to your message."

Fisher, taken aback at what seemed like such a close relationship between Laurie Mains and the lawyers from Davenports, said, "I will ring back."

He put the phone down quietly, sucking for breath. Just how far had this thing *gone*? Was the All Black coach *also* in on this? It was the first time Fisher had even considered the possibility.

By 10 o'clock that night, the lawyers still hadn't come and Fisher and Hobbs had retired to the latter's room to discuss things further. It was then that a rather chilling phone call came. It was from Bernie Allen, the Davenports lawyer. He sounded a bit upset. Sorry they hadn't made the meeting, Allen said, but they'd met with their "clients" and been clearly instructed not to have any further meetings with the Murdoch camp, or even the NZRFU. The lawyers were still available to act as a conduit of formal information to the All Black camp, he said, but that was all.

"So what do you think this all means?" Hobbs asked him. "Are we dead?"

There was a pause. A long one.

"Well," Allen finally replied, and Hobbs can remember the exact intonation and wording to this day, "if you previously had one finger on the window ledge, you're now hanging on by half a finger-nail."

Hobbs didn't sleep well that night.

It was just one of literally thousands of telephone conversations that took place because of WRC's existence at around this time. This one was between Ian Frykberg, in the ANA Hotel, and Sam Chisholm, now well installed in his St Ives house.

As Frykberg recalls it, "Sam said, 'This is a crisis, what are you going to do about it you bastard, you sold us this thing and now you can't fucking *deliver!*'

"I said, 'Look Sam, I accept that we have a fucking crisis, but I don't know what the extent of it is. I accept there is a crisis, we're on it, we are doing fucking everything we can!'

"He said, 'It's not good enough! Don't you ever fucking come back to News Corp with a deal again! Next time you come to News Corp you make sure you've got the deal *all signed!*'"

Truth be told, Chisholm *was* more than a little frustrated.

"They couldn't deliver what they promised to do," Chisholm says now. "That was the extraordinary thing, it was like building a house and then renting it off yourself … "

All up, as Frykberg remembers, "There were some very tense moments over a long period. Sure, I have had a long-standing relationship with Chisholm, but I'd have to say that this rugby deal placed a lot of strain on it on a number of occasions."

'Twould seem so.

The word was out. Jock Hobbs, through phone calls back to New Zealand, had got wind of something very interesting indeed. According to his contacts, Eric Rush was even then flying all over New Zealand, talking to provincial players and coaches, signing some players up for WRC, and at least getting promises from others that they would definitely look at the documentation he was leaving with them and get back to him if they were interested in signing.

Hobbs, ever a man for getting out there and among it quickly, took immediate action. Two phone calls later and the job was done.

From that point on, for the next two days, the marketing department of the NZRFU back in Wellington kept phoning all the provincial Unions and telling them to be on the look-out for Rush. If he contacted them, then the basic message was "don't do anything until you've heard from the NZRFU first".

A large map of New Zealand was even got out to track exactly where Rush had been and where he was likely to go next. Brendon O'Connor, who was in charge of the effort, at last picked him up on their radar screens at about two o'clock in the afternoon. A phone call to a leading Manawatu player revealed that Rush had been there and had left two hours previously.

Another look at the map, and it was obvious. Hawkes Bay. A single call to one of their leading players, and … *bingo*.

"Rushie left just a few minutes ago," their informant told them.

There was never any question of sending out an "All Points Bulletin" on Rush, or hauling him in — it was Rush's perfect legal right to go wherever he wanted to go and say whatever he wanted to say. It was the aim of the NZRFU marketing department, though, to at least try to put the provincial players in a holding pattern, and get them not to do anything rash until further contact could be made during the following week and an alternative proposal put to them.

A lesser version of the same episode would take place in Australia the following day, when the NSW Rugby Union Football Director, Matt Carroll, sent out a faxed letter to Sydney club officials. The letter included this paragraph: "Please be advised that the Union has confirmation that Troy Coker has organised meetings of players … to sign the players to Turnbull's rebel circus."

This ol' Rugby War was heating up …

Chapter eight
Three days in July

Sydney Town, Friday, July 28, 1995.

There is a special buzz in rugby towns the day before major Test matches, and on this unseasonally warm winter's day Sydney was in full grip of it. But this time the buzz had a rather jarring, jangling note to it.

The morning's newspapers had brought more news that something called the World Rugby Corporation had signed up most of the players due to play in the following day's Bledisloe Cup encounter between the All Blacks and the Wallabies. All three, *The Sydney Morning Herald, The Daily Telegraph Mirror* and *The Australian*, claimed the same thing — that the players were going, going, gone.

Simon Poidevin read the stories while sitting at the kitchen table of his seaside Coogee home, slowly shaking his head at each succeeding paragraph.

It wasn't so much that there was a lot of new information in it from his perspective, but rather seeing it there — black on white in the newspapers — really brought home the fact that the whole wretched thing was *actually* happening.

What's more, Wallabies and All Blacks whom he'd played with and against, many of them his personal friends, were signing in droves.

Time to move. On his way to work he passed the hotel where the All Blacks were staying, just 200 metres down the road from where he lived. Then a few more twists and turns, and he was onto Alison Road, heading towards the city and another day of phone calls and meetings to try and thwart the perfidious rebels.

Coming in the opposite direction at exactly the same time, Geoff Levy quite possibly passed Poidevin in the traffic. The lawyer was heading towards the All Blacks' hotel, on a mission. Enough of this nonsense. To this point the All Blacks had been quite happy to talk the talk, now it was time for them to walk the walk.

"What I knew," Levy says now, "was that there was a real possibility that these guys were going to be banned, kicked out of traditional Test-match rugby, and I needed two things that morning. I needed a personal assurance from them that they really had the stomach to keep going if that happened and, more importantly, I wanted their signatures on release forms, to give force to the contracts they'd already signed.

"All the international players around the world were talking to each other, and all the other players assumed the New Zealanders were in because the New Zealanders had told them they were committed, but technically, *legally*, they weren't."

With this in mind, Levy had arranged to meet with five of the most senior All Blacks and one of their most senior officials in a private conference room on the ground floor of the hotel, after they had completed their morning training. Such were the times that Levy was again, uncharacteristically, het up. After a few preliminary remarks, he was ready to roll …

"Okay guys, this is enough!" he remembers beginning. "I need you guys to all sign these forms, so the contracts have legal force. Because technically, legally, these contracts still aren't signed."

The word back from those senior All Blacks was that Geoff should just calm down a bit, that there was nothing to worry about, that they were all still with him all the way; in any case, in the minds of most of the All Blacks, they already had signed.

"No, I want things 100 per cent kosher," Levy says he replied. And so it went, to-ing and fro-ing.

The All Blacks said Levy would just have to trust them. Levy said that wasn't good enough, he wanted *all* the All Blacks who'd already signed the contracts to sign the release forms.

The most senior All Black on site said that that was out of the question, as doing such a thing the day before a Test match would mess with the psyches of the younger players and put way too much pressure on them. But, he said, "I guarantee you we'll do it before we leave."

"Well, you've *got* to do it before you leave," Levy recalls replying, "and it has to be done before the Bledisloe Cup centenary dinner tomorrow night because if you don't [commit to it] before then, they might try to get to you at the dinner and all this crap will go on, you know?"

The senior All Black on site made reply:

"Alright, we'll give you our undertaking that we'll arrange it. We'll get the boys as soon as they've showered onto a bus, and you tell us where you want to meet the bus and we'll get them all to sign the forms for you."

Levy agreed. But just a second before you go there, lads ...

"Okay," he remembers telling them, "I'm prepared to understand you don't want to go and stuff up the psyche of the young guys, but you five big guys, you're the senior players — I need you to give me your commitment here and now. I need *you* to sign the release forms."

One of the players initially declined, saying he wanted to think about it, but the other four signed on the spot. So did the official, when Levy prevailed upon him too, to make the commitment. The deal was done.

"I think they wanted to prove to me," Levy says now, "that I shouldn't have a lack of confidence in them. They wanted to prove to me that it didn't matter what happened, they'd made their commitment to me and that was it."

After a "thank you" and a firm warning that they had to be mentally prepared to be banned from the game, because at that stage he felt that was really on the cards, Levy left, feeling a lot better.

B.J. Lochore had arrived in Sydney. He'd been rung in the middle of the night at his farm in Wairarapa, north of Wellington, and told that he was urgently needed on site to try and keep the lines of communication between the NZRFU and the All Blacks open.

The most deeply respected figure in the New Zealand game, B.J. had been particularly requested to be there by Jock Hobbs, who wanted him to be on the sidelines at the All Black training session, just in case any of the players wanted to talk to him. And if they didn't that was okay, too.

In the rather poetic words of Rob Fisher, "B.J. could look players in the eye and make them feel embarrassed because they knew what he did not know."

Again the tables were set up in the defensive wagon-train formation, again in the spacious rooms at the top of the ARU's offices in North Sydney. The people around the table were trying to ward off the attack that had been launched by the World Rugby Corporation, and this meeting on Friday afternoon was to determine just what the scope of this attack was, what damage it had already done, and how best to counter it.

Around the table sat Ian Ferrier, Richie Guy, Leo Williams, Louis Luyt, David Moffett and various other officials of the international Rugby Unions, while it was Ian Frykberg who had the floor.

"Listen!" he said, once he had their full attention. "We have a full-blown crisis on our hands. There's a few things you blokes have got to realise, *immediately*. You've lost all the All Blacks, you've lost about 50 of your provincial players in New Zealand. In Australia you've lost all your Wallabies except maybe one or two, plus 30 state players! In South Africa you have lost *150 players!*"

Consternation around the table. Disbelief. Replies that it couldn't possibly be as bad as Frykberg was making out, because such and such player, who they'd known for 10 years, had looked them in the eye and told them that he hadn't signed and nor had the others.

"I'm telling you," Frykberg remembers continuing, "whatever they are saying to you, however long you've known them, they are NOT telling you the FUCKING TRUTH! We have got a *crisis!*"

Louis Luyt, who had flown in a couple of days before for further talks on SANZAR business, still didn't want to hear it. The way participants at the meeting remember it, he simply couldn't believe even at this late stage that his Springboks, let alone so many provincial players, would ever have signed with Turnbull.

In the first instance, he refused to even countenance Frykberg's contention that there was "a crisis", and insisted on making a phone call to South Africa to check it. Whoever it was that Dr Luyt called definitely had his or her finger on the pulse, because after a 30-second conversation in Afrikaans, the Chairman of SARFU snapped his mobile phone shut and said with a heavy affirmative nod, "We have a crisis."

More earnest discussion followed, but the meeting had to be cut short because some of the gentlemen there had an even more pressing engagement.

Sam Chisholm had summoned the Chairmen of the three Unions for his own crisis talks, and it was definitely a good idea not to be late.

At least Frykberg had warmed them up for what was coming …

At 5.30pm, at Chisholm's house, they gathered. In his living room, around his coffee table, the three Chairmen, plus David Moffett, Jim Fitzmaurice, Bruce McWilliam and Ian Frykberg sat, a little nervously. Chisholm had something to say, and he said it with great force — most specifically to the national Chairmen.

A synopsis of his remarks could be boiled down to this:

"Listen, you blokes, you've got to get your arses into gear on this, get out your chequebooks and start paying your players a fair dollar. By offering them the money you have been, you're jeopardising this whole deal!

"We did a deal, and you're not delivering what you *promised*. You have sold me rights which you can't deliver! *You can't deliver!* I've told you and told you and *told you* about getting the players on board, and you simply HAVEN'T DONE IT!"

An angry Chisholm is a sight to behold, with his voice getting raspier and more intense with every word. One of the Chairmen came in for a particularly withering blast.

"I'm sorry to have to tell you this, but your players just *don't like you*," Chisholm said. "They think you're a joke. You've got to get with it, get moving!

"I mean it," he continued to all of the Chairmen generally. "We're tired of this! If you don't get serious, and I mean right now, then the whole thing will fall through and the deal will be *off*.

"It is a sheer indictment of you all that Turnbull has been able to make the progress that he's made!"

It was a magnificent harangue, more a verbal cyclone than a speech, and it would have taken a very strong man to voluntarily put himself in the way of it.

As a matter of fact, though, Louis Luyt was just that man. After Chisholm had been going at them for 15 minutes solid, Luyt remonstrated with Chisholm, saying in his thick South African accent, "You must stop speaking to us like this. We are not school children. If you must say these things, get your lawyer there to send us a letter."

Chisholm paused momentarily, stared briefly at Luyt, told him to "calm down", and then sailed on regardless — a battleship that had hit a very good-sized whale indeed, but remained entirely undamaged.

On the subject of Dr Luyt, Sam Chisholm was most insistent and specific. It was CRUCIAL that the South African Chairman get the World Champion Springboks signed up on contract. Whatever it took, Chisholm didn't care, but Luyt had to get them signed! They would be absolutely pivotal to whether or not the Unions around the world were going to be able to maintain control. Louis, you've got to get to it! Got to get the Springboks signed!

Dr Luyt again argued the toss.

"I said," the South African chief recalls, "'Look, for every one of those guys we have a replacement, in some cases better … '"

Chisholm didn't want to hear it. He wanted the Springboks, the same ones who'd won the World Cup in such sterling fashion, and he wanted Louis to go as close as he could to matching the payments that WRC was offering them. Frykberg would even go along to South Africa with him, to help with negotiations.

Eventually the storm passed. As was Chisholm's way, after the strength of the message had been delivered and everyone had been seen to *get the message*, he suddenly became quite pleasant again and a normal discussion ensued as to how best to proceed from this point.

The meeting broke up at about seven o'clock, with Luyt in particular agreeing that he would indeed — upon his return to South Africa the following day — open the coffers and start shovelling some serious money the Springboks' way.

He even made the crucial call from Chisholm's house, organising for the 13 Transvaal Springboks — who were always going to be pivotal to whatever deal was done — to meet him in his Johannesburg home on Sunday at 10am.

Nice morning. The day of the second Bledisloe Cup Test, in Sydney. Outside, the sun was shining, the birds were singing, a very gentle sea breeze was coming from the east.

Inside, no one gave a single solitary damn about the weather. At least not inside the main conference room of The Rocks' Parkroyal Hotel, which lies in the shadow of the Sydney Harbour Bridge.

For it was there that an emergency meeting was being held of the New Zealand Rugby Football Council. All 19 members of that Council had made the trip to Sydney for the game, but they were now hearing something to burn their ears and freeze their souls.

Jock Hobbs had the floor, and he put it in no uncertain terms:

"Unless we take action, and take action immediately," he said, "this might very well be the last time that this body meets as a significant force of New Zealand rugby."

His words were left hanging in the air for a moment.

Nigh on a century of All Black history looked back at Hobbs, nodding with grave eyes, as they perhaps realised for the first time just how *truly* grave the situation was.

The decision taken that morning — to launch a counter-attack against the forces of WRC — was the obvious one. Perhaps more importantly, they also agreed to give Hobbs and his negotiators total authority to go at it full throttle in whatever way they saw fit.

It was one of the most senior of the councillors, John Sturgeon, who rammed that through. After Jock Hobbs had finished speaking, Sturgeon picked up the cudgel for him:

"Okay you guys, you have heard the situation," he said. "If you have got any concerns at the approach that these blokes are taking, let's have it out on the table now — otherwise you've got to back them. Let's not have anyone coming along and whinging later on if there is something you don't like about it. We've got to back them to do what they think is right, without having to refer back to us all the time."

All those in favour say "aye".

Aye, aye …

"I was glad they all supported us," Jock Hobbs says now, "but I was still feeling pretty grim about the whole situation."

At least, though, there was one tiny chink of light, which appeared shortly after the meeting was over. Earlier in the morning, Hobbs had been contacted by a solicitor from Dunedin, Warren Alcock, who had said he wished to speak to him "on an urgent matter", and they had arranged to meet that morning after the council meeting was over.

Alcock, a 31-year-old who himself still plays a goodish brand of rugby down in Dunedin, arrived in the company of another legal-beagle, Michael Fisher from Auckland. (Confusion reigned supreme in the Rugby War, but, for the record, Michael Fisher is not even on the same family tree as Rob Fisher.)

Together, the two lawyers told the trio of Hobbs, Rob Fisher and Richard Crawshaw that they represented 50 of the leading provincial players in the country — from Otago, Waikato, Counties and Wellington. All of their clients had received offers from the WRC, true — but they all still wanted to be All Blacks at the end of the day and at this stage were still loyal to New Zealand rugby.

Their clients had kept their options open, but what the two wanted to know was just what the NZRFU might be offering their clients. Should they follow their desires and *remain* loyal?

Although he is not a particularly demonstrative man, Hobbs could have hugged them then and there.

"It was the first break," Hobbs says, "something to grab hold of."

And he did just that, with both hands. With occasional input from his two fellow negotiators, Hobbs spoke rapidly for the next hour, setting out the position of the NZRFU *vis-á-vis* provincial players. He gave them a copy of the NZRFU standard contract. No, he acknowledged, it might not necessarily be quite the same terms that WRC was offering, but it was sure, it was *guaranteed*, it was the best thing for New Zealand rugby; it was not some airy-fairy scheme like the one the WRC circus seemed to represent.

The lawyers nodded, listening, and the men of the NZRFU were delighted. Between them they laid down the platform for further negotiations. At last, here were some people from the players' side of things who were prepared to *talk* to the national Union. To this point, Hobbs particularly had had a very strong sense, in spite of himself, that a decision had been taken, that was that, and the New Zealand Rugby Football Union simply had been left bleeding and dying in a ditch.

Hobbs promised to have another meeting with them on the following day to further discuss things, but for now they had to go and get down to work. Together, they urgently needed to refine the letter that was to be given to each of the All Blacks at the conclusion of that afternoon's Test match.

This letter communicated to the All Blacks the essential aspects of the contract they were being offered, including the specific amount of money for each player. As a sweetener, they were promised they would automatically get a 75 per cent advance on the first year's payment within seven days of signing, plus $NZ10,000 for every one of them for that day's Test match, *plus* $NZ30,000 for the coming tour of France. The letter also included the reasons for the NZRFU wanting their team to sign.

It was a tricky business to get the balance of such an important communication right, and all three men were totally absorbed as the time for kick-off approached.

He was a well-dressed figure, walking along New South Head Road away from Rose Bay, in Sydney's east, and in the general direction of the Sydney Football Stadium. And he was perspiring freely — as one who has walked a long way does. Beside him was a small boy, perhaps 10 years old.

Every now and then they talked about this and that. Mostly they kept walking, edging their way closer to the stadium. The man was in a singularly pensive mood. Often entirely lost in thought. The sun kept pelting down, surprisingly hot for winter.

It was actually a bit of a pain to have to walk that far, but it had to be done. Geoff Levy was determined to watch the Test match at the ground, but he was far more determined still not to break faith with the Jewish Sabbath. His beliefs strictly forbade him getting in a car between sun-up and sun-down on a Saturday and that left only one way to traverse the 15 kilometres that separated his home from the stadium.

He and his son kept walking.

At 2.20pm, when the All Blacks and the Wallabies were getting ready to file out onto the lush turf at the Sydney Football Stadium and do battle for self and country, Hobbs, Fisher and Crawshaw were getting near to polishing the final wording on the last page.

Inside the All Blacks dressing-room at that time, the atmosphere was as intense as ever before a Test match, but, if it's possible, the New Zealanders were even more motivated than usual.

"We felt," recounts Laurie Mains, "that this may be the last time the *true* All Blacks played, and certainly we felt we knew that it would be the last time an [essentially] amateur All Black team played, so it gave us an extra focus. We wanted to go out with a big one and … "

And that'll be the knock on the dressing-room door now. The All Blacks, led by Sean Fitzpatrick, filed out the door, down the tunnel, and out into the sunlight of that momentous winter's afternoon.

Back in the hotel room where Fisher, Hobbs and Crawshaw were feverishly working away, they didn't even have the television on for the kick-off.

Searching for the right words to finish the whole letter off with, they decided on the ones that had been previously suggested by B.J. Lochore:

We realise that you have been placed under tremendous pressure by the circumstances surrounding offers from both the NZRFU and WRC.

We very much regret this, and we have endeavoured to reduce the pressure as much as possible. We are conscious of our duty towards you and the other 150,000 rugby players currently playing in New Zealand. We are also conscious that we must act responsibly so that all New Zealand rugby, including All Black rugby, continues to be strong, and your sons have the same opportunity to wear the Silver Fern that you have had.

It was perfect. They signed ...

Yours faithfully,
Brian Lochore. Jock Hobbs. Rob Fisher.

It was 3pm, and the job was done. Richard Crawshaw jumped into a taxi and headed to the stadium with all the letters in his briefcase. He arrived there, a little after half-time, meaning the letters would be ready for the All Blacks when they came off the field, handed out to them by B.J. Lochore.

Finally, Fisher and Hobbs turned on the television set to see what was happening. The All Blacks were going well. Jonah Lomu was killing 'em.

The usual way of things in rugby speeches after Test matches is for various dignitaries and both captains to mouth well-rounded platitudes as most of the crowd go on their merry way in the distance. This was different, and everyone knew it.

At the end of this Bledisloe Cup Test — a magnificent match won again by the All Blacks — virtually no one left. First up in the now fading sunlight of late afternoon was the ARU President Phil Harry, speaking to a crowd gripped by a strong sense of melancholy that this was the living end, that for better or worse, come what may, the essentially amateur era had just faded away before their eyes.

But if it was out with the old, the real question was, just what would the new era look like? Would it be one at least run by the traditional bodies, with their rugby roots embedded deep in the rich soil of the century past? Or would it be run by a totally new crowd, formed maybe last Tuesday for all the crowd knew. Was all the paper talk true, about this thing called WRC? Phil Harry spoke:

"I would also like to say a few words to the spectators both here at the ground, and watching on television," the ARU President said after a couple of preliminary remarks. "This is the end of the season and in many ways is the end of an era. Let me say this … That sort of spectacular, passionate game between two nations is *something that money can't buy*. Thank you."

The italicised words were, particularly, met with warm applause from the crowd — creating the atmosphere for what came next.

Then to Phil Kearns who, like most of the Wallabies, had taken Harry's last remark as a specific dig at their whole presumed involvement with WRC. After his own opening comments he came to the line that will be long remembered.

"To all Australian supporters here today, we thank you. It's been terrific, your support," Kearns said, with his voice rebounding all over the still-packed stadium. "*And whatever happens in the future, we hope you and the Union support us*. Thank you."

Around the ground, there was a sudden stunned silence. On this lovely winter's day, after a splendid game of traditional Test-match rugby, one of the most admired figures of all had just said that it was all over.

"*Whatever happens in the future, we hope you and the Union support us*."

As innocuous as those words might appear here, black on white, *there* it was different. In the atmosphere of that ground, under the circumstances of all the headlines, rumours, and innuendoes that had been swirling for the past few days, Kearns' words were taken as confirmation that it was all true, that the buggers had gone! Snaffled in the night by we knew not what!

It was nothing less than a public relations Chernobyl, and immediately that Kearns had finished, the stunned crowd broke up into a series of twisted knots and straggled on home. Whatever the way was to break the news of WRC plans to the rugby public, and confirm that the Wallabies were, almost to a man, right behind it, this was not it.

There is no doubt that the whole concept of the WRC had its charms, its vision, its own internal logic, even its clear advantages over the Murdoch arrangement — at least if someone really would be prepared to back it to the tune of the hundreds of millions of dollars it would require to make it work.

But there is equally no doubt that at that time the WRC was seen as a nefarious underhand organisation with enough "cloaks and daggers to keep the Royal Shakespeare Company going for decades", as one British newspaper put it. They had not yet been able to sell themselves to the public, were still seen as the wilful destroyers of the code, and here was the Wallaby captain publicly endorsing and aligning himself with them!

For Kearns personally, while he was not involved in WRC to anywhere near the extent that others were — and genuinely believed he was acting for the good of the game and the team — it was unwise in the extreme to forever be remembered in the public mind as the bearer of that traumatic news.

At around 6pm on that Saturday night, a 14-year-old schoolboy living in one of the most prestigious streets in Sydney's eastern suburbs looked out his bedroom window and saw something unbelievable. Truly, ruly, *unbelievable*.

Within moments he was on the phone to one of his schoolmates, whose father happened to have very close links to the Australian Rugby Union.

"The All Blacks!" he said excitedly. "They're walking down my street and going into one of the houses. I promise you it's them. I saw Jonah Lomu and all the others!"

The news was out, as surely as if a telegram had been sent to every single Australian and New Zealand rugby official. After the Test match — and before the enormous post-Test dinner that was planned — the All Blacks had got straight onto the team bus and headed for the impressively opulent Vaucluse house of Kerry Packer's chief lieutenant, Brian Powers, to meet with Geoff Levy.

They each now had their letters from the NZRFU, and many of them were still reading them when the bus got stuck on the way down the twisted crescent where Powers lives.

They were ushered into the spacious basement of Powers' house, where a few drinks, nibblies and Geoff Levy, Powers himself, David Leckie of Packer's television station Channel Nine, and the lawyers from Davenports — Bernie Allen and Chris Morris — awaited them.

The reason for Leckie's presence there was the same reason that the venue was Brian Powers' house. At that time, some of the All Blacks still had lingering doubts about the WRC's financial *bona fides*, and were not convinced that Kerry Packer was actually backing it.

"[Geoff had said to us]," one of the individuals there that night recalls, "'That Packer *is* involved and to prove it, I will take you to the Managing Director's house and we'll have key guys there and you'll see them with your own eyes — flesh and blood.'"

And, good as his word, here they were. To this point, there had been no solid proof that the Packer organisation was going to back the concept. Their name had not appeared on any of the documentation, the All Blacks had never sighted an official Packer representative, but you couldn't do much better than to be standing in the basement of the Managing Director's house, for getting proof that the Big Boss himself was with the program.

The formalities were sparse. Bernie Allen made a brief but thorough speech about the legal implications of what they were about to sign, making it clear that they would be legally committed to WRC from this point, and then the All Blacks got to it.

A further inducement to the All Blacks signing en masse was the *guarantee* of $NZ100,000 for each and every signature. Well over $NZ2 million had been deposited in a trust account with Davenports, and Levy says his intention was that the players understand that if they signed with WRC and not with anyone else, then they would get their $100,000 whatever happened on November 22 — even if the competition wasn't actually launched. If it was launched, they'd also get their $100,000, but it would be deducted from their contractual payments.

Even with an inducement like that, some four players declined to sign there and then. One of those, for the record, was Jonah Lomu. The players who didn't sign had indicated earlier that they weren't going to, but coach Laurie Mains, in his words, "only agreed to let the players go provided we all went".

And all did go, but not all went inside the house. The All Black coach, as a matter of fact, had remained in the bus up the road with Colin Meads, talking quietly, and becoming increasingly agitated.

"I was very unhappy about it," he recalls.

The problem was, where *were* they? It seemed to Mains like his team were taking forever, and presently he could stand it no more.

"I actually did go into the house at one stage and pressed — not the panic button — but I did say, 'Listen guys, we have got to go, we cannot show bad manners.'"

They left, and headed back to the dinner. In the darkened bus, with some players talking quietly while others were lost in thought, Mains pointedly did not ask anyone what had happened inside.

"I did not want to know at that time," he says. "It was only [the following day] before we left, that Sean, without giving me names again, told me numbers of who had signed. I didn't want to know names."

The approach of Sean Fitzpatrick for one, incidentally, impressed Mains greatly during this time.

"Out of this whole thing, my respect for Sean and Mike Brewer rose dramatically," he says. "They made some very mature decisions about what to tell me about and what not [to]. They were very sensible and protective of me, in keeping me away from the nuts and bolts of it and not dragging me into it, and I was very happy about that."

The bus continued on to the dinner.

"When the going gets weird, the weird turn pro." Such was the most famous rule of that great American writer Hunter S. Thompson's career, and he certainly would have been in his element that Saturday night on the occasion of the Bledisloe Cup Centenary dinner out at Sydney's Hordern Pavilion.

Weird, wired, way out — with some 600 people, including the present and past legends of the game from both sides of the Tasman, gathered into the one room with the intention of celebrating 100 All Black/Wallaby Test matches.

It was either a curious quirk of mathematics or perhaps just the cosmic order of things that the centenary of Tests should have been completed that very afternoon. For it was clearly the end of an era in every other way.

If the general buzz in Sydney on the previous day had been low and wide in pitch, the concentrated buzz in this room on this night was high, tight and discordant.

Everyone but everyone was talking about the World Rugby Corporation, contracts, who'd signed what, who hadn't, what Murdoch's forces might do to counter-attack, what the Phils — Kearns and Harry — had said in their post-match speeches, and what they really meant by them.

Andy Haden remembers one of the few lighter moments of the night. "Players who had just come back from the signing session were winking and you know, waving their arms as if they were flying," he recalls.

At least *they* were having a good time. Elsewhere the mood was rather more tense. Eye-contact was being avoided, people were taking circuitous routes to get to their tables, so as to avoid seeing people they simply didn't want to.

It was in this kind of atmosphere that the formal part of the evening began, with the room darkened as the waiters came out with the evening's fare. At about 8.30pm, a little after the entrée was served, one of the men from IMG, Bill Anderson, came up to Ian Ferrier, seated at the main table, and broke the news to him.

"I've just been talking to Phil Kearns," he told Ferrier, "and he *has* signed a contract."

Ferrier looked back at Anderson, unflinching, not speaking, trying to comprehend the seemingly incomprehensible. As absurd as it seems in hindsight, even at that late stage Ferrier was *still* refusing to believe, in spite of everything, that Kearns had actually signed anything. But now there could be no further doubt.

"I felt like I'd been kicked in the guts," recalls Ferrier now. "Phil had told me on at least four occasions that he hadn't signed, and now here was confirmation that he had. I felt very, very angry, and very let down."

(Kearns acknowledges that the situation of having to deny their commitment was "extremely difficult", but adds that "we were not the only ones telling porky pies".)

Around the room, the buzz had turned up even higher in pitch, and alcohol was just beginning to loosen previously controlled emotions — and other people were moving from table to table with the latest rumours and revelations.

The evening raced on. After a video presentation reviewing the history of the 100 Tests between the Wallabies and All Blacks, the Chief Executive Officer of the ARU, Bruce Hayman, gave a thundering oration about the fact that, "you can't replace 100 years of fierce rivalry and national pride with created teams which lack support and purpose, and which are motivated only by the dollar".

He added an impromptu suggestion that, "the older All Blacks and Wallabies must help the current generation through this difficult time".

At speech's end he was met with deafening applause from some sections of the room, and an extremely stony silence from others. The battle lines of the Rugby War were, even then, clearly forming up for the first time, for all to see.

With the conclusion of the formalities, many of the boiling passions that had been building up were now really allowed to explode up and out. And they did. Groups of people were talking animatedly all over the darkened room, while other little huddles whispered conspiratorially. Some older players from both nations did indeed try to approach the incumbent players, meeting with only mixed success.

There were some areas of calm, though, even quiet sadness. In one corner of the room, Sean Fitzpatrick was speaking quietly to Rob Fisher. The two went back a long way, from the days when Fitzpatrick had been an extremely promising under–21 player at the Auckland University Club, and Fisher had been one of the club officials. But now the All Black hooker had something quite difficult to say.

"Fish, whatever happens," Fitzpatrick told him with obvious heartfelt sincerity, "I just hope you and Helen and Bronnie and I can remain friends."

Fisher took it calmly enough on the outside, saying, "Of course, Sean, I mean, we are mates, and whatever happens that won't change," while inside he was outright staggered.

Fisher went straight back to his table to recount the comment to his wife, Helen, saying, "Well, that doesn't sound too bloody good, does it?"

Helen Fisher agreed entirely, and informed her husband that as a matter of fact she had just been told much the same thing by Bronnie Fitzpatrick.

Somewhere there, as they discussed it, Simon Poidevin walked past. On a mission. The red-haired breakaway was *everywhere* that night. Out and about — transparent fury, high-octane intensity — keeping himself in check … but only just. For the most part, he tried to talk to the Wallabies he felt he might have the most influence on, while he contented himself with simply glaring at those he thought to be lost causes.

In the latter category was Phil Kearns. For most of the night the two had been like caged lions, angrily circling each other without ever actually coming to grips.

Kearns, for one, had no actual desire to, knowing it was a futile exercise. At one point he really had had enough, though, and told a mutual friend through gritted teeth, "You're a mate of mine, and I know you're a mate of Poidevin's, and I want you to tell him to BACK OFF! *Or else.*"

All about him at that moment, the room was starting to seethe, sway, break up. The atmosphere was increasingly angry, devastated, uncomprehending and resentful all at once. There was an over-whelming disbelief that *it should have come to this!*

It was in the midst of the fray that Ian Ferrier was again approached, this time by Rob Fisher.

"They've gone," Ferrier remembers the clearly dejected Fisher telling him. "They've gone. I think we should hold out the olive branch to them." Ferrier looked at him aghast, taking his words to mean that Fisher wanted to sue for peace.

"Don't be ridiculous," he said, and stormed off.

(For the record, Fisher says that Ferrier had misinterpreted him. "What I meant was not that we should surrender to them at all, but that whatever else happened we should do everything to ensure that we didn't end up with the same situation that Super League was in, with players split into two entirely different camps.")

The evening raced on.

In one corner of the room, Peter FitzSimons, a journalist with *The Sydney Morning Herald*, was seen to have a stand-up drag-down screaming match with his good friend and former coach, Bob Dwyer, over the whys and wherefores of the whole WRC saga.

Their voices kept getting louder until something had to break, and it did. Almost simultaneously, they stormed off in opposite directions. It was about typical of that extraordinary night, as there were many similar altercations around the room.

Around midnight, Poidevin was standing near the exit, ready to take his leave. Phil Kearns and his wife, Julie, walked right by him, without saying a word, without acknowledgment.

It really *had* come to this.

Somewhere to the west, high over the Indian Ocean that separates the Australian and African continents, Louis Luyt was winging his way home — formulating just exactly what he would do on the morrow when he landed.

On the other side of the aisle, and three rows back, Ian Frykberg was doing exactly the same.

Sunday. The campus at Sydney University, just a few kilometres up the road from the Central Business District, boasts one of the most beautiful and historic rugby ovals in Australia. The oldest rugby club in the southern hemisphere, it is also, not surprisingly, the most traditional in ethos and *feel*.

It was to this oval that three of the most powerful rugby potentates in the country retreated on Sunday afternoon to watch University play Easts and review their position. The mood of NSWRU President Peter Crittle, ARU President Phil Harry and NSWRU Chairman Ian Ferrier was generally sombre, though at least uplifted a little by the timeless scene before them.

"I was just glad under the circumstances," Ferrier says, "that rugby like this was still going on."

Out on the field, the 30 players drawn from the two clubs were going through their paces, playing for nought but the thrill of the game, as the timeless spires of Sydney University were visible over the tall leafy gum trees on the eastern side of the oval.

The three close friends talked, the way you do in the middle of a crisis — with passion, a little bit of desperation, although also semi-enjoying the fight, ready to go for it.

That morning Ferrier and Harry had addressed a meeting of the Wallabies back at the Darling Harbour Parkroyal, where Ferrier particularly had hammered away at what he saw as WRC's lack of financial credibility.

As a man who had made his fortune working as a receiver of choice for extremely sick companies, he was in his element talking forcefully about the economic realities of becoming involved with what he called "a two-dollar shelf company" which, in his opinion, was being run by "snake-oil salesmen".

"I put the view to them," Ferrier recalls, "that they were dealing with the Devil ... They were dealing with people who lacked substance. They were dealing with snake-oil salesmen, with people who were playing charades with them."

And as soon as the following day, Ferrier had told the players, the ARU wanted to see the players one by one, and put before them their counter-offers. Surely, the players would then see the clear difference between the benefits of staying with the establishment that they could trust, which was *guaranteeing* them the money, and wandering off with a two-bit organisation that might be promising the moon but would wind up delivering them nothing.

It all seemed to go well, bar one bad moment. Ferrier had been just about to wind up when he asked, "Is there anyone in the room who is in a legal position where they can *not* sign an ARU contract?"

Silence. Players looked around the room to see if anyone was going to 'fess up, when Tim Horan suddenly stood up ... and went to get himself a glass of water.

That Horan was a *riot*. Ferrier moved on, relieved more than somewhat.

Mere oration, however, was never going to win this fight, as Crittle, Harry and Ferrier knew, and as the University-Easts rugby game proceeded before them, the three administrators decided on a basic plan.

Firstly, they would play with "a totally straight bat", the way Ferrier tells it, essaying to be as open and honest as they could at all times with the players, and hopefully standing as a delightful contrast to what they saw as the nefarious ways of the WRC.

Secondly, they would not resort to high passion.

"I think you could say what we most wanted," says Phil Harry, "was to avoid at all costs what happened with Super League, where each side trumpeted their signings and the whole thing was torn apart in the process."

Unlike the famous Vietnam War quote from a US military man — "We had to destroy the village in order to save it" — the ARU officials wanted to have something worth saving when it was all over.

In essence, that afternoon they decided to do a "WRC" on the WRC. Taking a leaf out of the way Ross Turnbull had done it to them, they would not trumpet each Wallaby that they signed, but rather go after them quietly until they achieved their own "critical mass" of Wallabies returning to the fold, whereupon they hoped that WRC's plans would be scuppered, at least in Australia.

(The irony in the whole situation at this point was that while the establishment side of the Rugby War had all the money but no players, the WRC side had no money but *most* of the players.)

Johannesburg. Sunday morning. Louis Luyt was strong on his feet, and so powerful of personality that none of the mighty Springboks — indomitable only a month before on the field against the All Blacks — dared to stand up to him, at least not face to face.

At a meeting at Luyt's house that Sunday morning, he addressed 11 of the 13 Transvaal Springboks. In harangues at the World Champions, he likened Kerry Packer to a "financial midget", and maintained that the Australian media magnate simply did not have the funding to go through with his proposal.

For all that, though, he was here to tell them that SARFU *would* match the money that Packer was offering them. They could either take that and accept it, or they would have to face the inevitable consequences.

He said that while there seemed to be a lot of people who were fondly imagining that both SARFU and the Transvaal Rugby Union would do a deal with WRC, and would even let them play at Ellis Park, he could assure them, as Chairman of the former and President of the latter, that neither body would *ever* cut a deal with WRC, and "if we have to put a 'C' team of Transvaal players on the field, then *we will*, and the people will come and watch them".

Dr Luyt's son-in-law, Rian Oberholzer, was in the room at the time, carefully monitoring the reaction of the players to Dr Luyt's words.

He is of the impression that "this really got to the younger players particularly, when they realised that if they went with WRC they could never play for either Transvaal or the real South Africa again. They couldn't be Springboks again, and that is what they wanted most."

Whatever. Dr Luyt continued, hammering away at the rugby players and, by one account, "doing a lot of shouting along the way".

For the record, Dr Luyt denies rattling the windows, but does at least acknowledge that he was not in the most temperate of moods.

"I am not disposed to ever being meek and mild," he says.

Within hours of the meeting finishing, Ross Turnbull in London had a full report of what was said. In his daily fax back to Geoff Levy's office in Sydney, written in his billowing hand, he made clear his own consternation at the fact that the meeting had taken place at all. It read …

When I asked Harry Viljoen WHY they attended the meeting in the first place (after our discussions re forming a committee like the All Blacks) … he said, "Because South Africa is different to other countries, and the boys are scared of Dr Luyt."

Now at that meeting Harry Viljoen says that Luyt has offered the 10 Transvaal Springboks the same contract as WRC but with 10% deposit payable on Thursday/Friday next.

AT THAT TIME — FRANCOIS PINAAR [sic] MUST HAND OVER THE WRC CONTRACTS.

A little later in the long and rambling fax, which covered a number of other issues, Turnbull is magnetically drawn back to the one thing that was really doing the WRC cause the most damage in South Africa. Dr Louis Luyt …

Basic Problem. Luyt treats the players like a bunch of schoolboys and they accept it. (THEY SEEM TO ENJOY IT.) Might be something to do with the Afrikaan mentality.

What then was the way forward? As Turnbull saw it, in this same fax:

[Harry] SAID AT THE END THAT IF YOU CAN PROVIDE ME WITH SOME FORM OF LETTER OR PROOF THAT PACKER WILL DELIVER, HE CAN SETTLE DOWN THE PLAYERS AND HE WILL FIGHT LUYT.

LUYT WON'T GIVE IN — HE WILL KEEP FIGHTING. (WE ALWAYS KNEW THIS.)

He got that right.

Chapter nine
The empire strikes back

Around the rugby world, the reaction to news of the WRC push was uniformly one of outrage. It varied in degree and manner of expression, but it *was* outrage.

Auckland's *Sunday News* headline on July 30, the day after the Bledisloe Cup was PACKER BASTARDS!

David Kirk, the All Black captain of 1987 who was the first captain to lift the World Cup above his shoulders in triumph, sounded the general theme in his newspaper column. The former scrum-half was almost Cromwellian in his grandiloquent anger:

"To the older players and some coaches and administrators who are leading the charge to the WRC," Kirk wrote, "I say 'go'.

"Get out, leave, remove the stain, the blot you are on the spirit of rugby. Take whatever money you can get, from whoever you can get it, but leave before you do any more damage."

His fiercely expressed attitude resonated well with the rugby public of New Zealand, for whom, generally, news of the WRC concept was some 10 kilometres *past* the "Welcome to Anathema" signpost.

Generation after generation of All Blacks had entered the pantheon of the terrestrial gods, all for the simple fact that they had worn the famous black jersey in battle. And that had always been reward enough. While it might now have been grudgingly accepted that something more than that was going to be necessary to keep them together in the modern sporting age — and the Murdoch deal had been accepted on that basis — any thought that the heroes in black would willingly lay down their jerseys and don new ones in return for a higher dollar was simply stomach-turning.

And the people said so, in letters to the editor, on talk-back radio, to each other in clubs and pubs around the land. The opinion polls showed that 88 per cent of New Zealanders stood shoulder to shoulder against the whole concept of WRC, or at least against what they thought that concept was. They were not to know — even at this late stage of proceedings — that a specific part of the WRC plan was for the Unions to be included in the professional structure.

Similar anti-WRC sentiments were expressed elsewhere in the rugby world.

Across the Tasman, in *The Sydney Morning Herald*, Peter FitzSimons was every bit as worked up as Kirk.

"What can you guys be thinking of?" he asked rhetorically of the Wallabies in his back-page column. "Rugby is your *mother*, dammit. For the past two decades she's nurtured you, taken care of you, taught you, been proud to call you her own, and held chook raffles so that you could travel around the world.

"She's allowed you to walk taller down George Street than ever you would have dreamed, and now that she has come into a large amount of money [from SANZAR], you are *guaranteed* to enjoy enormous amounts of her largesse as one of her favourite sons.

"If you make a decision that that is still not enough, that you want instead her to whore for you, too — to earn the very last buck for you she can and to hell with the consequences — then you will be deserving of your fate."

In South Africa, similar perhaps over-heated commentary was apparent. There were simply no commentators supporting WRC and their grand scheme. It suggested the obvious question, though. How did the powerbrokers of WRC react to this tide of anger that kept coming at them? Was it not obvious at this point that there was going to be no laying down of arms by the rugby authorities, that it was totally out of the question that they would ever be accepting half-shares in "franchises" that they already owned outright?

"If they had looked at it in a strictly business sense with an open mind," Geoff Levy maintains, "they would actually have seen that even with their so-called half share, they would have got more money for the game with us than they were getting on their own. But our problem was a very simple problem. We needed credibility.

"And the only thing we could do at that point in time for credibility in the press was to talk about who had been signed, how many had been signed, where they have been signed and we had a choice. We could either blurt that all out in breach of confidence and be dishonourable — or we had to just take it on the chin in the press quietly and just make sure that we had the product that would sell itself when we were ready to launch.

"Even if the thing had to fail, that was life. We could not in any way give up our loyalty and credibility with the players. But at the end of the day, we felt that if we'd got all the players and the players still wanted it, the Unions would [have to] follow because they can't play a great game without the greatest players."

It was one of a few one-on-one conversations that Francois Pienaar and Dr Louis Luyt had that tumultuous week.

"I never said, 'we *need* you'," Dr Luyt recalls. "I said, 'Why didn't you come to me, you have always come to me with your problems. To win the World Cup and to be treated like a [hero] … and all of a sudden you are selling out your country.'"

Dr Luyt felt, he says, "very betrayed".

And one other thing besides, surprising as it may seem for such a notoriously tough, and sometimes abrasive, man.

"I was hurt," he says simply.

Wallaby captain Phil Kearns took a phone call on the Monday morning at his office, where he worked in a managerial role for Tooheys brewery. He was still feeling extremely sore from having played a full-on Test match only two days before, not to mention the extreme emotional turmoil of having now publicly taken the lead in something so clearly controversial as the whole WRC concept — but for whatever reason, he listened to what the bloke, a former Wallaby team-mate, had to say.

It was one of the many similar calls that would come his way that morning, afternoon, and indeed over the next few tumultuous weeks — just as his parents and wife would also be hassled. His interlocutor in this case put it to him succinctly, and with no little amount of passion.

"It's very simple, Phil. You're the Wallaby captain and you're standing at the crossroads at the head of your troops. Straight ahead lies honour, glory, the Wallaby jersey, and enormous riches *guaranteed*.

"To the left lies dissension, civil war, enormous bitterness, pissing on the Wallaby jersey and only the *possibility* of slightly more riches. If you are seen to steer them to the left, it won't be forgiven and it is a decision you will regret for the rest of your life."

Somewhat taken aback at the ferocity of the attack — though he really would get used to blasts of similar ilk in the weeks ahead — Kearns replied, "It's not that dramatic, Fitz. You don't understand, you simply don't understand, you don't understand the full picture."

Back in Ian Ferrier's offices on Sussex Street, at that very moment, Ferrier and Phil Harry were trying to do just that. They were essaying to elucidate just what level of attachment the players really did have to WRC, and then knock that level down a few pegs.

Ferrier had been appointed as the official negotiator of the ARU, while Harry was there in his role as President and also, in those early stages, as a witness to everything that was said.

At 11 o'clock that morning, they were due to talk with their first Wallaby, and endeavour to secure from him a signature committing him to the establishment.

The money they were offering was good. Whereas for the 1995 season, Wallabies had been reimbursed to the tune of $A25,000 — $A80,000, through a variety of trust funds designed to preserve their amateur status, those numbers had gone forth and multiplied. At a meeting held in Leo Williams' Brisbane offices a couple of weeks earlier, rugby officials had put figures against the names of all members of the World Cup Squad. The ante had been upped from Williams' original offer of $A220,000 for those Wallabies who played a full season, and had now gone up to $A250,000 for the best of them.

Not bad dosh.

Each session began with the question, "Is there anything you have signed which prevents you signing a contract with the ARU?"

This was a legal mechanism to prevent any later accusation that the ARU was inducing players to break legally binding contracts, but for whatever reason in the two weeks that these interviews were being conducted, there was not a single Wallaby who said that yes he'd already signed another contract, so he couldn't sign with the ARU.

Presumably those who had signed with WRC were under the impression they could answer thus because their contracts hadn't yet been lodged.

Harry and Ferrier also continued their attack on the financial credibility of the WRC scheme, and handed each of the players a document to that effect. By this time, some of the WRC financial feasibility documents, as well as a copy of the original concept, had been leaked to ARU officials, who vigorously attacked the exposed financial props which the players were presuming would hold the whole WRC structure up.

"The more we looked at it," Harry says, "the more we became convinced that they [WRC] simply couldn't pull it off.

"We had our own people look at their figures because we'd recently made a detailed bid to stage the 1999 World Cup — so we had a lot of internal data available — and they all said that their figures were way off-beam."

Harry is backed in this contention by David Moffett. While Chief Executive of the NSW Rugby Union, he had not only spent long hours over the three previous years organising such things as buses to collect NSW players from Johannesburg's Airport and hotel beds long enough for the tallest of the second-rowers, but he had also pored over the WRC data — and it was his firm opinion that much of the WRC feasibility study was in "fantasy-land".

"The biggest problem, in my view," says Moffett, "is that while WRC had a guy like Ross Turnbull who would be looking at the broad picture and someone like Levy who was a lawyer, they didn't have anybody with any idea of rugby administration in their organisation.

"So the first time that we saw their document, which purported to have players flying to South Africa and back within two, or two-and-a-half days, we knew it was quite ludicrous because they firstly, obviously, hadn't even looked at an airline timetable."

Ross Turnbull, in reply, maintains that his numbers did stack up, and as to the charge that it wasn't sensible to have players going back and forth to South Africa in two-and-a-half days, he is even more dismissive.

"Listen," he says firmly. "These guys would have been professionals, they would have coped with all that. This is what the amateur officials could never understand, that they were now dealing with real *professionals*."

Levy also weighs in heavily on the subject of finances.

"I don't know where they got their figures from, because we certainly never gave them our data, and what is more, the WRC financial feasibilities had been prepared in consultation with the resources of Ernst & Young, and in my opinion as well as of people in the Packer organisation, they were reasonable."

The first rule of rugby politics is that power off the field is in direct proportion to power on the field — and it holds for the international game particularly. Just as the New Zealand Rugby Football Union had been the most influential in the world from 1987–91, when they were world champions, and the Australians had laid down the law about which way the code should head from 1991–95, there was no doubt that the most important battleground of all in the Rugby War was South Africa.

For whoever boasted the Springboks on their books, boasted the World Champions, and would boast the most credible competition, if indeed it came to a point where there would be dual competitions running the following year — with the establishment international competition going head to head with the rebels.

The short answer, at that time, was "who gets the South Africans wins", and both sides clearly realised that. Late on the afternoon of Monday, July 31, Brian Powers was on the phone to a journalist acquaintance from *The Sydney Morning Herald*, engaged in a passionate discussion as to the rights and wrongs of what his organisation appeared to be attempting to do.

The strong contention of Powers was that far from driving the whole thing, his organisation was prepared to accommodate a player-led revolution if *they* made it happen, and ... and ...

And the journalist interrupted. At that very moment a wire-service story had popped up on screen claiming that the Springboks had signed back with Louis Luyt. The journalist informed Powers of this fact, who promptly signed off, saying he'd have to check with his own people in South Africa to see whether or not it was true. They had both previously agreed that with the South Africans went the whip hand in the clash.

Within an hour Powers was back on the phone, sounding a little relieved, saying he'd checked and it simply wasn't true.

And he was right.

The day before, while the Transvaal-based Springboks had listened intently to what Dr Luyt had to say at his house — and even tentatively agreed that they would return to the fold — they were still a long way from signing contracts. The leading members of the side remained in firm contact with the WRC side of things as they tried to decide which way to jump.

As ever, close to the pivotal point of action, Ian Frykberg was ensconced in his Johannesburg hotel room (the Sandton Sun, just for a change) also making calls, taking calls, monitoring just how far Louis Luyt had progressed in his plans to bring the Springboks to ground.

He also received one important visitor. Francois Pienaar came to Frykberg's room on that same Monday afternoon. He looked very much like a man under extreme stress, and he spoke like one too.

Pienaar had come to touch base with the News Corporation version of things, and his basic message was that he and the Springboks were simply sick of the enormous pressure being placed on them by both sides.

"We're *rugby players*," the Springbok captain told Frykberg, "we just want to play rugby. We don't need all this."

Frykberg gently talked him through it. That was all his side of things wanted too, he told him — all they wanted was for the players to play rugby. His side didn't want to own their souls the way the WRC did, and make them go through enormous traumatic changes. They just wanted the players to do exactly what they had been doing, with the only difference being they would also be getting an enormous amount of money.

Frykberg also pushed the point with the Springbok captain that he had a higher duty — to rugby generally, rather than just to the elite level of the game — and even if WRC did come up with the money to pay the elite, the real question was: what was such a traumatic split going to do to the game at the junior level, at grass-roots level around the world?

Pienaar left, with Frykberg having the clear impression that "we were making headway".

They called it "the War Office". It was the Wellington boardroom of the Kensington Swan law firm — the solicitors for the NZRFU — and for the remainder of the Rugby War it would serve as the nerve centre for the establishment counter-attack against the forces of WRC in New Zealand. One side of the room was dominated by a large whiteboard, while on the other side a panoramic window looked out upon Wellington's Lambton Quay and a small slice of Wellington Harbour.

In the middle of the room was a large oval table, upon which sat a large conference-call phone complete with speakers. It was in this room on that Monday morning that two of the key generals of the counter-attack had a meeting, initially sitting at the large oval table that dominates the room.

Jock Hobbs did most of the talking early on, while the senior partner of the firm, Brian Gunderson, did most of the listening.

"We've got to get out there *immediately*," Hobbs told Gunderson, "because WRC could launch on us at any moment. We've got to get as much of our message to the provincial players as we can before the WRC balloon goes up. We can turn this situation around, but we've got to be meeting with the players *by tomorrow* to do it."

Gunderson listened, nodding, and gradually came around to the Hobbs point of view — that the plan to move all over New Zealand with roving bands of negotiators to talk to all the leading rugby players in the land and put before them the essence of the NZRFU offer was something of absolute prime urgency and should be fast tracked.

It was decided …

Gunderson swung his staff into action to make it happen, working closely with the staff from the NZRFU, as the War Office buzzed with activity for the rest of the day and on into the night. There would be three principal groups of negotiators touring the country, starting that very night.

The first would be headed by Ian Abercrombie, the CEO of the All Blacks Club (a body which had been set up in 1992 to raise money for the team and distribute that income to the players) — and it would be his role to maintain contact with the All Blacks.

In the meantime, the two other teams would be doing the real meat and potatoes work of getting to the provincial players. One would be led by B.J. Lochore and would endeavour to see all the players in the top half of the North Island, while Jock Hobbs would embark on a scorched earth tour through the South Island and the bottom part of the North Island, hopefully wiping out WRC bastions as he went.

Their weapons were two-fold, the way they saw it.

Firstly, a "sell" of the NZRFU — a presentation on just why it was the best thing for rugby in the country if the national body remained in control of the game and was not exposed to the whims of corporate pirates. The players should get it right out of their heads that there was any chance that the NZRFU would ever negotiate with the WRC. That would never, EVER happen, the players would be told.

The second part of the presentation concerned details with respect to the contract that they would be offered as a result of the deal SANZAR had struck with Murdoch — and just how much they could expect to receive as they got to progressively higher tiers of the game.

By eight o'clock that night, everything was in place and Jock Hobbs was already on his way, bound for Christchurch. B.J. Lochore was heading for Auckland.

Here is your holy mission. We want you to go out and bring the boys home.

Did someone say cavalry? For the WRC — *vis-á-vis* the increasingly shaky position in South Africa — the cavalry was indeed on its way, in the form of Ross Turnbull and James Packer. Truth be told, the younger Packer was more a devotee of rugby league, but by this point the exercise had moved well beyond the realms of individual likes and dislikes. This was *business*, and it was something that James Packer had been learning for the previous 27 years from his father and his father's most senior advisers.

So now that Packer's company, PBL, had formally taken out an option on taking control of the World Rugby Corporation, the younger Packer had joined the fray for the first time, and in the first instance had flown to London to meet with Ross Turnbull to discuss just where it would be best to proceed from this point.

That much became obvious quickly. To South Africa, where the principal pillar of the whole WRC edifice was clearly in danger of being knocked out. Both men hit the ground running from the airport, doing everything possible to make sure that the World Champions remained faithful to WRC's version of the revolution.

While Turnbull busied himself with liaising with crucial players like Pienaar, centre Hennie Le Roux and winger James Small, it was Packer's job to see if he could bolt down Johann Rupert to be part of the whole deal. Johann Rupert, or "the other Rupert" as he is sometimes known, was to the South African business world what James Packer is to Australia's — which is to say son of the richest and most powerful man on site.

The Rupert family's fortune was invested in such diverse companies as Cartier, Dunhill and Rothmans, but for the purposes of the WRC it was the family's hold on the South African television network M-Net that was most crucial to the success of the WRC venture.

M-Net generally, and Johann Rupert particularly, had been extremely distressed by the deal between SANZAR and Rupert Murdoch from the beginning, in that it had cut them out of one of their most valuable television products without even the slightest consultation. After a long relationship with the South African Rugby Football Union, the folk at M-Net had woken up one morning to find that the rights had simply been sold to someone else. They too, were not well pleased, and were an obvious potential ally for the World Rugby Corporation to have on side.

For what was clearly needed to calm the jittery Springboks at this point was cash. *Provable* cash, BANKABLE cash. It was all very well for the South Africans to be on the promise of all this wonderful money, but where was it? The word from the Springbok camp was that unless they could see their money guaranteed by WRC, then the Springboks really would go and sign back with SARFU.

(True, via the good graces of the money loaned to them by PBL, the World Rugby Corporation had been able to deposit two million rand into a trust account with a South African law firm — to cover any possible loss of income that individual Springboks might suffer between then and November 22 — but this had proved insufficient to allay the fears of the South Africans that the concept was inadequately bankrolled.)

To come up with the far more serious money that was needed, Turnbull and James Packer had come up with a plan whereby, if M-Net would guarantee the salaries offered to the Springboks, they would get in return a guarantee of the television rights for 10 years when WRC was up and running in 1996. It was not a straight-out swap, according to Turnbull, but that was the essence of the deal.

Before getting stuck in, though, in one of the few moments when he talked to the media in the whole affair, James Packer told the South African newspaper *Business Day* on the day he arrived:

"The response we have had from the players — internationally — has been very positive. If there has been a concern among the players it is because of misinformation given to them. However, once we talked to them, the concerns have been dispelled."

Packer, the paper reported, acknowledged SARFU's attempts to keep players loyal to their cause, but questioned the tactics used.

"It is my perception bullying tactics have been used when dealing with the players, and that is unfortunate. It is not the way I know business to be done in the '90s, and in any corporation you expect people to be open and forthcoming ...

"I also understand Dr Louis Luyt has got very personal about my father, and that in itself is unnecessary."

And with that, the interview was over. The younger Packer busied himself with opening negotiations with M-Net, while Turnbull focused on the Springboks.

The phone calls were flying. Kearns to Fitzpatrick, Fitzpatrick to Pienaar, Pienaar to Kearns, Kearns to McCall, McCall to Pienaar, Fitzpatrick to Hennie Le Roux, all of the above to various combinations of the others a dozen times over. It was all primarily communication to work out just exactly how they were all situated.

There was even, in the middle of it all, "a bit of counter-espionage". At one point, Rod McCall in Brisbane received a frantic message that Francois Pienaar was going berserk, because he'd just heard from John Eales, who'd said the whole thing was falling apart in Australia, that all the Wallabies had decided to return to the establishment and renege on their WRC contracts and WHAT THE HELL WAS GOING ON?

McCall calmly dialled Pienaar's mobile phone number and when it was answered, handed the phone over to John Eales. McCall listened to Eales' end of the conversation.

"Francois, this is John Eales ... no, no, no, the *real* John Eales!"

The Australian second-rower was able to assure Pienaar that whoever he'd been speaking to, it certainly hadn't been John Eales, and in any case none of those claims were true.

So who did make the call?

McCall and Eales still wonder.

Oh, and one more crucial phone call, around this time. To Ian Frykberg ...

"I was having talks with M-Net as well," Frykberg recalls, "and one day M-Net said, 'look, James Packer has asked us to lend them five million American dollars'."

Frykberg made a few phone calls himself immediately afterwards. Quite a few.

Back in the War Office, officials from the NZRFU were monitoring the progress of the negotiating teams as they made their way around New Zealand. Despite the plan of getting the word out to the provincial players, this scheme by no means precluded also going after the All Blacks — who were also present as the presentations in each province were made. Winger Jeff Wilson, for example, was every bit as much an Otago player as he was an All Black.

The question back at headquarters was just how much focus should be made, meantime, in going after getting *specifically* the All Blacks signed, and in just what manner.

Up on the board, in one session chaired by Rob Fisher, the three major strategies that could be pursued were listed:

1. *Go after all the All Blacks equally.*
2. *"Cherry-pick" the key All Blacks. (As in contract the linchpins, so the rest would have to follow.)*
3. *Ignore the All Blacks and isolate them by focusing entirely on the provincial players.*

Rob Fisher decided to get the opinion of Sam Chisholm. Chisholm, whose morning and evening rituals frequently included strapping himself into or out of commercial jet-liners, was by now in Los Angeles — but such was the importance with which Chisholm viewed the Rugby War that Fisher was able to get through to him almost immediately.

This was a time when the television executive was on the phone virtually around the clock, ceaselessly trying to determine just how far Turnbull had penetrated the international rugby landscape, and how the not inconsiderable forces of News Corporation could best be positioned to counter-attack.

His advice to Fisher on this occasion was to absolutely, totally, and no mistake about it, still vigorously pursue the All Blacks — "We bloody well want the ones that played in the World Cup" — but by all means continue to make all efforts to get the provincial players signed up, as that could only put pressure on the Test players.

A small advantage for the NZRFU in all this was that it was a proven matter of recent history that when the top side disappears — as they did in 1986, when most of the All Blacks went on a rebel tour of South Africa under the name of the "Cavaliers" and were promptly banned — it takes only a short time before another great team arises from the provinces to replace them.

The team that took over from the Cavaliers became known as the "Baby Blacks" and there was some expert opinion to the effect that they were actually better than the more experienced campaigners they replaced.

Jock Hobbs knew all this only too well, for he had been a Cavalier himself, going against the wishes of his Union to do something he wanted, in return for what has ever since been rumoured to be a large amount of money.

The fact that the man leading the fight against WRC in New Zealand was once a rebel himself would open Hobbs up to the charge of hypocrisy.

"On that subject," Hobbs says in reply, "I would say two things. Firstly I was wrong. I shouldn't have been a Cavalier, shouldn't have gone against the wishes of the Union.

"And secondly, it was not the same thing at all. The Cavaliers tour was just a one-off affair, it was not something that was going to change the entire face of rugby as we knew it. It was *entirely* different to what we were dealing with here."

It was getting close to deadline at *The Sydney Morning Herald* offices, late on the Tuesday night. Greg Growden, the paper's leading rugby writer, was working furiously, getting the final paragraphs written on what would be one of the rare heart-warming moments of the whole Rugby War.

The headline was MERRICK MAY KNOCK BACK MONEY. The story beneath it contained a small and wonderful sliver of what had been — that had somehow survived into the new age. Growden's article concerned Steve Merrick, the still incumbent Wallaby scrum-half, who had been plucked from the total obscurity of a Singleton coalmine and rugby team only two months before, and now found himself offered something like $A200,000 from both sides.

And was likely to refuse them both.

Sure, he had talked to the ARU and WRC out of simple politeness, and heard what they had to say. But now he'd damn nigh made up his mind. He'd do neither.

"I've done everything I've ever dreamed of in the past four weeks," he told Growden. "I wouldn't be disappointed if I broke my leg and couldn't play again."

Soooo …

"I'm off," the scrum-half finished. "Hoo-roo."

Hoo-roo, Steve.

They were small, but there were at least some signs that the total black-out of the major Unions against WRC was starting to break a bit.

In South Africa, the President of Western Province, Ronnie Masson, was one of the first to moot the possibility of breaking ranks, announcing to *Business Day* on August 2 that he fully intended to meet with WRC representatives, saying that "options like Packer's can only be a healthy development for the game of rugby union".

This very successful businessman was also very critical of the way the whole Murdoch deal had been done.

"I was very outspoken as to the way things were done when the deal was first announced, and said so at the time," he was quoted as saying. "I can also assure you that to date I still do not know what is going on, and it has placed the Unions in a difficult position when dealing with players.

"Players want to know how they will benefit and their questions must be answered. We [administrators] must realise the players are the game and not us. The players are also not, by nature, rebels. All they want to do is to be looked after and it is for the Unions to do that."

Back in Australia, Ian Ferrier was still hard at it in Sydney — negotiating with the NSW-based players — just as the two Queensland officials, Dick McGruther and Terry Doyle, were doing the same in Brisbane with the Queenslanders. Phil Harry had gone south to handle the Canberra end of things, in the company of the two leading officials there.

Before Harry left for Canberra, one of the more interesting sessions he and Ferrier had was with the Wallaby captain, Phil Kearns, on the Tuesday afternoon at two o'clock.

The mood in the room was understandably a little tense. There was gentle, careful discussion about the situation, with neither Kearns nor the administrators succumbing to the temptation to descend into expostulations.

Ferrier and Harry repeated their view that any Wallaby would be crazy to align himself with the WRC, while Kearns maintained that he was doing what he thought was right for the team, and right for rugby.

At the end of the interview, Kearns was not actually offered an ARU contract, the only Wallaby not so offered. The reason?

"I didn't want to put Phil in a position where we asked him to sign and he refused," says Ferrier. "I thought it way better that he take away just our document, without a salary offer on it, to look over, think about, and then get back to us.

"But I thought if we asked him, he would have said 'no', and we would have been further back down the track than when we started."

Kearns left the building, being photographed in the corridor outside Ferrier's offices by a *Daily Telegraph Mirror* photographer looking in a singularly pensive mood.

In New Zealand, Jock Hobbs was covering territory, moving along the highways and byways of that spectacular country, essentially covering the same territory that Eric Rush had a week before, trying to undo Rush's damage to the establishment cause.

On occasion, *frequent* occasion, it was more than passing tough. Snow up ahead. Wind from the side. Oncoming traffic. Keep going, on and on, listen to the car-radio, monitor what the news services were saying about it all. On one of those days, Hobbs flew from Dunedin to Wellington to Napier, drove then to Taupo. The following day to Palmerston North to speak to the Manawatu team, then to New Plymouth to talk to Taranaki. He drove back through the howling southerly all the way, arriving home in Wellington at three o'clock in the morning. A few hours sleep and he was at it again, from seven o'clock in the morning.

"It was three days, but it felt like three years," he recalls. "The schedules were really demanding, just going from province to province making the presentations, and the whole time thinking that at any moment WRC might launch against us."

That sense was exacerbated by things he heard on the car-radio. The situation was now such that even so generally cautious a man as Laurie Mains felt free to give at least reserved support to WRC. Mains was pulling no punches when he had spoken to Radio New Zealand, shortly after his team had returned from their win in Sydney.

"Often it takes revolution to get evolution," he said. "Maybe there'll be a bit of blood let … but at the end of the day I've got no doubt the people of rugby around the world will come out of it stronger and the sport will be very much stronger and more united."

Mains went on to say that his charges had bitterly resented the fact that no one had talked with them before their services had been put on the block and sold to Rupert Murdoch.

"There is a genuine concern among the players that decisions are being made and they are not being consulted," he said.

This concern was not expressed, at least not publicly, by Sean Fitzpatrick, when he was asked the following day where he stood in the whole saga. "Now that we have got the Bledisloe Cup out of the way, we can weigh up our options," Fitzpatrick was quoted in the New Zealand press as saying. "We have committed ourselves to nothing."

It was a very guarded statement, such were the sensitivities of the times. Now, at liberty to say exactly what he feels, Fitzpatrick is categorical about what he and his team-mates found most attractive about the WRC concept.

"The globalisation of it, the players having a say, and the [whole thing being] run professionally," he says without hesitation.

Not that, the way he tells it, it was ever an absolutely clear-cut case between the two options.

"The biggest thing for me," the All Black skipper says candidly, "was whether we were doing the right thing or the wrong thing. I felt that we were doing the right thing."

On the morning of Thursday, August 3, the Rugby War was fairly evenly poised. On the side of the "rebels", as they had become known, the WRC had enough signatures to open a sports memorabilia shop — 407, in all, from around the world.

That was the good news. The bad news was that signatures without mega-money to back them were mere cannonballs, without the big solid gold cannon needed to fire them.

The WRC camp was still a long way away from securing the $US100 million they needed to activate the contract — roughly $US100 million short in fact. (While the Packer camp had taken an option on the rights to WRC if it got up, there was never any question of them actually writing the cheque for $US100 million. As Brian Powers explains now, "We were *never* going to back it to that extent. We might have gone as high as 25 million, but that was it.")

On the side of the "establishment", on the other hand, there were just the slightest of cracks beginning to appear in the otherwise fairly united front of the players around the world. And, most importantly, they had the weight of the rugby public's sentiment still firmly behind them. They also remained confident that WRC simply would not be able to come up with the enormous money required.

The agenda of WRC on this Thursday, therefore, was two-fold. It was firstly to shore up the unity of the most crucial sets of players — those from New Zealand, South Africa and Australia — by holding a video hook-up between the three countries and letting each group see before their very eyes how committed the others were.

It was hoped, particularly, that having the Springbok leaders see just how committed the Wallabies and All Blacks were to the cause would give them some extra backbone to resist what in their minds was clearly the terrifying vision of Louis Luyt.

To add to the pressure put on the Springboks, particularly those from Transvaal, it had been made clear that if they had not signed the contracts with SARFU by the following Friday at 5pm, then the offer would be withdrawn. Sign then, or forever hold your peace.

And the second item on the WRC agenda was even more important. James Packer had received an affirmative from M-Net, and a meeting was set up for that very afternoon at five o'clock at the M-Net offices to sign the document.

Notwithstanding the fact that no money had yet formally come through, the mood back at WRC headquarters — which is to say, Geoff Levy's offices — was very up-beat. So up-beat, in fact, that

Levy spent some time putting the finishing touches to a press release that had been worked up over the previous few days.

At the time Levy was working on it, he had every confidence it could be released as soon as the following day, once they had their hands on the South African contracts, and Ireland had also come to the party. Ireland, he had to admit, was proving to be a real problem — to that point there had simply been no contracts signed there at all. But apparently that would all be rectified shortly.

Up in Newcastle, Mick Hill was very much on the case, and he'd reported that Brendan Mullin was getting close to getting all the boys signed up at once.

But back to the dummy press release. A few excerpts from its fourth draft give a fair indication of how far things had advanced — and how right Jock Hobbs was in his sense that the WRC might launch at any minute, perhaps with simultaneous press conferences around the world where an array of the newly-converted Test players would be presented.

The dummy press release went thus:

The World Rugby Corporation (WRC) today announced the formation of a major international rugby union competition, beginning in 1996 and involving the top players from the leading rugby-playing nations.

While the transition to a worldwide competition will inevitably entail change, WRC and the players will make every effort to work with the current people and institutions involved in rugby at all levels, not only to preserve but to strengthen the game. To this end, discussions have already commenced with some of the existing Unions and major clubs in some of the countries involved.

WRC also announced today that Mr Kerry Packer's Publishing and Broadcasting Limited (PBL) has agreed to become a major investor in WRC. In confirming PBL's involvement, Mr ( ) of PBL said … "We are very pleased to be involved with WRC and its plans for a first-class international rugby union competition."

Francois Pienaar, Springboks captain, stated, "To us it is amazing that a game as big as rugby has not until now been able to compete on a financial footing with one as small as rugby league. We are grateful WRC will keep our best players in our game."

Phil Kearns, Wallaby captain, stated, "What we are looking for as players is simple — continued enjoyment from the game we love, fair remuneration and a say in the future running of the game."

Sean Fitzpatrick, captain of the All Blacks, said, "At the moment it is fair to say that if WRC had not emerged, half the current All Blacks team would have left, principally for rugby league. WRC's emergence has already helped preserve the game."

WRC will finalise its plans for next year's competition during the next couple of months. It will also be selecting entities to hold the individual franchises during that period. WRC expects to announce full details of its plan by then.

That same Thursday morning, Francois Pienaar took a call on his mobile phone from Sam Chisholm. It had been lined up by Simon Poidevin, who'd been working day and night to at least keep the lines of communication open with such crucial people around the world. And at this stage there was *no one* more crucial than Pienaar.

Chisholm, speaking from London, was at his persuasive best. The theme he pressed was that under no circumstances should Pienaar attend the video hook-up planned for that day. For all his general abrasiveness on matters of import, sometimes Chisholm could be gently influential …

"I told him it was the wrong thing for him, the wrong thing for the country, that it would be sending entirely the wrong signal," Chisholm recalls. He also pushed the point that the crowd Pienaar was dealing with, this WRC, had *no money*. It was all very well to sign for the promises of great riches, he said, but where were those riches? Had Pienaar yet seen a single solitary dollar from them?

No, he thought not.

The main thing, though, was that Pienaar had to realise that rugby people needed him to do the right thing, from the barefoot five-year-olds in the townships who were just starting to play the game, on up. Pienaar was the leader of the world's rugby players, Chisholm told him, and the world of rugby was *counting* on him!

"He was actually quite inspirational," remembers Bruce McWilliam, who was listening on Chisholm's end.

This was all, mind, nothing that Ian Frykberg, Simon Poidevin and others hadn't been telling Pienaar *ad nauseam*, but, for whatever reason, the Springbok captain at last agreed that he would not attend the video hook-up.

Beyond that the extremely agitated and jittery South African made no other firm commitments, though Chisholm made a particularly significant commitment *to him* — that whatever might happen in the future, News Corporation would indemnify him and pay all his costs so long as he signed the contract with the South African Rugby Football Union.

This was followed up by a faxed letter, organised by Bruce McWilliam, guaranteeing the same.

It was at Harry Viljoen's house. Ross Turnbull could barely recognise Francois Pienaar. Here before him was the Springbok captain, sure enough, but it was an infinitely different man from the one Turnbull had met a little under two months before.

Then, Pienaar had been a "magnificent looking man", whom Turnbull had felt privileged to meet. Now he looked almost as if he had wasted away, refusing to look Turnbull in the eye, sullenly refusing to speak to him, looking very jumpy indeed.

"He had transformed from a magnificent athletic business-type person to deal with, to a shaking bloody wreck," Turnbull says. "Like a frightened animal. Pathetic."

The two were standing in the office of the Viljoen family compound together with some of the other Springboks, making ready to head into the city of Johannesburg for the video hook-up with the other countries. There were a lot of things to discuss, but Turnbull's attention kept being drawn back to Pienaar.

"I just couldn't work out what had got into him," Turnbull recalls, "but obviously something or somebody had got at him. He was breaking up before my eyes."

But it was time. Time to head off to the city for the hook-up. "Do you want a lift with me, Francois?" Turnbull remembers asking him.

"No, it's alright, I'll go with James [Small]," Pienaar replied, with his eyes still averted from Turnbull's.

And now there's a funny thing. When they got to the studio, there was James Small alright, and fly-half Joel Stransky and Hennie Le Roux and Tiaan Strauss — and a whole phalanx of South African lawyers — but no Francois Pienaar.

"Where's Francois?" Turnbull asked Small.

"He had to go somewhere," Turnbull remembers him replying a little evasively, though for whatever reason the winger didn't seem particularly perturbed by it. Turnbull wished he could claim the same.

Time to begin. With the clicking of a few buttons, the wonders of modern technology would soon fill the television screen at the end of the table with vision of senior All Blacks in Auckland — Sean Fitzpatrick, Mike Brewer, Ian Jones, Eric Rush, Olo Brown — and, shortly, an equally senior collection of Wallabies in Sydney — Phil Kearns, David Campese, Warwick Waugh and Tim Kava.

The Australian contingent had come to the Comtech offices in the inner-city Sydney suburb of Alexandria after training with Randwick Rugby Club at an oval nearby and they were still in their tracksuits when they arrived, a little late. Other people at the Sydney end of the link from the very beginning were Brian Powers, Geoff Levy, head of Kerry Packer's Nine Network, David Leckie, and Tony Greig.

A video of the conference was taken at the South African end for use as a promotional tool to demonstrate to players in the South African provinces just how committed the Australians and New Zealanders were to the cause. The Australasians obliged, though their commitment stood in rather stark contrast to the extremely trepidatious noises the South Africans themselves made ...

A collection of "highlights" from the hour-long tape serves as perhaps the best historical record of all from the Rugby War, giving the precise temper of the times at the height of the fight ...

Geoff Levy is mine host for the show and, after a few welcoming remarks, he introduces Brian Powers, Kerry Packer's chief of business operations.

Powers: "We are firmly behind this competition and the reasons we are behind it are very simple. We think it is going to work financially, and we think it is going to be good for the game ...

"It is going to be a product we are going to be proud of. We are convinced that this is going to be the model for [an] international, professional sports League ...

"I think the player reaction is what really has drawn us into this. I'm amazed at the backing from players all over the world, the commitment of the players. I don't think anyone has any illusions about the pressure that you guys are going to be put under and I know everyone in South Africa is feeling that pressure right now.

"I think that a lot of people around the world have relied on you guys hanging tough and we want to give you all the support we can to make sure you do that."

David Leckie then spoke, pointing out that his Nine Network was the number-one network in Australia, that they were committed to sport generally and had "won seven of the last nine worldwide awards for the Grand Prix Formula One racing coverage".

"We think [WRC] is going to make rugby a hell of a lot better sport than it is now," he said. "It is that simple from us. We are not mucking around, we are not a 'midget' [as] I think we were called the other day. We are quite the opposite, we are very committed."

So far, so good. The two heavyweights from the Packer organisation had spoken and given a firm commitment that they were backing it.

So to the players, and what this video conference was really all about.

Sean Fitzpatrick was up first, from the Auckland end of the line.

"We are pleased to say," he said, "that … in terms of the New Zealand position, we have at the moment 64 players signed up, which includes 23 of the World Cup Squad that went to South Africa …

"It is not just the dollars that are enticing us, it is … the whole concept of the WRC proposal which we like.

"Our position now is we've rolled our dice. We have said that we are into this and we are totally behind it, so at the moment we are feeling the pressure probably as much as you guys are, but we want to make it work.

"One of our concerns is obviously the South Africans' position, and it was nice to speak to you on Monday, Hennie, and be reassured … and I spoke to Francois after I spoke to you, and he once again reassured me that you guys are totally behind it which was nice to hear."

It was good stuff from Fitzpatrick. In terms of launching something like this, you can't do much better than a commitment from an All Black captain that he and his men are with it.

But Fitzpatrick has one thing to add — a rather touching indication of the level of concern some of the senior players had that the rest of the rugby world was also taken care of.

"Our position in terms of the basic philosophy of the WRC," he says, "[is that] we don't want to break down any of the traditional infrastructure that is in place at the moment, we just want the game to continue and … and … "

And Mike Brewer finishes for him:

"And if it's possible and feasible [we want] to maintain the current infrastructure that we all know is one of the philosophies of WRC."

It was as good an indication as any that the key players really were genuine believers at this stage that the Unions would come to their senses and sign with WRC — just like they had.

So goodo, and moving right along. Now it is the turn of the Australians to give their commitment. We now cross to our Sydney studio where a still sweaty Phil Kearns has arrived from training with three of his Wallaby colleagues. Over to you, Big Phil …

"Okay," Kearns says, master of the situation, "we've got 60 players signed, sealed and delivered. The only point we are reiterating to everyone is just that we have to stay together and stick together and don't budge on that …

"I know Sean and I have spoken about this a fair bit and I've spoken to Hennie and Francois and as long as we stick together then we are strong, so that is our position. At the moment we will have our 90 players by the end of next week and that is our quota filled."

Great. Everything's going well. Well enough to return to Brian Powers to emphasise once again to anyone who might be even remotely jittery that WRC had *commitment* like the Sahara had sand.

Brian Powers: "If I can just make a comment, in response to the question from New Zealand, I think we are probably 24–48 hours away from wanting to make an announcement."

So, fine. So now to the moment that everyone has been waiting for. What is the true level of commitment out of South Africa? There have been all sorts of wild stories around about where they're up to, and as the cross is made to Johannesburg, the people in Sydney and Auckland all lean forward to hang on every word …

It is Hennie Le Roux who is the first to speak. After a couple of innocuous remarks about the wonders of modern technology, he gets to the point.

"Firstly, I would like to make apologies for Francois not being here," Le Roux says. "He is under immense pressure at this stage and I think he is getting ready for a couple of law suits that are being put on him from various people. Obviously, names don't have to be mentioned."

Of course not, Hennie, but get to the heart of it, man, we are *killing* ourselves to know if you blokes are still with it or not.

Le Roux: "We are putting in our best endeavours at this stage to ensure that the tables are cleared and the best contract on the table obviously wins the day, but at this stage we are very confident that we know which is the best contract."

WHAT!?!? Hang on, Hennie, we've got our arses on the line here! And you blokes are telling us the "*best contract wins the day*"!?!? Here's an idea, son, what about the ONE YOU SIGNED **FIRST** WINS THE DAY! The same one that we bloody well signed on the basis that you blokes were all backing it to the hilt!

No one in any of the studios actually liked to say anything, but the consternation on their faces is clear. Brian Powers is restrained in his reaction, although he and David Leckie do exchange rather thoughtful looks.

Soon it's Tiaan Strauss' turn. Perhaps the famous South African No. 8 will give a better commitment. We can only hope.

Tiaan Strauss: "Like Hennie said, I think we need a little bit of time at this stage to sort out the contracts coming from SARFU and also from the other people, and just get everything straightened out what is on the table and we want to really go into and make a business deal and make the best deal for the players."

!!!!!!!!!!!!!!!!!!!!!!!!!!!

Sean Fitzpatrick, in Auckland, could stand it no longer: "Hennie, it's New Zealand here, could we just clarify if any of you [have] signed a WRC contract?"

Hennie Le Roux: "Yes, in principle there are signatures on paper which are held with a person in trust, yes, definitely, I think most of the side, the squad has been signed up, and I think together we are looking at about 120–130 players ... "

Fitzpatrick: "So what you guys are saying ... to clarify it in our position ... what *we* have done is we've signed the contracts and we are totally committed to going with WRC. *Legally* we are committed and I think that, I'm sure the Australians are probably in the same position as us ... "

Phil Kearns: "We've got 60 signatures on paper, and as I say, 90 by the end of next week. So we have pen on paper, signed, sealed and delivered, as I said before."

The discussion proceeds thus, until there is a rather awkward silence from South Africa, whereupon Brian Powers jumps back into the fray, telling the players it's probably a good idea not to get into a legal discussion during this hook-up. He also gives an indication of his own organisation's thinking at this moment — that Murdoch would fall away if only the players hung tough.

"If you hold together for about another three or four days," Powers says, "this is going to be a fact that people around the world are going to realise [it] is going to work. They will lose their backing. The fellow who is telling you he has all this money doesn't have very much money. And if you all hold together, that will disappear and we will be in a situation ... to get a very quick peace with the Unions once they realise the players are stuck together. So without arguing legalities, I think that is the point everybody needs to remember here ... "

That and the fact that you South Africans bloody well signed like the rest of us, and now you're disintegrating before our eyes.

Presently, after a bit more chit-chat every which way, Hennie Le Roux then asks for advice from the other two teams on how they were able to withstand the pressure. After a few suggestions from other participants, David Campese weighs in, with a long and rambling speech the theme of which appears to be that it is better to maintain a deceptive stance of public neutrality even if privately committed to WRC.

David Campese: "I say, 'Look, I've still got to play rugby yet, I'll have a look at what happens when I finish the season.' But in the meantime, just play the game, get on with it and just say, 'Look, I want to play rugby.' You've got the Currie Cup, you've got other things on your mind, I mean basically rugby is a game to enjoy, you don't talk about contracts. When the season is finished you say, 'My solicitors have got the contract, I've got a few options, I've got Australia, some rugby league team in Australia wants to sign me up.' Just tell them bullshit, but don't get to a situation when they say, 'You must sign this now.' Just say, 'Look, I've got the Currie Cup to play, look I just don't want to talk about it yet.'"

Just tell them bullshit. It was to be this policy, taken by so many of the people involved, of systematically playing so fast and loose with the truth that no one knew who to trust any more, that would perhaps cause the most angst in the whole of the Rugby War.

All involved on the WRC side of the Rugby War agree that this was by far the most difficult aspect of the whole affair, though they are equally convinced that it was necessary.

As Michael Hill asks, "How else are you going to run a revolution? You simply can't broadcast your every move."

Geoff Levy agrees: "It was a very difficult thing. The reason [for denying one's commitment] was that once somebody becomes public that they'd signed, then it almost becomes very difficult for them not to come up public about everybody else who had signed. Whereas if you do that as part of a big group of people, there is a big difference.

"The other thing was that as part of the marketing [and] PR campaign that followed, we wanted to make it clear to the public that the players had given long consideration to both views — which they had done extensively — and ultimately when they did come out publicly in favour of WRC it would be seen as 'well, these players have given proper consideration to the pros and cons of it and have gone the WRC route and ... '."

And back to the video conference, where David Campese is still not done ...

"I know Louis Luyt," Campese continues, reaching for another way to give the South Africans some mettle. "I saw him on the plane on Sunday, on Saturday night here, 'cos he was heading on the plane back to South Africa. Like, he's an arrogant arsehole, so what you've got to do is don't cop any shit, guys. I mean, after rugby, I mean you've got to make a life of it, so get out there and do it."

Thank you, Campo.

Presently, Derek Dallow, the Davenports lawyer, proffers his own advice as to how the South Africans should proceed.

"Just talking on behalf of the players here," Dallow says, "I have been asked to just pass on to the South African players that to get the ball game really rolling with the World Cup Squad, what they did was five of them had had enough of all the talk and all the legalese and the contracts. They were committed, they believed in it, and they stepped forward and signed and said, 'We are unconditionally on board and we are totally committed,' and it was amazing what followed after that in terms of the rest of the World Cup Squad virtually followed into line and I think what the New Zealand group would like to pass on to the South Africans is that some of those Transvaal ones who are under pressure, if you really do believe in the WRC, make that move two or three or four of you who are prepared to step forward and I believe you will also get the others to fall into line."

There was more rambling as the conference wound down, but no basic change to the attitude of the South Africans. Despite making a few more positive noises towards the close, it was clear to everyone, in the words of one of the participants, "That the South Africans were just shot ducks, they were running scared, rattled, hopeless."

Sean Fitzpatrick for one, was extremely annoyed at the South African performance.

"We were thinking, they are not with us, they have been lying to us — especially Pienaar, after saying categorically that he was in. I had spoken to him a number of times and it just annoyed me that he wasn't at the video conference to start with, which made me think 'what the bloody hell is going on here?'

"[Pienaar] said that, 'Louis had put the pressure on, but that Louis' money could never buy him etc, etc.' If he had come out and said to me, 'Look, Sean, we have been offered this and there is no way we can't accept it, blah blah, blah' well, okay, but to [leave us] sitting on the garden path … "

And Fitzpatrick thought *he* was angry. Ross Turnbull, who'd been sitting in the South African studios and watching proceedings, aghast, was so angry he could hardly raise spit: "It was the most bloody pathetic performance by a group of sportsmen I'd seen. The [South Africans] were all over the bloody shop."

Turnbull had not said a word himself, feeling it was more a meeting of the players than officials like him, but he simply couldn't believe how "gutless" the South Africans had been.

He had more things than that to worry about on that afternoon, however. For starters, he and James Packer had a very important meeting that afternoon with M-Net to lock them in to guaranteeing the Springboks' WRC salaries, and thus hose down the whole South African problem.

James Packer had come through with his negotiations with M-Net, the documents had been drawn up, and at 5.30pm, after some final going-over of the contract terms, both sides — M-Net and PBL — were due to sign.

It is admittedly a difficult deal to understand, but Ross Turnbull's version of it goes like this: "At that point of time, Louis Luyt was running around South Africa saying, 'Packer's a peanut' or something, 'a midget' or whatever else, and he's got nothing. So the Springboks were concerned that Packer wouldn't or couldn't deliver.

"So we wanted this deal with M-Net, that was going to guarantee them their payments and, in return, M-Net got television rights for 10 years and whatever else ... "

Turnbull and James Packer arrived at the M-Net headquarters, and were ushered into the offices of Russell McMillan, the M-Net Sports Director. The mood around the walnut conference table was light and buoyant — businessmen doing a business deal that both sides were happy with, the way that Ross Turnbull tells it.

"We went through all the terms and conditions which James had sorted out with them the night before and we were all set to sign," Turnbull recounts.

The crucial clauses in the document were the following two:

4 UNDERWRITING.

4.1 *M-Net hereby agrees to underwrite the total fee payable to the Players arising from the Standard Players' Agreement, signed with the Players during the existence of these agreements, i.e. for a maximum of 3 (three) years commencing on 22 November 1995.*

4.3 *It is specifically agreed that M-Net's commitment in terms hereof is limited to the 26 (twenty six) Players forming part of the South African Squad chosen to compete in the 1995 World Cup and that the maximum commitment shall not exceed $US18.2 million at any stage ...*

Everything seemed fine. As near as Turnbull could tell the M-Net people were happy, and he fully expected them to reach for their pens to put their signatures to the contract — which was just as well, as he, James and their lawyers had dinner reservations for 7pm that night at the Portuguese restaurant at the Sandton Sun. From the moment the meeting had begun, Turnbull felt that it would be one hour maximum before the whole thing could be wrapped up and the deal sealed, as it were. (*Hallelujah!*) If they got to it, they would still have time to freshen up and change.

Then to what seemed like a minor hiccup ... Russell McMillan, who was running the show, said, in Turnbull's memory, that there were "a couple of points he wanted clarified by his board before signing".

Still, no problem.

"They said," Turnbull recalls, "that they would ring us back by 10 o'clock that night [at Harry Viljoen's house]. We left. James called his dad and told him what was happening. We went out to dinner with the lawyers, came back to the house by 10pm and waited for the call. The call never came.

"James slept [stayed] on the lounge by the phone waiting for the call, and the call never came through that night."

Or ever after, for that matter. As simple as that. As a matter of fact, the following morning, the M-Net people weren't even taking calls. It was as if the phone-lines had gone dead.

Ian Frykberg, who was monitoring the whole thing from his Sandton Sun hotel room, breathed more than a simple sigh of relief when one of his sources informed him of what had happened.

"I've no doubt," he says now, "that if M-Net had signed that document then and there, locking the Springboks in to WRC, and putting Johann Rupert in an alliance with Kerry Packer in backing the whole thing, they would have achieved a great deal of momentum. It would have been very, very difficult to stop."

Ross Turnbull couldn't agree more.

"If they'd signed," he says with certitude, "then it was *on*. We were one hour away from wrapping it up."

So just what had happened?

"I did talk to Johann Rupert," Sam Chisholm concedes. "All I said was that we would give 'sympathetic consideration' to dealing with him in future, if he co-operated with us now," Chisholm says.

Ahem. Another highly-placed source who was in close consultation with News Corporation at that time has it that what a very forceful Sam Chisholm really said to Johann Rupert was: "If you do this deal with these guys it will be war."

True or not, there could surely have been no more potent warning coming from an organisation of that size and power. But …

"No," says Chisholm firmly. "All I said was we'd give them sympathetic consideration."

It was a tiny little pub on the Taupo-Napier highway out in the backblocks of New Zealand, only five kilometres or so from the middle of nowhere. There was one barman, and one customer, both with the air of being every bit as lost and lonely as the pub itself. The clock on the wall read 5.50pm, as the sound came to them of a car screeching to a halt outside.

They looked up, only vaguely interested. This city fella then burst in, waving an impotent mobile phone that simply refused to pick up a signal this far out in the boon-docks.

"Can we use your phone!?!?" he burst out, without so much as even saying hello.

The barman nodded, without a word.

The fella then waved urgently to the man and woman in the car, for them to come in too. One of the newcomers looked familiar, maybe a little like Jock Hobbs, the former All Black captain. But the two locals kept their peace, still not saying a word, as this bloke picked up the phone and started shouting into it.

He was yelling urgently at some television journalist in Wellington, it seemed, something about how this journalist had to make it absolutely clear on the evening news bulletin that, hear this well, the Union would NEVER negotiate with WRC. The fella said that it was all very well for Laurie Mains to be saying that the two sides should sit down and talk to each other, as he was apparently going to be saying on the news that night, but that had to be balanced with the truth — that it simply wasn't going to happen! Not now, *not ever!*

And another thing! the bloke kept shouting. The journalist should see this WRC contract he'd just got hold of, 'cos you just wouldn't believe it, how full of holes it was, how there was absolutely no obligation on the part of WRC to pay the players a single solitary cent if they didn't get up. The journalist absolutely HAD TO get some of these points of view on the news, because it was crucial that both the public and the players realised as quickly as possible how shonky the whole WRC structure was.

The journalist resisted it seemed, saying it was too late, that that night's news had already been put to bed and you simply couldn't put any more stuff in now, no matter how newsworthy it might be.

"Just DO IT for me!" the fellow shouted just before hanging up. "It's VERY IMPORTANT."

So it really *was* Jock Hobbs! About 15 minutes after the fellow had slammed the phone down, he'd taken a seat in front of the television to watch the national news, and it had suddenly become like a mirror. For there he was up on the screen, filmed earlier in the day coming out of a meeting with provincial players — this same fellow who was still sitting in the bar watching the news with them! — and he at least seemed a bit happier that what he'd wanted had been put in. The journalist had come through for him.

The news was no sooner finished, though, than the three visitors had gone back to their car and roared off into the night — the money for the phone call left on the table behind them.

In the car, Jock Hobbs, NZRFU Marketing Manager Brendon O'Connor and a lawyer from Kensington Swan by the name of Anne Brennan, kept going hard to their next appointment — this time with the provincial players from King Country. Jock would hammer the same theme as always.

"The ding is on the table!" had become his catchcry — "ding" being his slang for money.

The former flanker would repeat the line endlessly, using great drama, pauses, body language, and occasional table thumping to ram home his point. The experienced litigator in him shone through.

"The ding is on the table. Those other people haven't got any money. Where is it coming from?" he would ask rhetorically.

"Just think about that for a moment! The ding is on the table *now*. It's in your hands, don't throw it all away based on shallow promises from people you don't even know."

It was persuasive stuff, particularly from a former All Black captain.

Beside him all the way through it, Brendon O'Connor found himself particularly impressed, and he wrote as much in a letter to an Australian journalist who had enquired of him what it was like.

"The experience of working with Jock in those extraordinary circumstances illustrated to me what it truly meant to be an All Black," he wrote. "The fact that a handful of players might have been tampering with a history, a part of New Zealand society and culture, seemed to hurt him personally.

"Jock put his reputation, standing and soul on the line, marked his line in the sand. Even though I am around about 30 years old and I have always followed the All Blacks, it took an experience like that to make me understand the passion and the courage that it takes to be one."

Other New Zealanders were equally impressed. At seemingly every port of call around the country, at every service station and stop, people would only have to recognise Hobbs and they would wish him luck, slap him on the back and tell him not to give up, they were right behind him.

Go, Jock, go.

Elsewhere, the beat went on. Back in Australia on the Thursday morning, Michael Hill had done what he did every morning — sent a fax to Nick Falloon, the Finance Director at Channel Nine, to give him a daily update of who had signed where.

Generally, those numbers were good, ticking over everywhere all over the world, with two notable exceptions — England and Ireland. In England, the "Carling Factor" still held sway, and even at this late stage they had only 10 of the World Cup Squad signed. But even that, even *that*, was fantastic compared with what was happening in Ireland.

There, of the World Cup Squad, they had a sum total signed of ... *none*.

"I just couldn't get any sense out of the Irish," says Hill. "Everything was always going to happen 'soon', or 'maybe tomorrow', but, of course, 'tomorrow' never came."

Finally, though, something definite. On August 3, he'd got a firm commitment out of Brendan Mullin that he and the senior players would be meeting in a Dublin pub that night, and maybe there'd be some signed contracts coming out of that.

It was Hill's firm hope that the senior players would become infused with some urgency for the whole thing, call a meeting of the whole Irish team for the following night, and get the whole lot signed, en masse.

All he could do, though, was wait for the following morning to call Brendan and find out what had happened ...

Chapter ten

The tide turns

"Well????" Michael Hill asked the following day when he at last got Brendan Mullin on the phone again. "Are the Irish boys ready to sign up?"

"No," Mullin replied in that exceedingly casual way of his, "this week is a long weekend so all the boys are going away."

"Brendan!" an exasperated Hill near shouted back down the phone. "These guys have got the chance to earn $US700 thousand over three years, and I know probably some of them are unemployed! I know it's a holiday weekend, Brendan, but geeeeeeez! Are they going to deal with it after they come back from holidays? I mean I'd have thought there might be a chance you'd even sign before you went away for the weekend ... !?!?"

"No, no," Mullin's voice came back as nonchalant as you please, "the boys are going to meet next Tuesday night, and we might have some news then."

Hill couldn't quite believe it. After telling Brendan he'd call him then, the Newcastle lawyer decided, in desperation, to ring a fellow lawyer in Seamus Connolly, the one who had been involved as

Mullin's solicitor. He would see if he could at least communicate to *him* the extreme urgency of getting the Irish contracts signed.

In some ways there was a whole organisation ready and waiting to launch if they could just do so without the glaring hole in their armour that an entire missing nation would be. After all, they could hardly announce the launch of the "World Except Ireland Rugby Corporation". Maybe, at least, Connolly could see that.

"No, I'm very sorry, Mr Hill," said his very polite secretary, "but Mr Connolly has gone to the Galway races."

"The *what?*"

"The Galway races ... for anybody in Ireland, you've got to go to the Galway races. Would you like the number of his hotel?"

... "Hello? Yes, I'd like to speak to one of your guests please, Mr Seamus Connolly."

"We're very sorry, sir, but Mr Connolly isn't in right now," came the soft feminine Irish brogue in reply.

"Well do you have a fax machine there? Can I SEND HIM A FAX?"

"Yes, sir," came back that lovely soft Irish lilt, "we have a fax machine, but we wootn't be turnin' it on, 'tis early in the mornin'."

It was 10am, Irish time. 1956, as far as Hill could see.

He gave up.

Instead, he made his next call to Warren Alcock in New Zealand. The phone calls and faxes between Hill and Alcock had been constant at this time, with the New Zealand lawyer still apparently keen to get his 50 provincial players signed up with WRC.

So to one of the seminal moments of the War. On the morning of Friday, August 4, the Springboks gathered in the Protea Hotel, in the Midrand, midway between Johannesburg and Pretoria. It was time for them to make a definitive decision about whether or no they were going to sign back with SARFU.

What had it come down to in the end? Consider yourself. You are now a Springbok trying to make up your mind between a WRC contract and a SARFU contract.

In the company of your team-mates, you've filed into this hotel conference room and the Chief Executive Officer of the Union has offered you the chance to sign a South African Rugby Football Union contract *guaranteeing* you the equivalent of $US250,000 a year for each of the next three years. You might also have an awareness that if you do not sign this contract by 5pm then you risk never being able to pull on a rugby boot in South Africa again. Or at least be denied access to run onto any playing field under the control of SARFU — pretty much every rugby ground that counts.

Meantime, you've also signed your deal with the World Rugby Corporation, offering you similar dollars. But while it's true that it seems like a terrific concept in terms of its global vision and fully professional nature, to this point you have not seen a single solitary rand from them. Not a dollar, not a cent, not a penny, not a peanut.

The minor matter of the fact that you've actually already signed a contract with WRC can be got around by the fact that Francois Pienaar is still holding that contract in his possession, and can give it back to you when you ask for it. As a matter of fact, he's got them in his car outside, and can bring them to you at a moment's notice.

Oh. And one more thing to think about. Tomorrow you are going out onto the field once more to play in yet another torrid provincial encounter of the Currie Cup, South Africa's premier provincial competition.

Stories of players "doing their knee" at crucial moments are legion in rugby circles, and every player taking the pitch knows it is quite possible he will suffer an injury that will mean he will never play the game again.

But if you sign the SARFU contract, now, this Friday morning, the riches are assured, and it simply doesn't matter what happens on the Saturday. The only condition placed upon you by Griffiths is that you must first hand to him your WRC contract. Then he will give you your SARFU contract to sign. After that is signed, it doesn't matter if tomorrow you do both knees irreparably, and break both of your arms for good measure. Financially, you will still be enjoying *rude* good health.

So which of the two contracts do you want your body tied to?

Tick, tick, tick …

And that's how long it took for most of the Springboks to sign, when it came right down to it. About three ticks.

When Griffiths had been asked to leave the room so the team could discuss it privately, a very subdued Francois Pienaar had spoken in favour of signing, and had only been countered by Hennie Le Roux and James Small, who had spoken against. It was at this point that the Springbok coach Kitch Christie had weighed in.

"I've kept out of it to this point," one of the players remembers their mentor saying, "because I've always thought it's your business what you do. But now I'm asking you to do what you must know is the right thing. I want you to sign with SARFU, for the team, for the country, for yourselves, for what we've already achieved."

The players voted overwhelmingly in favour of returning to the fold, and then Griffiths was allowed back in.

From there the players — less some five who had to leave in a rush to catch flights for their Currie Cup game the following day — were ushered into a room where Dr Luyt's lawyer daughter Corlia Oberholzer awaited them with the contracts. Nearly all of the remaining players signed.

Two notable members of the South African World Cup Squad who would prove reluctant to commit themselves were James Small and Chester Williams. Small eventually signed a full month later, with no recriminations against him for his delay.

Williams, who had not attended the meeting in the first place, simply decided at that point he didn't want to sign with *anybody*.

With the signing en masse of the Springboks, the whole WRC

structure had just had one of its principal and most impressive stanchions blown out from beneath it. WRC had started listing badly, even if it hadn't yet quite collapsed.

It was all dramatic enough, and seemed final enough, for Edward Griffiths to call a press conference at 1pm that day in Johannesburg and announce on national television that, "the threat to rugby in this country has been thwarted. We have faced the rape of rugby in this country and withstood it."

The news got out quickly. Back in Sydney, Simon Poidevin was in his Coogee Beach home, when he took a call from Ian Frykberg telling him the wonderful news. It had confirmed a conversation Poidevin had had late the previous night, when he had made one last try to get through to Francois Pienaar on his mobile phone. The Springbok captain had been incommunicado since disappearing around the time of the video hook-up, but Poidevin thought he'd try ringing one more time before going to bed.

Bingo. Pienaar's voice had come through Poidevin's phone, loud and clear, albeit hurried and frazzled from the first instant. He was at his office, with a gathering of the Transvaal Springboks, he said, the strain clear in his words. It was, to Poidevin's mind, the voice of a man who had simply had enough and didn't care what happened so long as the pressure stopped. For all the tension in Pienaar's voice, though, his next words were an anthem to the Australian's ears ...

"Alright, Simon, *alright*. We've had enough, the boys are all here and we're going to sign with the Union tomorrow. We've had enough, we've had enough."

They'd had enough. The way Poidevin remembers it, he would have done cartwheels right then and there, bar the fact that for all Pienaar's promising words, the Springboks hadn't *actually* yet signed with SARFU. And now they had. *Now they had!*

Outside his window, the waves pounded all the same, as they had for thousands of years past, and would for thousands of years to come.

The Springboks' capitulation to the establishment may not mean much in the finer scheme of things, when judged against the centuries, but in the here and now, for a certain section of the rugby world, it was a very very big deal indeed. Surely it was all over.

Surely, *surely*, Ross Turnbull would now have got the message that the game was up, that South Africa was a wasteland as far as his ambitions for the WRC went?

Not our Ross.

At 3pm that same afternoon he called his own press conference — his first since the beginning of the Rugby War — to say how profoundly shocked he was that the Springboks had reneged on their word.

"We expect our contracts to be honoured," he said flatly, before continuing.

"I think the atmosphere within the administration of rugby in South Africa is surrounded by threats, intimidation and misinformation. Rugby should be above that. Rugby players around the world have generously embraced the vision of WRC and have made commitments accordingly. We are moving ahead with full steam and we expect to be in a position to make important announcements favourable to WRC in the immediate future."

What Turnbull didn't say, but already knew, was that he was also going to take SARFU to court, immediately. WRC was going to ask for a hearing on the following day, Saturday, to get the national Union to stop bullying the South Africans into reneging on the contracts that he claimed they had lawfully signed. Of course, there was one small problem in that those contracts were back in the possession of SARFU — meaning it was entirely unprovable just who had signed what — but Turnbull went ahead anyway.

He was just like that.

This time, though, he would be going it alone. James Packer had decided to fly home to Sydney. Before leaving for the airport, he came briefly to Turnbull's room wished him all the best and, in apparent reference to the ongoing fights between the Packer and Murdoch camps, told him on the way out the door: "We're in the middle of fights over Super League and horse racing. We don't want any more."

It was the first of what would be many signs that the Packer organisation was not *actually* fully committed to the project. Turnbull felt a growing sense that WRC would have to regain momentum quickly or the Rugby War would be lost.

With that in mind, Turnbull, with his South African lawyers, worked on into Friday night preparing the affidavit they would file the following day in their effort to get an injunction granted. They included in the affidavit a copy of the document signed by Pienaar a week earlier, which was the nearest thing to proof positive they had that the contracts they had with the Springboks actually existed.

(Or, more likely by this time, *had* existed.)

The issue, as pointed out at the time by the Cape Town lawyer that Ross Turnbull engaged, Raymond Mallach, was this:

"We don't have all the contracts, but that doesn't mean they are not binding. What matters is if you can prove their existence."

What was also clearly required was some firm evidence of the circumstances in which the Springboks had been allegedly encouraged to break those contracts. It was in their failure to make any headway whatsoever in convincing some of the Springboks to give evidence to that effect that Turnbull realised just how badly the South African players had been spooked.

"When we were then going to the court case, two of these players were offered [by us] I think $US1.5 million each. *Unconditional* US dollars," Turnbull recalls. "They would have contracts guaranteed with the WRC and to be witnesses to this harassment in our court case. Unconditional guaranteed ... and they *still* didn't [want to do it]. Two of the Springboks."

That money, it should be noted, was absolutely not being offered as a bribe to the Springboks to give evidence, but as a guarantee that their financial future was secure whatever happened. It was money to be paid against their future earnings from WRC, and if that competition didn't get up, then WRC had the contacts to make sure that it would be paid out against their services. Perhaps playing for one of the Australian rugby league teams.

Whatever, even without any witnesses to go into court with, Ross Turnbull did what he did best — he kept going.

In Johannesburg, Dr Luyt admits to something more than surprise, when he heard that Turnbull was still out there, *still* going.

"I could not believe it," he says flatly. "I could *not* believe it."

He'd get used to it.

A t last, a genuine, *bona fide*, card-carrying *breakthrough*. With bells on, yet.

It was the best news for the Australian Rugby Union in the whole sorry saga to date. On the afternoon of Friday, August 4, the Wallaby no. 8, Tim Gavin, had gone to see Ian Ferrier and Matt Carroll in Ferrier's offices. Gavin had liked what he'd heard, had never been enamoured of the whole WRC concept anyway — and had never signed one of their contracts. This man from the country town of Cumnock, New South Wales, pretty much made up his mind then and there.

On his way out of the building, Gavin was intercepted by a waiting Channel Seven camera crew and, as was his way, said what he thought. His comments went out on the evening news bulletin, and then into the papers the following day: "I've enjoyed playing for my country," he said. "I've enjoyed playing for the NSW Waratahs, and I want it to remain that way.

"The blokes have got to make their own minds up, but I never saw WRC as an option. I'm very proud to be called a Wallaby. My ultimate decision to stay with the ARU had nothing to do with money. But I can see how some of the younger blokes could be swayed.

"It is such a tremendous honour to play for one's country. The build-up to a Test match — it's something money simply can't buy. I never played the game looking for a financial inducement. But, sadly, some of the blokes have been blinded by dollar signs. Friendships have certainly been strained.

"In some ways, I feel disappointed and disenchanted with some of the guys in the pro-WRC camp, but I still call them my friends."

At last, the Australian Rugby Union had one of the senior Wallabies publicly supporting them. At their own press conference shortly after Gavin had been recorded by Channel Seven, Ian Ferrier confidently predicted that: "By the middle of next week, I expect the whole of the Wallabies to be signed up [to the ARU]."

The ARU also put out a press release designed to dampen even the mildest speculation that they would *ever* do a deal with the World Rugby Corporation, or, as they called it on this day, "The World Rugby Circus".

"The proposal that the national and provincial Unions accept the notion of franchising — akin to a fast-food outlet — is both opportunistic and naive," the statement read.

"This response stems directly from the rather pathetic view World Rugby Circus has that the national and provincial rugby unions of world rugby will accept the imposition of WRC as the governing body."

It's called the Paris Cafe, and it wasn't far from the War Office. On Saturday morning, August 5, Jock Hobbs had a cappuccino with David Howman, a well-known New Zealand sports lawyer who, among many other famous sporting clients, acted for the All Black winger Jeff Wilson.

Which reminded Howman of something, come to think of it ...

"Now, Jock," began the lawyer, after some preliminary chit-chat, "I'd like to talk to you about Jeff's situation ... "

They talked.

If there was a moral atomic bomb in the whole of the Rugby War, it was exploded on that same Saturday morning in Sydney — in the form of an open letter from 13 past Wallaby captains, addressed to the current Wallabies, and the substance of it was published at the top of the front page of *The Sydney Morning Herald*.

It went like this:

STICK WITH THE ARU, PLEASE

To the current Wallabies:

We fully acknowledge you owe us nothing but we ask you to consider the following in the name of Australian rugby.

Please consider very carefully the steps you are about to take in the current situation rugby finds itself.

It seems to us that Australian rugby is standing at a major crossroads and its very future hangs in the balance, depending upon what you do.

From our perspective, it seems the choice between the traditional structure and the so-called rebels is the choice between an exciting new age for the game with all its culture and traditions maintained on the one hand and its polarisation at the hands of a very few on the other.

Remaining faithful to the Australian jersey will not only earn you the respect of the many people who hold it dear but it will stop dead in its tracks the bitter feud that is guaranteed to follow if you turn your back on it.

Some of you seem to take the attitude that the choice between the ARU and the so-called rebels is a choice between moral equivalents.

However, it is our view that whatever faults it may have, the ARU is a representative body of all of Australian rugby; of all the clubs from the Great Australian Bight to Cairns in the north, from Sydney to Perth.

The so-called rebels and their backers, on the other hand, it appears are out to make a dollar out of the game in a fashion entirely foreign to its traditional spirit.

We understand that many of the older players whose careers are nearing their end are pressuring the younger ones to hold the line, to act en bloc and go over to the so-called rebels.

Well, we are older players still and beseech you not to be swayed. We who are retired realise more than ever just what a precious honour it was to play for the Wallabies and we ask you not to take a decision now that you will surely regret for the rest of your lives.

Others have preceded you on the field and it is our hope that many more will follow. The millions who have watched, listened and read of your exploits and all who have had the good fortune to actually play have an equal stake in the game.

They, too, are deserving of consideration.

We believe the traditional game will continue and it would be a tragedy if all of us were deprived of your unquestionable talent and guts and the pride you have engendered in us all.

Good luck,
Simon Poidevin, Mark Ella, Tony Shaw, Peter Johnson, Geoff Shaw, Dr John Solomon, John Thornett, John Hipwell, Mark Loane, Paul McLean, Ken Catchpole, Alex Ross, Nick Farr-Jones.

The overall effect that such a letter had on the Wallabies cannot, of course, be measured. But it was significant. To have 13 such esteemed members of the Australian rugby community, from generations of players stretching back to the 1930s, so united on the one issue certainly whacked a cleaver into the certainty that some of the Wallabies had been feeling for the WRC cause to that point.

In the words of one of the Wallabies, who was as yet uncommitted with either side, "As soon as I read that, it set me to thinking what rugby was meant to be all about in the first place, why I'd started playing it, and by the end of the day I'd decided to sign with the ARU first thing Monday morning."

Other Wallabies, admittedly, were upset by the letter on the grounds that the captains were criticising them, without knowing any of the substance of the WRC concept.

But how could they? The WRC, at that point, had *still* not begun to sell themselves to the public.

That was being fixed. In Auckland, one of the copy-writers from the leading advertising firm, J. Walter Thompson, was just putting the finishing touches to a television ad screen-play that would be put into production as soon as WRC was launched. Excerpts read thus:

SCENARIO

Our cameras travel the country finding All Blacks; at home, at work, training, or relaxing.

Sean Fitzpatrick could be in a high-rise city office, Zinzan Brooke in a television studio.

Andrew Mehrtens may be practising touch finders in a deserted park one misty morning.

Jeff Wilson is out running in picturesque South Island countryside.

Ian Jones would be watching some little kids playing in a muddy game of rugby in a city playground.

Michael Jones is perhaps coaching some teenagers.

Walter Little is pumping iron in a gym. Frank Bunce could be spotting for him. Etc, etc …

Each makes a comment, no one remark is complete in itself, but they're edited together to produce a complete thought, a united players' view.

They're down to earth men who have tackled a tough issue and made their decision.

The pace is fast moving and purposeful, flowing from one situation to the next. We don't just see our All Black stars. Along the way, we see our country too.

We show New Zealand the commitment shared by rugby players the length and breadth of the country, and from all walks of life. Their pride and confidence in the move to support the Rugby World Championship.
Their belief that rugby is the winner.

AUDIO	VIDEO
"Hardest decision we ever made."	Sean Fitzpatrick looks up from his work at a desk in a city office building.
"The World Rugby Championship. We looked at all the options."	Andrew Mehrtens is practising touch finders in a deserted park.
"It's best for the game."	Says Frank Bunce, struggling with a bench press in a gym.
"Minor Unions, struggling clubs, everyone benefits."	Ian Jones is feeding out hay to a dairy herd.
"It's not just us, it's provincial players too, and guys right around the world."	Mike Brewer is just leaving a Canterbury shop.
"This is a players' thing. The players' initiative."	Says Zinzan Brooke in a TV studio.
"People think we want to take something away from rugby. We're adding something."	Michael Jones is putting a club team through its paces.

Voice Over: "Rugby's the winner." Animation forms The World Rugby Championship (logo).

And so on …

In a courtroom in Cape Town, on the afternoon of Saturday, August 5, a significant manoeuvre was carried out by WRC. Ross Turnbull had presented his 40-page affidavit, including a copy of the signed letter showing $US300,000 was promised to Francois Pienaar once he handed over the contracts.

Turnbull also claimed that Dr Luyt and other SARFU representatives had "brought enormous pressure to bear" on the Springboks to return to the establishment. He claimed that SARFU had "induced players" to enter three-year contracts, causing them to "terminate their agreements with [WRC]".

Turnbull claimed that on August 4, Dr Luyt and other representatives of SARFU had put an ultimatum to players that they would have to enter the agreements with SARFU by five o'clock that day, and deliver WRC agreements, or, "They would not play rugby in South Africa again."

The force of this threat had been such, Turnbull said, that Transvaal's Springbok flanker, Ian McDonald, had gone to the WRC lawyer "in tears", and begged that his contract be returned so that he could get it to SARFU in time. Ross Turnbull further claimed that he knew all this because Hennie Le Roux had told him so but, unfortunately, attempts to contact this Springbok to get him to file his own affidavit had failed.

Justice Van Reenen granted an injunction to WRC forbidding SARFU from having contact with any players in South Africa already contracted to WRC, at least until the following Thursday. At that time, he dictated, the court would examine the issue more fully, and SARFU could make legal reply.

Turnbull was thus free to go and talk to whom he pleased, while SARFU was placed in legal handcuffs for five days.

That night he flew back to Harry Viljoen's house in Johannesburg. An emotional Hennie Le Roux was waiting for him when he arrived.

"I'm sorry Ross," he told Turnbull tearfully. "I'm very, very sorry.

The pressure on us was just too great."

Turnbull shook his hand and told him not to worry about it, they'd both get over it.

There was to be no respite. Anywhere. That Saturday afternoon in Sydney, Kearns' club, Randwick, played a game down at Coogee Oval against their fierce local rivals, Easts. All the Test players, including Kearns, were back playing with their clubs that weekend. It was to be a torrid encounter, with no quarter asked or given, and such was the absorbing nature of the battle that for much of the crowd and surely many of the players, the tension of the times was forgotten.

Yet, it would return, it would always return. During one brief break in play it was Kearns' job as hooker to throw the ball into the lineout. In the long pregnant pause after he brought his arm back ready to throw, a sole voice rang out from the cramming crowd.

"Throw the ball in, Kearns … for the good of rugby."

Kearns' shoulders were seen to slump a little, as he settled himself, and then he threw the ball in, and the game continued.

On Sunday morning, Simon Poidevin was woken early, around 6am. It was Sam Chisholm, it was *always* Sam Chisholm — and it wasn't just Poidevin getting the calls. Now in his Los Angeles hotel room, Chisholm was ringing around the clock to all and sundry, harassing, cajoling, threatening, charming — through it all elucidating what was happening and the best way to proceed. In the room next door, his lawyer, Bruce McWilliam, was grabbing quick naps in the 15-minute gaps between his own phone calls from Chisholm.

On this call to Poidevin, Chisholm said that while he was only mildly concerned about the legal action launched by WRC in South Africa, he was genuinely concerned with what might occur if Levy and Turnbull pulled the same manoeuvre in Sydney and Brisbane, where the trickle of players coming back to the fold was as important as it was satisfying.

Now that the Springboks were out of the picture, Chisholm said, the real battleground had switched back to Australasia, and Sydney in particular, where the situation was at its most delicate, teetering on the edge of falling one way or the other.

With that in mind, Chisholm's feeling was that it would be a good idea to have lawyers posted around the Sydney courts on Monday morning to block any immediate injunction that WRC might try to launch to stop the ARU talking to players whom WRC had already contracted.

Poidevin, very much within the axis of power that was trying to turn the tide in Australia, promised that when the rest of Sydney had woken up he would make a few calls and see to it that it happened.

He then went to get the Sunday papers, and read with grim satisfaction an article in that day's *Sun-Herald* by the well-known investigative journalist, Alex Mitchell. It was headlined RUPERT ROUTS REBELS and carried the firm prediction:

For breaking ranks, Philip Kearns won't captain Australia again and Campese won't play for his country again.

Mitchell has a history of writing seemingly outlandish things that later prove to be absolutely correct, but as a matter of fact this did not seem at all outlandish. The common feeling among the rugby brethren then was that Kearns would not be accorded the privilege of running out at the head of the Wallabies again.

Francois Pienaar was facing similar fall-out in his country. On that same day, an article appeared in South Africa's *Sunday Times*, written by the most highly respected rugby writer in the country, Dan Retief, under the headline PIENAAR's CAREER ON THE LINE.

It began:

Springbok captain Francois Pienaar's career was last night in jeopardy following revelations that he agreed to accept $US300,000 to act as an agent for the Kerry Packer-backed World Rugby Corporation.

Pienaar could face accusations that he wilfully set out to denude South African rugby of its stars and may face disciplinary action ...

Just 42 days after South Africa's victory in the World Cup, Pienaar's reputation lies in tatters ...

Allegations made by WRC are the latest episode in a sordid tale of deceit which has seen South Africa's leading players locked in bitter pay-for-play negotiations ...

Pienaar's possible involvement as a key player is a damning indictment.

And so on.

No war is complete without a little hard-ball being played, and the Rugby War had at least its fair share. There is no better illustration of how bloody the battle would get than the situation of Simon Poidevin and Tim Kava — long-time friends and team-mates at the Randwick rugby club — but now very much in opposite camps.

Both received particularly stinging hard-balls of different varieties. In the case of Poidevin, it was the constantly repeated accusation that the reason he was riding this so closely was because he was himself on a success fee of millions of dollars from either News Corporation or CSI (the accusation varied), if it got up.

"Absolutely, 100 per cent not true," says Poidevin — and he is backed in this by howling laughter at the very thought from Sam Chisholm and Ian Frykberg on down.

But the accusation hurt.

Instead, Poidevin says, the reason he felt so strongly and was so heavily involved was, "because it was a situation of my credibility".

"I was involved early with drawing into negotiations Frykberg and Chisholm — both of whom were my close friends — and suddenly there was a large-scale ambush on that particular process. I also believed very strongly that WRC would be a disaster for rugby union."

He also notes that monetary considerations weren't entirely removed from the equation. "I have an occupation as a stock broker, and News Corporation are a very important company to dealings I have, but that's it."

And Tim Kava? This well-known lock took a phone call where he was threatened by a NSWRU official with no less than legal prosecution for his presumed involvement with the WRC side of things. As the player representative on the board of New South Wales Rugby Union Ltd, the allegation was that he had breached his duties and obligations as a director by acting in a manner contrary to the interests of that company.

Kava took independent legal advice — to the effect that he definitely had not breached any law — but resigned from the board anyway.

The Kava episode, Ian Ferrier acknowledges, though he was not the one who made the call, was "a regrettable mistake". This war would have its fair share of mistakes, on both sides, as people did and said things under extreme pressure that they might otherwise have steered a mile clear of.

Have spiel, will wheel. Ross Turnbull was out and about, all over the Republic of South Africa. Like Wile E. Coyote with a multi-pronged fist of pens, he was signing up players left, right, centre and wing-three-quarters. It was easy. The provincial players now had their noses seriously out of joint that the Springboks had cut a deal that simply did not include them, so they were more keen than ever to back the WRC.

There was even the first signs that public opinion might have swung against the establishment in general, and the Springboks in particular. The rallying cry of the victorious World Cup campaign had been "One Team, One Country". The joke at this time in the Republic was that the new slogan was "One team, One Million."

So Turnbull — in the company of the famous former Springbok

prop Guy Kebble, who'd signed up with WRC for the duration —
kept going strong, heartened.

On the Sunday he flew to Durban, and on that very day signed
up the balance of the Natal team who had not previously signed with
the WRC agents Turnbull already had on the ground there. Over the
next four days he signed up the leading provincial players of Free
State, Western Province, Eastern Province and Northern Transvaal.

"In four days," Turnbull proudly boasts now, "we entirely isolated
the Springboks."

"We weren't concerned," says Ian Frykberg in reply. "Once the
Springboks had signed up with SARFU, the battle in South Africa
was over, in my opinion. The Springboks were everything."

The fall-out from the Springboks signing with SARFU had
clearly done a lot of damage to the WRC cause outside of
South African borders.

Back in Newcastle, Michael Hill for one realised this when he
called Brendan Mullin in Dublin on Tuesday, only to find that the
Irishman had gone even colder on him.

At a time when Ross Turnbull's legal action in South Africa was
still outstanding, the Irish centre-three-quarter was quite firm in
saying, "We don't want to get involved in any litigation, we're going
to step back for a little while."

Hill had a sense that Mullin was using that as an excuse, that the
Irish really had lost interest in the whole thing.

At least, though, Mullin was contactable. Somewhere in
England, Brian Moore had gone to ground, and Hill could not raise
him for love nor money.

Things were beginning to look grim — the one bright point
being that at least over in New Zealand it looked as if Warren
Alcock really was getting very close to delivering the goods. Hill
had continued on the phone and fax to Alcock, and had every
confidence that he would soon be delivering into the hands of the

World Rugby Corporation no fewer than 50 signed contracts from top provincial players.

That was the only good point on what otherwise seemed to be an increasingly wavering bunch of international players.

So where was Kerry Packer in all this? Distant. Very distant. It was true that his grandfather, Herbert Henry Bullmore had once won a single cap for playing rugby for Scotland against Ireland, on February 22, 1902. And it was true that Kerry Packer himself had played a bit of rugby at school, with his biographer Paul Barry describing him as "quite good". But in this matter of revolutionising rugby, he was never emotionally involved.

Even though his company was now firmly a partner in the venture, with a clear option on taking progressively greater control if the competition was actually launched, at no time did Packer personally roll his sleeves up and get into it at the player level the way he had done with such success years before with World Series Cricket.

On that occasion, he had focused all his personal force upon *making it happen* and was able by personal intervention, to ram it through. A single anecdote serves to illustrate much of the whole.

At one point, in August of '77, many of the Australian cricket players, who were then on a tour of England, were themselves getting more than a little jittery about what would happen to their regular jobs, given that the news of the rebel cricket circuit had caused such a storm.

Packer had flown to London, and all the WSC players were ushered into his suite at the Savoy.

Doug Walters, the famous Australian batsman, who on this occasion had signed with Packer for five times the salary he had been receiving, takes up the story:

"There was an absolute bare minimum of chit-chat, and a beer for everyone, and then Packer took the floor," Walters recalls.

"He started saying that he was very glad we'd all signed, but said that he'd heard that a few of us were nervous about our jobs, and he was here to sort it out."

Which he did.

"Let's start with you, Rick McCosker, what do you do?" Walters recalls Packer asking.

"I work with the Rural Bank, Mr Packer, and I'm a bit concerned that I might lose my job, once all the news about the World Series breaks."

"That's no problem, I've got a pretty healthy account with the Rural Bank and you'll be right. Ian Davis, who do you work with?"

"I work for the Commonwealth Bank, Mr Packer, … and … "

"I've got a better account with the Commonwealth than I do with the Rural Bank," Packer interrupted. "You'll be right.

"Doug, what about you? … oh, you work with Rothmans. That's all right, I smoke enough Rothmans that you'll be right, too."

And so on, around the room.

"It was amazing," Walters says. "Within three minutes he'd been around everybody, and assured everybody that they'd be right … and we were."

And they were. It's possible that had Kerry Packer weighed in at this time with a similar speech to the wavering rugby players, the tide would have turned back to WRC again. But for whatever reason, Packer did not do so.

Ross Turnbull, for one, feels that it was a crucial liability.

"Without Packer there," he says, "we were always going to be up against it, when it came to settling the players' nerves."

Sometimes it wasn't just nerves. Jason Little, the most highly-regarded player in the Wallaby team, signed with the ARU on Tuesday morning at a press conference in Brisbane. This veteran of 36 Tests at the still tender age of 24, told the assembled masses that he'd made up his mind two Saturdays ago …

"It was a very difficult decision," Little said. "I had no strong

South Africa's hugely respected captain Francois Pienaar, triumphantly chaired around Johannesburg's Ellis Park by centre Hennie Le Roux, after his team had defeated the All Blacks in the 1995 World Cup final. It later emerged that Pienaar had been commissioned by the World Rugby Corporation to act as a link between the Springbok players and the rebel group.

Two memorable images from the 1995 World Cup. **Above:** England's fly-half Rob Andrew drops his dramatic last-minute goal that eliminated the Wallabies at the quarter-final stage. **Below:** Andrew again, this time diving bravely but forlornly at the ankles of the Cup's biggest sensation, the devastating Jonah Lomu, during the England-New Zealand semi-final. After this match, an enthusiastic Rupert Murdoch (who had watched, live on television, Lomu dominate the contest) called Sam Chisholm in London and said: "This is amazing . . . we've got to have that guy!"

Australian coach Bob Dwyer (with glasses, centre), flanked by assistants Bob Templeton (left) and Glen Ella during the second Bledisloe Cup clash of 1995, in Sydney. This would be Dwyer's final match in charge of the Wallabies.

Above: *Wallaby centre Jason Little, a prime target for Super League, WRC and the Australian Rugby Union.*

Right: *Michael Lynagh, who retired from international rugby after the 1995 World Cup, despite learning of the WRC proposal during the early stages of the Cup. Bob Dwyer had suggested the Australian captain delay his farewell to take advantage of the huge incomes star players would soon be earning.*

The first All Blacks to turn their backs on WRC and accept what Jock Hobbs was offering on behalf of the NZRFU were the Otago duo, Jeff Wilson (left) and Josh Kronfeld (below).

Right: *South African winger Chester Williams, the first Springbok to abandon WRC.*

Below: *Former England captain Will Carling, who (through his agent) showed scant interest in the WRC proposal.*

By the third week of August, 1995, a ceasefire in the Rugby War had been announced, after all the major southern hemisphere players agreed to support their respective Unions.
Above: In Auckland, Richie Guy (far left) and Rob Fisher look on as Sean Fitzpatrick signs the contract that tied the All Blacks captain to the NZRFU.
Left: Phil Kearns, leans behind Ian Ferrier to hear a comment from Geoff Levy during a press conference in Sydney, where details of the agreement between WRC, the ARU and the Australian players were made public.

Right: *Ross Turnbull, on the steps of the Cape Town Supreme Court, after hearing that, in the Court's judgement, WRC did not have a hold over South Africa's best players. Despite this ruling, and although very few shared his optimism, the indefatigable Turnbull vowed that the fight was not over.*

Below: *Wallaby scrum-half Steve Merrick, who made his Test debut against the All Blacks during 1995 but then chose to ignore the colossal money being offered to the game's elite players . . . to return to life on his farm in Singleton, in the Hunter Valley, two hours drive north of Sydney.*

thoughts one way or the other until the Second Bledisloe Cup Test, when I sang the national anthem in front of all those Wallaby greats.

"It reinforced just how much tradition there is in rugby, and how much the game means to so many people."

On the same day that Little announced his return, the utility Wallaby back, Patrick Howard, also put pen to paper to sign with the ARU. Clearly, a split was now beginning to open up in the Wallaby ranks.

It was, depending on the way you looked at it, either an extremely courageous decision by a leader knowing that it was *he* who had to take the lead — or an equally foolhardy one by a fellow who was needlessly exposing himself to a lot of guaranteed grief.

On Tuesday, August 8, an article appeared in the Australian magazine, *Sports Weekly*, written by the Wallaby captain, Phil Kearns.

It was the first time any of the Wallabies, let alone the captain, had actually stood up publicly and said what he believed in, at least in such strong terms.

"I don't believe the ARU's decision to sign a 10-year agreement with the Murdoch-backed organisation was in the best interests of the future of World rugby," he wrote. "It was about the interests of three nations — Australia, New Zealand and South Africa.

"In comparison, the WRC's plan is to develop the game worldwide. In sport, rarely is a 10-year deal agreed to. Five years, in most cases, is the maximum ... "

"It's our right as players, and our obligation, to make informed decisions," he continued.

"Do I sound as if I support the WRC? Well, yes, I have to say that much of what has been put in front of us has been attractive and, as I see it, the ARU, typically, has been blinkered on this."

The vengeful wrath that descended upon Kearns' head came as soon as the following day. A back-page piece in *The Sydney Morning*

Herald, written by Peter FitzSimons, called for Kearns to resign the Wallaby captaincy. FitzSimons wrote that while Kearns could express any opinion he damn well pleased, it was simply untenable to be expressing support for an organisation that was engaged in mortal combat with the ARU, while holding the most holy office bestowed by the ARU — which is the Wallaby captaincy.

Kearns didn't resign. But he was upset. As he told FitzSimons later, "I thought it was the height of hypocrisy for you to be writing that sort of stuff about me, when you'd already acknowledged that *you'd* signed with David Lord's professional rugby circus in 1983, AND you'd lived all those years in France making money for playing rugby over there."

But moving right along …

There would be some limited discussion within the ARU over the next couple of days about whether Kearns should be outright sacked. The Wallabies would be playing in two tribute matches for David Campese in the coming week, and the team had not yet been announced. Should the ARU seek retribution?

Bruce Hayman, CEO of the Union, was one who argued for it particularly strongly.

"I felt that he had made public utterances that were not worthy of the captain of the Wallabies," he says. "He had not shown loyalty to the ARU, of which he was the captain of the senior team. I advocated, when Tim Gavin came out and made a public statement of support, that Tim should be made captain and his loyalty publicly rewarded."

Perhaps wiser counsel prevailed, though, with Ian Ferrier for one insisting that any vengeful stance taken by the Union in those dark delicate days would be counter-productive in the extreme.

It was not just Philip Kearns who was coming under attack. The pressure that was brought to bear upon other players was extraordinary, although at least most of them were spared the hassles of being *publicly* associated with it. Being named in the newspapers as having even the slightest association with the World Rugby Corporation inevitably brought both public wrath and enormous media pressure.

The media. A little earlier in the piece, the best quote of the whole War emerged, and it came from the English hooker and WRC recruiter, Brian Moore, who said, "anyone who is fully informed is totally confused".

Yet, while it was hard to work out at that time just what the hell was going on in all the different countries, with all the claims and counter-claims of victory and defeat made by both the Unions and WRC, the real confusion was in the emotions of the players concerned. Upon one construction, the rebel players were the visionaries who had the courage to pursue a brave new world of rugby against a hide-bound establishment that had for too long denied them their dues … Upon the far more popular construction, they were sell-out bastards wilfully pissing on national jerseys that the people had loved through the ages and the players themselves had sworn fealty to.

Many of the players themselves, including droves who'd signed with WRC, weren't sure which was the correct way of looking at things.

In Australia, it was primarily Rod McCall who bore the brunt of these jitters. In the study of his Brisbane home, he sat aghast as one after the other of his team-mates called him, or came to see him and suggested that perhaps it would be a good idea to pull the plug.

"'Mate,'" McCall remembers them saying, "'it's not too late, mate, it's not that bad, let's just go back, it will be alright, everyone is going to get looked after, they'll do the right thing, no one will get hurt.'"

McCall would make reply in no uncertain terms.

"*Why* do you believe what the bloody administrators say more than what I say? What makes you think that they know better than I do what's good for rugby? You thought it was a great idea at first — great money, great concept — but as soon as the ARU put the pressure on, you fold like a faulty deckchair! What I want to know is when did it stop becoming a good idea?"

On a roll, McCall continued to go for them.

"Who says that because a guy's got grey hair, he is a better judge of what's good for rugby than I am?

"You're trusting people who have told *lies*, who have reputations for stuffing up. Why do you believe them more than you believe me? What's the attraction?"

"'Well,'" McCall remembers some of the players replying, "'at least the ARU money is there, and it's guaranteed.'"

"*Where* is the money?" he exploded. "Who has yet seen any of the ARU's money?"

More than just the rightness or wrongness of arguments about money, though, McCall felt strongly that once the decision to go with the WRC had been made — which it had — he and the other players were honour-bound to stick by it.

"If I was the only guy in Australian rugby who copped the blame for it, and I was never allowed near a rugby game again because of it," McCall declares now, "I still wouldn't have turned back and said, 'No, I'll change.' I'd made my decision.

"Other players made a decision and signed, and then they'd say, 'I didn't mean to sign.' These were *adults*, 25-year-old *men*, grown men who buy houses, drive cars, have babies, but sign things and then say, 'I didn't really mean to sign,' because they'd been put under pressure for doing something different and they couldn't live by their decision …

"And that really grated against me."

There was another player, one of the Wallaby icons, whom McCall was talking to at this time, who was also getting extremely shaky in his commitment to WRC.

This particular player was one respected around the world as clearly the best in his position. And, though he had signed with WRC earlier, he was now having what could fairly be described not only as second thoughts, but third, fourth, fifth and sixth thoughts.

McCall, in hour-long conversations — daily — attempted to talk him through it.

"I said, 'You made that decision, do you know how many people's lives are connected with this? You are a trump card, the game couldn't go on without you. If, when I'd asked you, you'd said no and given me all the reasons [why] and stuck by it, I would have lost interest in chasing it because I don't think the game could go on without you. I would have torn up the contracts I already had and forgotten about it.

"'But you didn't say no, you said yes and everything has fallen into place because of it. Players around the world have confidence in it, because they know you are a part of it, they've put their arses on the line because they know you're with them, that you've made your decision.'

"'But I'm now not comfortable with that decision,'" McCall remembers the player replying.

"'Mate, it's too late. You made it and you can't make a decision like that that affects so many people and just walk away.'"

At the end of one these conversations — with McCall almost frustrated beyond measure at the ongoing Wallaby wobbles all around him — the two decided the best thing to do would be to get all the Australian players together for the one meeting, and decide once and for all what they were going to do.

McCall picked up the phone and three calls later it was done. A meeting would be held on the following Thursday, in Sydney at the Darling Harbour Parkroyal, where they all stayed before Test Matches at the Sydney Football Stadium …

McCall was more than somewhat glad that a final decision would be taken.

"I could see what it was doing to [that player], I could see what it was doing to me and, more particularly, my family — who just never saw me — and at that stage I was wondering myself whether it was all worth it. What I wanted was to just get it out on the table, and make a decision one way or another.

"We had to finish it."

Jock Hobbs had simply not stopped. For the past three weeks he had been working night and day in the War Office and out and about in New Zealand in an effort to win the day for the NZRFU. He had barely seen his four children, or his wife, Nicky.

At last, though, he felt he was genuinely close to a real breakthrough. Although they had not yet signed any All Blacks, the move to get the leading provincial players signed up was progressing well, and continued negotiations with Warren Alcock, David Howman and Mike Fisher had brought them all to the point where they were close, *very close*, to signing those players to contracts.

But now this …

It was Wednesday evening, August 9. Out in the foyer of Kensington Swan, the well-known television reporter from TVNZ, Peter Williams, was waiting. He was ready to do a cross to the nationally broadcast *Sports Night* program, and he had brought news that their lead item would be Andy Haden claiming quasi-victory in the fight, that WRC now had 60 contracts signed by leading players.

Williams was offering Hobbs the chance to make reply, and the former tearaway flanker had no problem with that. What he did have a problem with was the voice coming out the speaker-phone in the middle of the conference table.

It was Richie Guy's voice, and the Chairman of the NZRFU was telling Hobbs not to go on television and refute the claims.

"I don't want you to do it, Jock," Guy said simply.

Hobbs' flabber had never been more gasted.

"Why *not?*" he demanded. "I have to refute it, Richie, because the players need to know that we are going to win this battle. It's very important to us at this crucial stage of negotiations."

"Well, Kevin Roberts is in Sydney looking at some of the WRC books," the Chairman replied, "and they might not show them to him if you go on and refute this claim."

Kevin Roberts? What the bloody hell was Roberts doing in Sydney looking at WRC books? Hobbs had no time to think about that now.

"Richie," he said quietly, "I've got to go on and refute the claim or the players we've almost got over the line will suddenly think they've backed the losing side. I've got to go on, and I *am* going on."

Hobbs was as good as his word. Looking straight down the gun-barrel of the live cross, Hobbs began, "Thank you, Peter. Nothing of what the WRC says stacks up … "

And he was away, hammering at the whole rebel concept for the next 10 minutes. He was passionate, articulate, and convincing.

Richie Guy, in his farmhouse living room, watched the whole thing and switched off the tube when it was over.

Maybe Jock had been right after all …

In Dunedin, way down on the far south of the South Island, Josh Kronfeld couldn't sleep properly that night, the same way he hadn't been able to sleep much for the previous few weeks. The agony of wanting to make the right decision without being quite sure what it was, was really starting to get to him.

Tossing and turning, the star new boy of the All Black forward pack kept going over and over in his mind the whys and wherefores of the whole WRC saga. The pressures on him were enormous. On the one hand, he desperately wanted to be with the other All Blacks. On the other, he wanted to *be* an All Black, first, last and always.

And to his way of thinking, there was no guarantee whatsoever of ensuring that other than by staying with the national body. In muffled, troubled conversations with close friends, he would say, "I don't want to be just a seven-Test All Black, I want to be a *great* All Black. I want to play lots of Tests."

In another suburb of Dunedin, not too far away, his friend Jeff Wilson was in a similar position. They'd each had long conversations with their respective lawyers, David Howman and Warren Alcock, but neither was still quite decided about what to do.

"Just remember, boys," the editor of a Scottish newspaper had told a few Wallabies at a post-Test function in Edinburgh in 1988, "when you're dealing with the press, it's like making love to a porcupine …

"You're just one prick against a thousand."

Boom, boom.

This man knew of that which he spoke: that when the press were united on a particular issue they could do some terrible damage to a person or cause — and in this instance sports commentators around the world remained very much against WRC. The first flurry of perhaps emotionally overwrought and negative articles had been followed up by more deeply thought-out commentary … which nevertheless remained negative.

As Geoff Levy remembers, "It used to upset me to read the things in the newspapers, especially when I used to see how wrong they were, and how they just didn't understand what we were doing."

As a matter of fact, in the entire media world it sometimes seemed that there was only one commentator with the nous to see what WRC was trying to accomplish, and to courageously embrace it — Alan Jones, the Sydney radio broadcaster and former Wallaby coach.

It was particularly brave of Jones to give this support, as there were many doubters who thought it would be inconsistent for him to take any such position. When Super League had been launched six months before, Jones had been so publicly outraged that a long-standing organisation like the Australian Rugby League should have come under attack that he had quickly been installed as an "official spokesman" for the ARL, and had been vociferously pushing their cause ever since.

But forget all that. Jones, possessed of a marvellously malleable mind, was a master at keeping his opinions moving with the times, entirely un-weighed down by whatever he might have said before, or even contemporaneously, and he was as good as his reputation now.

An article had even appeared in Sydney's *Telegraph Mirror*, beneath the headline "THE ARU IS 'DOOMED TO DEFEAT'", where, upon being interviewed on the subject, Jones railed against the obtuseness of the administrators and implied that they always had this coming. The rugby administrators, he said, "are faced with a battle they can't win".

Jones told the journalist, Jon Geddes, that WRC *would* pay the money on November 22, and was most supportive.

Ross Turnbull, for one, was gratified by this support from his long-time friend, but not at all surprised. For he had already talked to him quite a lot on the subject. Turnbull knew that Jones personally supported the WRC proposal, as he had long been a proponent of the modernisation of international rugby union.

But there was an added bonus.

"He wanted … to be the next coach!" Turnbull says with an uproarious laugh. "There was no doubt that Alan would have been very interested in getting back involved, but there would be no way … "

It was just like any war. An inevitable result of the long and bloody battle was that the landscape around the combatants was changing all the time.

One of the surest signs of this came on August 9, in Scotland, when perhaps the most conservative Rugby Union in all the world announced that amateurism should be on the way out, and professionalism adopted.

After a meeting of the Scottish Rugby Union in Edinburgh, the SRU's Vice-President, Fred McLeod, announced to a waiting press the position his board would be formally submitting to the International Rugby Football Board when it met in Paris later in the month.

"I believe that the word 'amateurism' should be totally removed from the Laws," said McLeod. "There is a clear desire to move towards a professional game where there is a payment for playing in addition to the other benefits already available."

That night, pigs were seen flying before a blue moon, as beneath them Hell was freezing over solid. That the Scottish Rugby Union should be taking this position was a particularly potent sign that win, lose or draw, after this battle the rugby game would never be the same again.

In the bad old days of Beirut, the surest tension-indicator was said to be the sale of window glass. If it seemed that the fighting would flare again, nobody replaced their smashed front windows …

The equivalent in the political arenas of Washington DC is late-night pizza sales. As politicos around the American capital kept working through the night during both the darkest days of the Watergate hearings and the height of the Gulf War, all records of pizza sales were broken.

In the Rugby War, in New Zealand at least, it was the consumption of instant coffee at the War Office. Never in the history of the Kensington Swan was so much coffee consumed by so many over so few days. For the War Office was filled, almost around the clock, by lawyers and officials trying to nail the deal down — all of them powered through the night by adrenalin, desperation, a sense of duty that they were "fighting the good fight", and by the constant consumption of caffeine.

After Hobbs had done his live cross to *Sports Night*, he'd gone straight back into the War Office and got down to tin-tacks with everyone gathered there … both in person and on the phone.

Warren Alcock was on the line from Dunedin and Michael Fisher from Auckland. Both had senior provincial players with them. This was to be the final wrangling over the wording of the contract that the 50 provincial players would hopefully be signing the following day — before a big press conference was booked in at Wellington Airport for 5pm.

Warren Alcock opened: "Now Jock, about that clause on the second page … "

There were still significant legal issues to be ironed out. Alcock wanted a clause taken out which let the NZRFU off the hook from fulfilling their side of the contract if ever the Murdoch deal fell through.

Hobbs stuck to his guns. If the Murdoch deal fell through, then there simply wouldn't be the money to pay these players. That much was obvious.

Alcock also wanted an assurance, black on white, that if ever the WRC and NZRFU did a deal, then his players would formally be included in that deal. Hobbs repeated, for what seemed like the 100th time, that the Union would NEVER do a deal with WRC. But allowed the clause in.

The clock whirred around, the coffee cups were emptied and filled again. And again and again. They were close to agreement, they were a long way from agreement. Things looked good, things looked bad. The coffee kept going. Matters progressed at the pace of a sickly centipede on a bad day.

By 3am they could at least see the end, if not quite daylight. Warren Alcock, for one though, had had enough.

"There are two things I'm good at doing at three o'clock in the morning," he said, "and talking about contracts is not one of them."

His line went dead. Just like that.

Never mind. From Alcock's side of things, he was basically happy with the contract as it now read. The others kept ploughing.

Chapter eleven
August 10, 1995

Sussex Street lies just on the western side of the small ridge that acts as the spine of Sydney's Central Business District. It is long, wide, and newly popular with the pin-stripe brigade for its easy access to the very heart of the CBD, while still maintaining a neat distance from the noisy hurly-burly of the downtown craziness.

It was along this low side of the ridge that is Sussex Street that much of the Rugby War in Australia was fought. Ross Turnbull's office at Ernst & Young lies at the northern end, while Ian Ferrier's building is 300 metres to the south. Diagonally over the road is *The Sydney Morning Herald*, while just beneath the *Herald* are John Singleton's offices, where Geoff Levy was able to secure his first bit of seed money.

It was particularly appropriate then, that the site chosen for the pivotal players' meeting of the Rugby War in Australia, was also at Sussex Street — down the southern end at the Darling Harbour Parkroyal Hotel. The word had gone out for all interested rugby players to turn up for the meeting which was to start at 8.30am sharp, and they came in their droves. From Brisbane, from Canberra, from Sydney.

There was an obvious tension to the morning, right from the beginning. That had been apparent from the moment that Phil Kearns arrived and was asked by one of the many waiting reporters how he was feeling on this brisk morning.

"I'd be a lot better without you parasites of the media," was Kearns' reply, before disappearing into the confines of the hotel.

This was an odd assessment from an Australian captain who was himself making a fair living from writing a column for a weekly sports magazine, doing television work with Kerry Packer's Channel Nine — and doing nightly radio reports on 2UE for free — but it was a fair reflection of the times. Kearns was never normally like that, but neither was the situation.

Distrust, distress and dissension were the constant companions of seemingly everyone involved in the whole saga. At least, though, Kearns was able to make his way into the meeting without being barred. Others were not so lucky.

Jason Little and Tim Gavin, for two, were shocked to find that one of their former Wallaby team-mates was standing at the door barring the way to any who were said to have already signed with the Australian Rugby Union.

"Sorry, Jason, Tim, you can't come in. WRC players are having a meeting for an hour or so and then we'll let the rest of you in," he told them.

So they waited. Extremely annoyed at such high-handedness — who the hell said this bloke was in charge of the shooting match anyway? — but they waited, with three or four other players who had not yet committed themselves to WRC.

Downstairs, James Erskine, the head of IMG in Australia, was arriving. Buffeted by the demands of both sides, Kearns had turned to Erskine for advice. The two had a professional relationship insofar as IMG acted as Kearns' agent, but the two also enjoyed a close relationship beyond that. Kearns trusted him.

In the previous few days Erskine had met with the Australian captain several times, just as he'd met with Sean Fizpatrick once, Geoff Levy once, and with Phil Harry and Ian Ferrier several times.

Clearly, Erskine's position within the whole saga was an extremely delicate one. His business relationship with the Australian Rugby Union was cast in concrete. In return for the guarantee of some $A42.5 million, his company had the marketing rights for the Union over the next five years — meaning it was very much in his interests that the ARU survive and prosper in the coming years.

Although there had been a previous agreement between Geoff Levy and Ian Ferrier that they would not attend the meeting, and instead let the players sort it out, Geoff Levy had been called by some of the players with the news that Kearns had invited Erskine, and decided he should attend so as to balance what he clearly felt would be the pro-ARU position of the IMG boss.

So Levy, too, was waiting in the foyer when Erskine arrived …

"You!" Erskine recalls Levy saying. "I don't know how you've done it, James, but you've weaselled your way into this meeting."

"I haven't weaselled my way into anything," Erskine says he replied. "These guys have to be told the truth, and at the end of the day, Geoff, you haven't told them the truth. These guys believe there's enough money to pay their salaries, and there isn't."

(Levy, for the record, denies Erskine claiming to him then and there that WRC had no money, but remembers Erskine telling him that he was going to attempt "to portray the pros and cons of WRC as he honestly saw it". Levy says he replied that in his opinion the IMG man "only saw it through ARU/Murdoch tinted glasses".)

Whatever the conversation, at its conclusion, Erskine turned on his heel and went up to the first floor to wait his turn in the lion's den. After an hour or so it came, when he was invited, with all the non-WRC-aligned players, to come in.

The scene Erskine found inside was an obviously troubled one. Some 60 players were ranged around the room, together with one or two agents, and lawyers who were firmly entrenched in the WRC camp. In one corner of the room Phil Kearns was holding a phone up, on the other end of which was the All Black captain, Sean Fitzpatrick, keeping track of how things were progressing.

After clearing the room of all agents and lawyers — bar the one lawyer whom he was asked to allow to stay because he was "with the players" — Erskine began.

Or was about to begin. Before he could even open his mouth, Tim Kava had jumped to his feet and broken in.

"I hope you are going to tell this group before you start, all your conflicts of interest … "

Erskine would have none of it.

"Listen, pal," he replied in an equally aggressive tone, "do you want to read my speech for me or do you want me to do it myself?"

Kava backed down, for the moment, but the tone was set. Erskine maintains he had planned to acknowledge his conflicts of interest anyway, and proceeded to do so.

"My conflict of interests as head of IMG are that we've got an option to do the next World Cup. We have a contract with the ARU, and I also have a contractual arrangement to act on behalf of some of the top Wallabies.

"So, look, I'm not going to be able to give you both sides of the story. I think it's going to be quite obvious which way I think you should go, but I'm not saying what I'm saying because it's necessarily in my interests.

"My contract's going to stand up anyway if half of you end up playing for WRC and half of you end up playing for the ARU. There is still going to be, believe me, an Australian team that goes on that field next season."

Then to perhaps the most dramatic moment of the meeting. Motioning to the lawyer in the front row on the left, Erskine paused and said, "Excuse me, I know you, I think you're the lawyer from Brisbane, aren't you?"

The fellow, Eddie Kann, silently acknowledged that he was, and then Erskine continued.

"Now, all you guys have signed contracts, or the majority of you have signed contracts with WRC. You guys have signed the contract. But are those contracts in trust with a lawyer acting *for you*, because Phil Kearns thinks they are, and everyone else I talk to thinks they are, or are they in trust with a WRC lawyer, which means they've been exchanged and you have a binding agreement?

"Now," Erskine continued, turning to the lawyer. "Are you holding the contracts for the WRC or are you holding them for the players?"

As Kann recalls now: "I acknowledged that in respect of the holding of the contracts, I was holding them as the agent of WRC."

There was no question of Kann having withheld this fact from the players. As far as he was concerned all the players had known this — and, as a matter of fact, he felt he'd made it quite clear, at the meeting of exclusively WRC players held prior to Erskine's address.

But he does agree that around him at that moment there were clear signs of consternation and surprise from some players. Somewhere along the way, the fact that the contracts held by Kann had passed from the possession of the players to the possession of the WRC had escaped the attention of a number of the young men in the room.

And, in fact, in an odd twist, Kann *was* representing both WRC *and* the players. A legal letter from him to WRC, sets out his position, in this passage:

"Whilst this firm holds the contracts as agent, of and for and on behalf of WRC Pty Limited, they are held without prejudice to this firm's right to continue to act for the players on whose behalf it currently acts and on behalf of whom it may act in the future."

This was legalese for the fact that while Kann was holding a contract for WRC, therefore making the contract binding, if a client of his (as in one of the players) wished to argue the toss over something in the contract, then Kann reserved the right to act on his behalf.

The bottom of all bottom lines?

To the consternation of many of the players, it appeared that they were now legally and contractually bound to the WRC, correcting their erroneous impression that they were *not yet* legally bound.

It was at this point that one player put up his hand and tried to limit the damage:

"Well, *I* knew they were being held for WRC."

"Well, it sounds to me like you're the only person," replied Erskine. This was a clear exaggeration, but still …

Still the James Erskine Demolition Derby had a way to go. For the next 90 minutes, Erskine kept hammering away at the credibility of the WRC, doing, in the words of Rod McCall, "a *total* demolition job".

And you were saying, Mr Erskine?

He was saying that the whole essence of the WRC contract was based on very dodgy financial premises. He told the players that he acted for athletes and sports-people all over the world and he'd never seen anything like the contract that the Australian rugby players had signed. Didn't they understand that standard procedure in this sort of thing was for the athletes to at least receive 10 per cent downpayment on the amount they were due to receive? So what had they got? Ten per cent? *Five* per cent? ONE per cent even?

No. They'd gone and done it, hadn't they, they'd signed themselves away and weren't getting a brass razoo in return.

Well, he said with a heavy sigh, it wasn't for him to criticise, but he really just couldn't understand it.

"So maybe you don't like the ARU. Maybe you do think they're pompous. Maybe you think they're old farts. Well at least there's not 57 of them like in England. I've only dealt with nine of them here …

"But even if they are old farts, so what? We're talking *business* here, guys. Get that through your heads. It doesn't matter that you don't like them. The thing is, they will sign contracts now that you know they're going to honour. They'll sign you to big money. Do you *really* think they're going to wait around to November 22 to see if WRC comes good with the money or not, and then, if they don't, offer you the same money they're offering you now?"

"They'll have to!" interrupted one belligerent player.

"*Bullshit!*" Erskine fired back. "It just doesn't work like that and surely you've got the brains to know that."

Erskine also took particular aim at WRC's financial prospects. His own estimate, he said, was that they would likely make a loss of \$US80 million in the first year, a 40-million loss in the second, and somewhere between a 30-million loss and breaking even in the third year. Erskine further claimed that he'd shown his estimate and reasoning to Brian Powers, and the PBL boss had agreed with him.

With those figures in mind, Erskine put the proposition to the players. If they were prospective franchise holders, would *they* sign up to be a part of such a loss-making machine? Well, *would they*?

Well, then, who the hell did they think was going to put up that money? He'd talked to the Packer crowd, Erskine said, and they'd said they wouldn't. As to the WRC company itself, it was worth all of two dollars, so there was an obvious shortfall there.

He also took particular aim at the way the whole WRC push among the players was working, claiming that it was being led by older players, and lesser players — whose only chance of big money out of rugby was from WRC. The young players and better players, he said, should look at the whole thing judiciously and question whether or not they were being pushed in a direction that was not in *their* best interests.

On and on he went.

It was, as McCall says, a complete demolition job. One person who seemed visibly upset by it was Phil Kearns, who'd asked Erskine to come and speak to the team.

"In hindsight," Kearns says, "I guess I was naive in having him there. In getting him there, my intention was for him to say 'this is one side, this is the other side, and boys, make your own decision', I didn't expect him to go at it the way he did.

"I was disappointed, I was upset."

Whatever, the job was done.

The boss of IMG finished his speech thus, softening a little.

"Anyway, that's it. I have given you my honest opinion. Take it or leave it, as you see fit. For your sakes, whatever you do, draw a line in the sand and then end the whole thing bloodlessly, because no amount of money is worth losing your mates. After all, you can play it for nothing in heaven anyway.

"Thank you."

This last reference to heaven was a rather stilted attempt at humour — a reference to rugby being known to its aficionados as "the game they play in heaven" — but the mood was way too heavy for anyone to even snigger.

After Erksine had at last wound up, Tim Kava suggested forcefully that now that they'd heard from Erskine, they should get Geoff Levy to give the counter-arguments. More earnest discussion between players followed, concerning whether such an address would be appropriate, and if so whether Ian Ferrier and Phil Harry should also be allowed in to make it fair all around.

Eventually the doors were thrown open, and Levy was allowed to make his statement first, to be followed by Ferrier straight afterwards. There ensued brief speeches from both men, where they warmed to themes that the players were now well familiar with, before an all-in question-and-answer session took place.

Little headway was made on either side during this session until one of the players asked a question about the legal enforceability of the contracts that the players were being asked to sign, or had signed with both parties. Would the ARU ever sue to enforce the contract, Ian Ferrier was asked.

"No, of course not," Ferrier replied. "The ARU is not in the business of suing players. But I do suggest you ask the same question of Geoff."

It was surely a difficult moment for Geoff Levy. At a time when the players were under pressure from all sides to return to the fold, he couldn't say that the players were free to go, that the contracts they had signed, the contracts on which he was in the process of building a rugby empire on, actually meant nothing. But nor, under the circumstances, could he say, "Yer, damn right, we'll sue your pants off."

He ended up taking the middle ground, saying "We will enforce our contracts, unless the whole lot of you together decide that you don't want to be a part of it. We would never force the whole body of players to do something against their will."

With partly that in mind, the players' group decided to form a seven-man committee to analyse both sides of the equation and get back to the group within two weeks.

All up, the meeting had clearly been a good one for the establishment and Ian Ferrier was delighted — albeit with one part disgust.

The delighted part was that while exiting in the company of Phil Kearns, he'd been able to talk to the Wallaby captain for the first time properly all day, and unveil to him the news of the ARU's own "critical mass".

"Phil," Ferrier said as they walked, "we've signed 14 of the Wallabies ... "

Kearns stopped momentarily, and turned, searching Ferrier's face for signs that he might be joking.

"Is that true?" he asked.

"It's true, Phil, we've signed 14 of the Wallabies."

"Well, that's it then," said Kearns, who had always maintained that the players were either one-in-all-in or forget it. "It's all over."

Ferrier took his words to mean that the Wallaby captain had accepted the inevitable, and lost interest in going on with it ...

Ferrier's sense of disgust remained, though, because of a conversation that had taken place just before leaving.

"A [person representing a tiny group] of the players approached me just before the end," Ferrier says, "saying, 'If you give them another $50,000 each they will stand up and say they've signed, and destroy the meeting.'"

Ferrier, shocked to his core that any Wallabies should so conduct themselves, says he told the fellow to, not to put too fine a point on it, "Fuck off."

"It was just absolutely incredible to me," he says now, "*unbelievable* that anyone could ever make an offer like that."

Geoff Levy, had he known, would no doubt have been equally shocked to know that players for whom he was holding contracts should have been so prepared to do the cause wilful and public damage in exchange for money.

But Geoff Levy had other things on his mind as he came out of the meeting. One of them was the media scrum that suddenly started converging on him.

"What went through my mind," Levy recalls, "is that I had a choice. I could either run for it with my head covered like the guys you see on television coming out of court, or I could face the music."

Levy faced the music and it was, as he says, "the first time ever they had anybody who was a somebody from WRC they could speak to".

As the press gathered around, Levy gathered himself and let it rip. One of the *Herald's* reporters covering the meeting, Michael Cowley, had the clear impression that, "He was a man who had been bursting to say something for a long time and now had his chance."

So, Levy was asked, who will be televising your competition if you can get it successfully launched?

"We haven't entered into any arrangement with anybody as to who will and who won't get the TV rights," Levy replied. "There has never been any suggestion that we wouldn't deal with Rupert Murdoch or Kerry Packer, or anyone else in the world.

"If Mr Murdoch puts the right deal for rugby to us and it is the correct deal and is the best deal, there is nothing to stop us wanting to do business with Mr Murdoch."

Levy was going well, sounding confident and obviously committed to what he clearly saw as a very fine cause. He, for one, did not see what had just gone on with the players as in any way damaging. But it was at this point that Levy made a bad error in terms of the public relations war that was then raging between the two sides, for the hearts and minds of rugby people.

"What's in it for WRC?" he was asked by one of the pressing journalists.

"Oh, over the next few years, lots and lots of money," Levy replied honestly. "What will happen is the players will get more money, the game will get bigger, people will come to the games, and over time, the sponsors will get more money out of it, the investors will get more money out of it, the players will get more money out of it, and the crowds will get more enjoyment out of it."

Mistake. Bad mistake. While seen in full context the remarks were reasonable, it was not however in the context that the remarks went out on the electronic sound-grab media. The line that made the evening news was the "lots and lots of money" one.

There is a story that circulates in New Zealand, that one of the recent All Black captains was finished from the moment he appeared on the national evening news fielding a call on his mobile phone *while in a rugby dressing room*. It painted him as "just another Aucklander yuppie scum" in the words of one New Zealand journalist, and his captaincy never recovered.

Perhaps the same might be said on this occasion. Levy was being honest in saying that money was one of the primary motivations — they weren't a charity, after all — but it simply didn't wash with the wider rugby community.

They were already deeply shocked by the events of the previous week, and this line confirmed their worst fears ... that it was all simply a sell-out of the sacred jersey. It excited much negative comment in the days to come.

In Cape Town, the hand-to-hand stuff in the court case between SARFU and WRC was just getting under way. In response to Ross Turnbull's affidavit on the previous Saturday, Dr Louis Luyt now put forward his own.

In it, he respectfully submitted that WRC was not a serious business proposition to begin with.

"*It is a foreign company with no assets,*" Dr Luyt claimed. "*Its share capitalisation is just over 5 rand [$2], yet its affidavit is replete with ambitious promises of grand schemes.*

"*Not only is the applicant clearly unable to finance any of these ambitious projects, but no indication is given to this court of anyone who might be able to sponsor the applicant or its intended projects.*"

Further in his affidavit, Dr Luyt claimed:

"*Each of the South African players who signed the WRC recruitment documents had since told Francois Pienaar, who was given a mandate by WRC to recruit players, that they had decided to withdraw from the document and that they had no intention of reaching an agreement with WRC.*"

It went on ...

"*Pienaar had not signed any of the documents which had been signed by the players, and had no intention of doing so. No binding agreement has been entered into between the players and the applicant.*"

On this day, the proceedings had started late in the afternoon and only went for a very short while, until Justice Van Reenen adjourned to the following day.

Ross Turnbull and Louis Luyt once again came face to face, this time on the steps of the court house.

"How are you going, Louis?" enquired the Australian.

"Better than you at this stage, I think," replied Dr Luyt, before quickly moving on.

J ust down from the Kensington Swan law offices, in Wellington, there lies Old St Paul's Anglican Church. It's not Notre Dame, but it does have its own air of sweet peace. At about 3pm on that Thursday afternoon, a sole figure could be seen sitting in the pews about half-way up on the left. Not praying, just sitting.

It was Jock Hobbs.

Sitting, thinking. Though he was not a religious man, particularly, it had become his practice over the previous few hectic days to occasionally come here to get some moments to himself. On this afternoon, he was confident that everything had pretty much been done that could be done. That morning, after they'd finally concluded negotiations at about 4am, almost everyone had gone home to snatch a couple of hours sleep. One solicitor, Martin Dalgliesh, stayed on through the night, continuing to prepare things so that when the rest of the staff of Kensington Swan arrived at 7am everything would be ready for them to get all the contracts drawn up, with all names correctly spelled and so forth. Then the challenge would be to get the contracts into the hands of the leading provincial players around the country — making sure that they were happy with the terms and, most importantly, ensuring that every player concerned *signed* them.

By mid-morning, one solicitor had been dispatched to Auckland. He was to proceed from there, to take a set of contracts to the players from the Counties team and another to Hamilton for the Waikato side. To the south, another solicitor was on his way to Dunedin to get the contracts to the Otago team, while at least the Wellington provincial players could simply come into the offices of the NZRFU and sign their contracts right there. Similarly, the Hawkes Bay team had been taken care of by Hobbs himself, and they already had their contracts.

The bottom line?

At the time that Jock Hobbs was sitting there, he was hoping and praying that no fewer than five senior provincial players (most of whom were the team captains), one from each of the leading provinces in the country, were flying their way to Wellington Airport where at a press conference at five o'clock that afternoon they would tell the country what they *and* their teams had done, and why they had done it.

They would be joined at the conference by the entire Otago team, which would be on a brief stopover at Wellington Airport, on their way from Dunedin to play a game against King Country at Te Kuiti.

Hobbs was hoping to be able to reveal another coup as well. All the while that negotiations had been taking place with Warren Alcock and David Howman about the provincial players, he had also been talking to them about the possibility of signing up their two star clients — Jeff Wilson and Josh Kronfeld — both of whom were also in the Otago team, and on the flight. Nothing had been locked in yet, but both players appeared to be close to signing. He hoped.

But enough already, it was time to head to the airport. Hobbs roused himself from his pew and headed for the door, the light from the stained glass window falling briefly across his face as he left.

That afternoon, Geoff Levy met with the Lion Nathan boss, Kevin Roberts, and agreed to let him see the WRC "books", showing how the finances of the whole thing would work.

Roberts' presence there was a result of a meeting that had taken place the previous Monday evening at his Auckland home. Attending were Richie Guy, Rob Fisher, Sean Fitzpatrick, Laurie Mains, Richard Crawshaw and Colin Meads. Roberts knew all of them equally well, got on with them, and was perhaps the best man in all of New Zealand to bridge the gulf that separated the administrators from the team.

Around his living room, a general discussion took place about the whys and wherefores of the whole WRC scheme, and whether or not it actually had business legs. The result was that all parties agreed that the process of reconciliation, of finding common ground, would be immeasurably advanced if Kevin Roberts — who knew the international rugby landscape *and* had a first-class business brain — could look at the WRC books, and work out whether or not it was all "smoke and mirrors".

It was a good idea. From the point of view of the All Black team, they knew that Roberts could be trusted to give them an accurate assessment of the business plan, and it would be good to know soonest if they were pinning their hopes on nonsense.

Ditto Richie Guy and Rob Fisher. Their claimed motivation in having Kevin Roberts go to Sydney was that at this stage of the game any intelligence was good intelligence, and it would be very valuable to know just exactly what they were up against.

One thing, though. And Richie Guy is absolutely clear on this. In no way, shape, sense or form was Roberts there officially representing the New Zealand Rugby Football Union.

"He was an interested party who both sides trusted totally, and he wanted to do it so it was okay with us. But he was *not* our emissary."

For the record, Laurie Mains begs to differ.

"He was a quasi-emissary of the NZRFU," Mains says flatly. "What we were trying to do [that night] was to get the New Zealand Union to open their mind a little bit, to see that they actually had *two* options. They now had Murdoch and they had WRC, and if the players had gone WRC, they needed to keep their eyes open to taking that option as well.

"Richie [Guy] wasn't warming to it at all, but the others were taking a much softer approach to it. I am not suggesting that they said they would support WRC — that is not correct — but I think they weren't as openly against the possibility that if WRC came off, that New Zealand rugby would probably have to go with them.

"That night I found out that [they] were sort of accepting up to a point that … if they did lose, that maybe they could go with it."

Roberts himself refuses to be drawn on just whether or not he was an emissary of peace from the NZRFU, saying only: "I was going to see Levy because I thought it would help both sides, and I said I would come back and try and fashion a solution that includes rugby union."

His main concern, from a personal point of view, was that he was not there representing Lion Nathan in any way, shape, sense or form.

"Absolutely not," he says strongly. "But I *am* a New Zealander, the All Blacks are a passion of mine, I like the guys, I love the things that they do for New Zealand and I didn't want the game to be ripped away from the people, the provinces, the rural areas."

So it was that Kevin Roberts, private citizen, a regular man-off-the-street, was ushered into the Sydney office of Geoff Levy at about 3pm on that Thursday afternoon.

Line by line, Roberts went through the details of World Rugby Corporation's business plan, challenging Geoff Levy as he went.

"I thought they were a bit optimistic," he says now. "And I said so. Geoff showed me all the numbers, showed me all the backing, told me all the story, took me through all the meetings, took me through their strategy and I said 'there are some financial assumptions in here, that I don't think are going to play'."

Like …?

"Like attendances, ticket prices, sponsorships, TV rights, all of the income stuff that I thought would be quite tough — I thought the revenue side of the equation was tough and the costs very high. I didn't think that people would pay the kind of money they wanted. I didn't think they would get the attendances they had budgeted — and I didn't think they would get the sponsorship dollars."

There were other things he liked, though.

"The actual concept I thought was good," acknowledges the brewery chief, "and was visionary. It's just I thought they would have a lot of trouble with the execution."

In the end, if WRC was not quite *all* smoke and mirrors, Roberts at least came to the conclusion that there was a fair amount of smoke there.

"I thought it was possible that if Kerry Packer backed it fully it might work on a limited scale, but what I saw there I didn't think quite stacked up the way they wanted it to."

From Levy's office Roberts went to the Channel Nine studios at Willoughby on the other side of the Sydney Harbour Bridge. He met there with Nick Falloon, the Finance Director of Packer's PBL, which had taken out the Loan and Option agreement with WRC.

The two talked, not as adversaries on opposite sides of a bitter struggle, but as businessmen who operated on the assumption that while business was business, it was always a good idea to know if something was going to be bad business before fully launching. Roberts, in any case, had been punctilious throughout all his dealings in the Rugby War never to let raw emotion enter into it.

"I thought that was destructive and damaging in this whole thing," he says, "and whenever I could, I tried to take heat out of the situation."

In this case there was no heat to begin with. Falloon had been heavily involved from the Packer side of WRC from the beginning, but was genuinely interested in Roberts' perspective of where the All Blacks stood in all this.

"The bottom line was Falloon had just been talking to Packer," Roberts recalls, "and he said to me, 'Mate, Kerry has said all along he will only do this deal if everybody is a willing participant. If the players are willing and the Unions are willing he is willing, but he does not want a split.'"

Which was Roberts' cue. Operating from a position where he knew perhaps better than anyone just where the All Blacks were positioned at that moment, he was genuine in telling Falloon that there was "no chance whatsoever" that WRC would be able to secure *all* the All Blacks.

"You simply won't get all the players," Roberts remembers telling Falloon with conviction. And whatever the mood of the New Zealand councillors at his home the previous Monday evening,

Roberts went on here to make a strong case that when it came right down to it, the NZRFU would never sue for peace.

"And you won't get the Union," he went on to tell Falloon. "The New Zealand Rugby Union is going to fight it. They are going to fight it in the media, they are going to fight it in the trenches, they are not going to lay down. This is *rugby*, this is too important to our country."

Falloon's response?

"He said that the Packer organisation would pull out, subject to certain guarantees being given to the players."

Another nail in the coffin of WRC?

This one appears to have been more like a bolt.

The two left it at that, with Falloon assuring Roberts he would get back to him within hours, he hoped, to confirm a meeting with Brian Powers for the following day to discuss it further.

Roberts was to be proved prescient, particularly in his sense that not all the New Zealand players would back WRC when it came right down to it. A few hours before his meeting with Falloon, the Otago rugby team had taken off from Dunedin. Each player had been given his contract before take-off and the players read them as the plane droned north. One by one they signed. All of them except Josh Kronfeld and Jeff Wilson.

Sitting together, apparently still unsure what they were going to do, the two young All Blacks bided their time, going over every last little thing in their minds. They walked off the flight together, knowing that this was it. There up ahead of them at the gate was New Zealand's leading sports lawyer, David Howman, waiting for them. Every step took them closer to him. He had a briefcase. He had their letters of intent committing them to the NZRFU, ready for them to sign if they chose to.

An emotive conversation then ensued. It was all about timing, Alcock and Howman said. Now was the time to do it. If they signed now they would be national heroes in New Zealand the following day. If they signed now, they would be helping to save New Zealand rugby. There was no doubt that that is what the public wanted to see, and there was equally no doubt that the deal they were getting was a good one.

While it was one thing to have loyalty to a large group like the All Blacks, they also had to have loyalty to themselves, and as their legal advisers, they had to tell them that the NZRFU's was clearly the best deal for them.

Above Alcock's head, the public address system kept squawking his name, asking him to call his office urgently. He ignored it. Standing just a few metres away, watching the whole thing, was a lawyer from Kensington Swan — sensing that this was very much a time to keep his distance and give these two crucial players as much space as possible.

At the press conference that was just starting 30 metres away from where they stood, Jock Hobbs sat up the back and watched with quiet satisfaction as one by one the provincial captains and leading players announced to the waiting press that, indeed, they and their teams had signed up with the NZRFU.

Hobbs was more keen than usual to stay well away from the limelight on this one, wanting to send a clear message to the rest of New Zealand rugby that this was a *players*' decision, done for the good of rugby. Finally, back with Howman and Alcock, it was over. After some 20 more minutes of discussion, Kronfeld and Wilson looked at each other. Then Kronfeld, trembling with a powerful but nameless emotion, reached for a pen. He signed. Wilson signed.

A minute later, David Howman sidled up to Jock Hobbs — who had now moved near the podium to make a few brief announcements himself — and handed him the confirmatory letters.

"They signed," he breathed.

Hobbs paused momentarily and, ever the lawyer, checked briefly to confirm that it was true.

It was.

"And, ladies and gentlemen," he suddenly boomed into the microphone, "we have some further terrific news to reveal this afternoon ... "

"Sure," Geoff Levy was saying to one of his associates over the phone, "I think Erskine did us some damage, but most of it we were able to neutralise."

Then his secretary interrupted him. Brian Powers was on the line. He would quite like to have a chat with Geoff at PBL headquarters, if Geoff was free.

Geoff was free, if a little worried at the slightly reserved tone in Powers' voice. In the company of his partner, David Gonski, he set off to walk the kilometre or so that separates the two offices, and was half-way up Castlereagh Street in the mid-winter cold of a particularly blowy evening when his mobile phone rang. It was Andy Haden, and he was clearly very annoyed.

"Geoff? You'll never guess what those bastards have done now. Kronfeld and Wilson have signed with the Union ... !"

Levy kept walking, talking, all the way to Powers' office on the third floor at 54 Park Street. By the time Levy and Gonski got there, the PBL boss had already heard the news himself and was feeling grim. It surely only confirmed what he already knew ...

Powers had already talked that afternoon to Sam Chisholm, who had told him his feelings on the matter. And then some.

"I said to him," Chisholm recalls, "'Look, forget it. It is a waste of everyone's time. You're *not* going to win.'"

Another source has it that he put it in stronger terms still, but the judgement was now, obviously, entirely correct. The roll-call of problems was overwhelming. The Springboks had reneged on their WRC contracts, the Australians were wavering, England still had only 10 players of their World Cup Squad signed, legal advice had been received that indicated that the Federation Francaise de Rugby had the overwhelming weight of French law on its side — in that any such "rebel" organisation as WRC was outright illegal in that country. And Ireland *still* hadn't turned on its fax machine.

All up, it was plainly not going to be possible to do this thing without there being an enormous split in the ranks of world rugby. As gently as he could, Brian Powers communicated to Levy that PBL was losing interest, in fact had *lost* interest.

The upshot of his remarks was that while PBL didn't want to leave WRC high and dry, they were going to get out. The best they could do was not to make public their withdrawal for a short while, so as to give Levy and Turnbull time to find new backers.

Levy left. Not angry, simply extremely disappointed that it all seemed to be fading away.

In Newcastle, Michael Hill was stunned when he heard about the signing of Kronfeld and Wilson, and even more staggered to know that the large bloc of players he had been counting on for WRC had now declared themselves for the NZRFU. He was not, though, oddly enough, at all aggrieved at Warren Alcock for having led him up the garden path during all those weeks of negotiations. Even more oddly, he actually sounds a rather admiring tone when discussing it now.

"I'll tell you what Alcock did," Hill says. "He played us off a break, and in the process he did a bloody good job for his clients."

Chapter twelve
End game

Finally, on Friday afternoon, in his Cape Town court room, Justice Van Reenen delivered his verdict. The injunction against SARFU preventing it from negotiating with its own players would now be lifted, and the matter "struck from the roll", as not urgent to be settled immediately.

In short, the way it seemed to the press, WRC had lost. Outside the court room, though, a South African media contingent that had been expecting to see a beaten and bruised Turnbull were staggered to see the ever ebullient "Mad Dog" bouncing around, ready to go again.

Try as he might, the former prop just couldn't spot any defeat in the judge's decision.

"The application was merely removed from the urgent roll," Turnbull rumbled. "This was in no way a defeat for us."

And actually, the man of the moment really didn't feel all that bad about it.

"Through that initial injunction," he says now, "we'd achieved all that we wanted to in having had room to manoeuvre with all the provincial players. We didn't need any more injunctions because we'd already got them all signed up under contracts."

Things were starting to break in New Zealand. In the War Office, several incoming blips of good news were starting to show up on their radar screens.

At around 11.45am, Jock Hobbs took a phone call. It was Colin Meads, ringing in his capacity as All Black manager. He was as friendly to Hobbs as ever, but had called with a specific purpose. The All Blacks wanted to talk, he said. They wanted to meet with Jock next Monday morning. Would Jock be available to have a chat?

Jock would indeed be available. Only too happy. They made a time, and a place, and they left it at that. Three senior All Blacks, however, didn't even wait until the Monday, but called Hobbs that afternoon, separately and independently.

One player said he felt that he'd been "misled", while the other two were more interested in simply coming to terms. Whatever, all three said they thought it would be a good idea to talk to the NZRFU. Jock thought it was a good idea too …

In Johannesburg, Ross Turnbull put the phone down after talking to Geoff Levy, and was clearly aggrieved. Levy had just informed him that the Packer organisation wanted "out". Turnbull had had some warning of it the day before when a phone call from another highly-placed source within the Packer camp in Sydney had rung him to say that he thought PBL had "a different agenda" from WRC and that Ross should return home to Sydney immediately to try and sort it out. But it was still a shock.

As Turnbull wrote later, in a diary he kept of the whole affair:

Geoff Levy tells me that Packer wants out. He is not going to exercise his option, which expires next Monday. Geoff has negotiated one week's extension. I am shocked by this news. I had assumed that he already has exercised his option — just by his behaviour. Packer was running the show …

"Packer" in this instance was a term for the Packer organisation, rather than Kerry Packer himself — who remained distant — but the bottom line was that the Packer backing was backing out. Fast. Time was clearly of the essence.

Without Packer, the men of the World Rugby Corporation were left with only one chance. That was to go once again to Johann Rupert and see if he would replace Packer as their backer. After all, they were firm in their belief that the concept still stood up, they had over 500 signatures from players all over the world and most of the heavy lifting work had already been done. All they needed was someone with a lot of money to come in and reap the rewards.

There was, of course, the minor problem that Johann Rupert's M-Net had already pulled out of the arrangement once. However, even if an agreement had been engineered between News Corporation and M-Net, a source within the offices of Johann Rupert's lawyers was able to confirm that nothing had yet been signed.

So it really was time to have another go at getting Johann Rupert and his mega-millions on board. And just where would that august gentleman be right now? Enquiries revealed that he was on holiday, up in the north-east corner of South Africa, on safari at a game park reserve.

Harry Viljoen, who had previously done some business with the magnate, had his mobile telephone number and made the call. Rupert listened to what Viljoen had to say for a while, but then rather peremptorily interrupted to say he was watching the USPGA golf in California, and wasn't interested in discussing it at the moment.

Still, he would be interested to hear from WRC representatives, perhaps on Sunday at 7pm, at which time they could arrange a meeting for early on the following week. Viljoen and Turnbull got to work. They began to prepare a formal business plan to show Johann Rupert when the meeting came.

Every sport has its own culture and, of course, the two — sport and culture — feed off the other. While the World Rugby Corporation to this point had been amazingly successful in getting the top players around the world to sign contracts — the culture as a whole simply refused to be so lassoed.

And it wasn't just that the rugby union public remained clearly against it ...

From the beginning, Levy and Turnbull's plan required the rugby union administrators around the world to see sweet reason — to see either that the WRC scheme was truly visionary and should be embraced or, alternatively, to see that they were so heavily out-gunned in terms of player manpower that they simply must wave the white flag so as to salvage what they could.

This did not transpire. Why? In part, because the WRC were uniformly dealing with *rugby men*, and it is a point of honour among rugby men, NEVER to give in to intimidation. The ethos runs strongly through rugby veins that you should never back down and, at the very least, it is taken as given that if you can't actually beat an intimidatory opponent you must at least try and take a piece of him home with you.

Thus, with the possible exception of some slight wavering among *individuals* in New Zealand, at no point in any of the WRC manoeuvres did it ever seem even remotely possible that the national Unions around the world would give in to them. In this, it seemed, Ross Turnbull had misjudged things. Right up until that Friday, August 11, the stance of the key southern hemisphere Unions, particularly, had been uniformly implacable against every WRC advance.

But then a strange thing happened.

On that very day, both the New Zealand and Australian Rugby Unions suddenly appeared to go into a placatory mode — with an enemy who seemed clearly beaten bar one or two last desperate rolls of the dice.

The making of peace in New Zealand began when Kevin Roberts arrived back in Auckland to give a summation of his trip to Richie Guy and Rob Fisher.

That summation ran, in the memory of Rob Fisher, "that the WRC really was mostly smoke and mirrors, but with the right backing some sort of smaller type operation could be made to work, and therefore we needed to be concerned".

Roberts was dealing from strength. Before getting on the flight home to Auckland, he had gone to a brief meeting at Brian Powers' office, where the PBL boss had got to the point thus:

"Well, Kronfeld and Wilson have gone, so what you told Nick Falloon last night was right — we never were going to get all the All Blacks.

"I have spoken to Kerry and he said we are going to pull out on Monday. We are not going to renew our option so long as they (the Unions) take care of the players and give them what they want — take that message back to New Zealand."

However, the fact that the Packer organisation was probably going to pull out still gave absolutely no guarantee that Geoff Levy and, more particularly, Ross Turnbull, wouldn't find another backer meantime.

With that in mind, Roberts wanted both Sean Fitzpatrick and Richie Guy to meet around his dining room table later that same night, to reach an agreement and kill the whole thing stone dead on the spot.

Guy and Fitzpatrick, after a couple of phone calls, agreed they'd be there. Roberts got busy in the interim, calling Geoff Levy in Sydney. Levy's attitude, according to Roberts, was that while he reserved the right to look for another backer and was in the process of doing that very thing, he would be much more disposed to pull out himself if the New Zealand Rugby Union would agree to four basic things. Roberts jotted them down, and was ready to talk turkey when Fitzpatrick and Richie Guy arrived.

The mood between the NZRFU Chairman and the All Black captain when they met that evening was one of tired equanimity. It was good news to both that someone looked to be close to finding a way to put this whole infernal thing to rest, and both were in a mood to listen to whatever Roberts had to say.

Roberts said this: he wanted them to sign an accord — which they could draw up on the spot with pen on paper on the dining-room table, and his wife, Rowena, could then type it up on the home word-processor for them.

The accord, framed with six separate points, called on the NZRFU Council to agree to:

1. Review the "governance structure" of the Union in line with the Boston Report as a matter of priority, and strongly recommend an independent Player Representative be elected to the governing body — this representative to be elected solely by the players.

   (The "Boston Report" had been drawn up several years before by an independent consulting group, and was a veritable blueprint for streamlining and modernising the structure of the game's administration in New Zealand. It called for such things as reducing the number of councillors from 19 to nine.)

2. The Player Representative would also be granted full access in relation to its financial affairs, and players generally would be allowed input as to the structure and length of forthcoming tours.

Clause 3 read verbatim thus: *"Consult with the Players' Representative as to the distribution of up to 66 per cent of the television proceeds receivably [sic] from Newscorp. This arrangement to be reviewed with the Players' Representative in three years time."*

4. Confirm there will be no retribution against any person who signed a WRC contract.

The finish of the accord read:

This agreement is subject to WRC confirming that they will release all New Zealand Players from any contractual arrangements currently in force.

The Chairman of the NZRFU pledges his full personal support to all these proposals.

Signed, etc.

Both men read it, and liked it. There remained one significant hurdle, though. Both Richie Guy and Sean Fitzpatrick were still concerned that the All Black team that they had both been so assiduously working at keeping together — albeit on different sides of things — might still be prey to the forces of Super League once this was all over.

It was Super League that had been the primary cause of this to begin with, and both would feel a lot better if they could be sure that once the smoke had cleared on all this, they didn't *remain* a threat. This was a particular bone of contention with Sean Fitzpatrick, who had long been jack of the continuing spectre of rugby league raids on this best of all possible teams.

No problem. Roberts picked up the phone and dialled Sam Chisholm's number. It was very late, Auckland time, but still the top of the morning in London, where Chisholm presently was. Roberts explained the situation, and Chisholm, in his inimitable gravelly fashion, said he would "fix it".

Within five minutes, Roberts' phone rang. It was John Ribot, the Chief Executive of Super League, who had just got off a plane in Brisbane. Ribot sounded chastened and just a little shell-shocked, almost as if his ears were still ringing from some loud noise that had just been pounding on his ear-drums.

"Kevin," he began, "I have just talked to Sam and I understand — let me tell you now — as of this minute, Sam has made it very clear to me that Super League aren't going to be going after any of the All Blacks."

Ribot said that while he could not answer for individual clubs, which were independent entities organised under the Super League umbrella, his organisation was out of it from this moment forth. Roberts asked him to tell that to Sean Fitzpatrick personally, and Ribot was happy to.

The All Black captain listened for a few minutes and chatted briefly along the way, and then handed the phone back. He was satisfied. The deal was done.

Roberts put the phone down ... and picked it back up again when it rang only a few moments later.

It was Chisholm.

"Did he call you?"

Yes.

"Did he tell you?"

Yes.

"Are they happy?"

Yes.

"Good."

(*Click.*)

And goodbye to you too, Sam.

Fitzpatrick and Guy were both satisfied. They both signed the accord. Hark the herald angels sing and hold the phone, but it looked as if a rough peace had suddenly materialised in New Zealand. Richie Guy would still have to get the council to ratify the agreement that weekend, but he didn't feel that would be too much of a problem.

In Australia at that time, the mood was also starting to lighten up. Earlier that same afternoon, Brian Powers and Nick Falloon had gone to Ian Ferrier's offices to meet with Ferrier and Phil Harry, to see if they could thrash out some kind of a peace deal. The essence of their proposal was similar to the one that Kevin Roberts outlined to Richie Guy and Rob Fisher.

PBL would agree to back out if the ARU would accede to the

basics of the players' demands — many of which had been formulated by James Erskine in the previous few days in his continuing search to come up with common ground — and they also wanted the ARU to agree to hold joint press conferences at which they could be present.

In the words of another of the insiders on this whole peace process: "They [PBL] wanted to be able to back out easy, they wanted to do it with high integrity, they wanted it with grace. They didn't want a public black eye. And if there was going to be a public black eye, they wouldn't let go. They wanted to make sure that the players and the Unions — everybody — went home happy with them."

Correct, says Harry. "It was all quite affable. They didn't see their group as being defeated in any way because they were never really in there."

Well, PBL *were* in there, even if formally they had only been a part of the whole thing for a little over two weeks.

At last, a Saturday evening at home. Talking to his wife, getting reacquainted with his children. It was Jock Hobbs' young son, Michael, who picked up the phone when it rang at around 6pm.

On the line was one of Jock's fellow NZRFU councillors, asking if he'd yet seen the fax of resolutions that had been circulated by Richie Guy and endorsed by Rob Fisher that would be put to the vote by the Council the following day. Hobbs, unsuspecting of what was coming, said no, but he'd be interested to know what those resolutions were.

Then it came out. Hobbs, shocked, listened as the councillor outlined something that Hobbs says, "Smacked to me of a deal having been done with WRC."

Hobbs had no hesitation in telling the councillor at the other end of the line that if those resolutions were passed, "then I would resign and that he should let Council know that."

Why was Hobbs so adamant?

"Because," he says, "it simply wasn't necessary to do any deals with WRC. The Council wasn't so much at the coal-face as I was, so maybe they didn't know that. But it really put me in a very, very difficult situation.

"I had my own reputation to think of. I had been out in the media, saying that there would be no agreement, no compromise, no meeting with WRC and here it looked like some form of agreement or meeting had taken place without my knowledge."

The hell with it. Geoff Levy, in Sydney, could wait no longer. It was very late on Saturday night, and he had just returned from a dinner in the city. The last couple of days had not been great for the World Rugby Corporation. A preliminary contact with the Reg Grundy organisation — an international television production house which, ironically enough, specialised in soap operas — had come to nought, and that left them back with Johann Rupert once again.

Without Rupert on board it was now obvious that there was simply no one else to bank-roll WRC, and Levy for one simply wasn't going to wait around until Sunday evening to talk about it. So it was that at two o'clock early Sunday morning, on the balcony of his Rose Bay home, with the moon shining off Sydney Harbour in the distance, Levy dialled Johann Rupert's number.

"*Ja?*" Johann Rupert answered.

Levy was off. For the next half-hour, he spoke to the "other Rupert", trying to convince him that WRC was presenting to him on a plate a wonderful business opportunity. Levy talked in urgent, though quite hushed tones — his four children and wife were sleeping inside — but he felt confident that the South African billionaire was at least listening to him.

Johann Rupert denied outright, in Levy's memory, that any deal whatsoever had been done with News Corporation, and emphasised that he had an enormous regard for the Packer organisation. Levy replied that he was glad to hear both things, but what he really wanted now was for Johann Rupert's organisation to take over the Packer position.

At the end of it, Johann Rupert, somewhere way out there in the African wilderness, made no commitments — but promised that he'd liaise with Harry Viljoen the following night and organise a formal business meeting with Turnbull and Viljoen for the Monday morning. He also agreed that Levy could fax him a plan where the details of the proposal could be set out more fully.

You beaut, and good night.

Jock Hobbs was back in the War Office on that Sunday morning and *appalled*. And he didn't mind showing it. He had now read the proposed resolution closely and made up his mind even more firmly that he would oppose it with everything he had.

The long preamble to the formal resolution noted that "an independent person" had looked at the WRC books and reported back that the whole scheme could be viable if the right backing was found. It said that while Kerry Packer had an option to fund the proposal, which expired the following day, he had agreed to pull out so long as the communiqué was passed by midday on this day, and what's more he would use his influence with WRC to get them to drop the concept.

"Packer believes he has a 70 per cent chance of achieving this," the preamble read, before getting to the clauses that had been agreed on two days previously at Kevin Roberts' house.

Jock Hobbs blew up, big-time. The whole thing really did smack of some deal having been done between the NZRFU and WRC, and he wanted nothing at all to do with it if that was true.

In a tense phone conversation with Richie Guy, who was back on the farm, Hobbs said that unless he got a formal letter from the Chairman, affirming that the NZRFU had done no deal with the

WRC then he would resign forthwith, and take no further part in proceedings. He wouldn't even meet with the All Blacks the following day in Wellington as was planned.

Hobbs got the letter from Richie Guy half an hour later, coming out of the fax machine. After all, no formal deal had been done with WRC. From the Chairman's point of view, it was all about "finding the best way for WRC to finish".

Meantime, two of the councillors whom Hobbs was closest to had been busy, calling and faxing other councillors, telling them why Jock didn't think this resolution should be passed. When the final vote was tallied, just before midday, it was 10–9 against.

Kevin Roberts was staggered when he heard what happened. It might be that he got the wrong end of the stick, but he also got a clear impression of just *why* the resolution had not passed, and what the current feeling of the Council was. He immediately got Geoff Levy on the phone in Sydney.

"We've had problems," he said. "They won't pass the resolutions, because they don't want to give amnesty to everybody involved, just the players. But they'll [apparently] agree to everything else … "

"Is Sean happy with what they're doing?" Levy asked.

"Sean is happy," Roberts replied. "Here he is. I'll put him on."

Sean Fitzpatrick and Geoff Levy then had a brief conversation, where each affirmed that the other was desirous that the whole thing finish. The issue of not getting amnesty for all was regrettable, but it was way too late in the day for the whole fragile peace to be split asunder on that issue alone.

It was left at that. Levy made no formal commitment to Roberts, when he came back on, to press the self-destruct button on WRC there and then.

"But I thought he was still basically satisfied," Roberts says. "I had the impression from talking to him that Turnbull was still gung-ho to keep going, and he felt obliged to give him his head, but that he was [basically] happy."

Was Roberts worried that Levy would stitch up a deal meantime?

"Not at all," he says firmly. "I thought in general that while the concept had a lot of good points, they'd find it very hard to get somebody to write the cheque they needed — particularly when that person knew that Kerry Packer had already pulled out of it, and that they'd be up against Rupert Murdoch."

And he was right, incidentally. Levy really did want to get out himself by this stage.

"Emotionally, at that time," Levy acknowledges, "I'd had enough, and it was obviously a losing battle. I was exhausted and I wanted out, but I also wanted to ensure that I could help Ross and give him one last chance to get an investor. I didn't really think Ross could do it, though … "

But, by God, Ross really was going to give it a burl. It was time. It was seven o'clock, Sunday evening in South Africa, the designated time to call Johann Rupert.

Harry Viljoen waited until about a minute past the hour, so as not to appear ridiculously over-eager and then dialled. Out of range. He tried again. Still out of range. Viljoen kept trying throughout the evening until at last, at around 10pm, the voice of Johann Rupert came through loud and clear.

The billionaire was brief. Of course he'd be happy to talk to Viljoen and Turnbull, but not right now as it was not convenient. But if Viljoen called him at 8.30 the following morning, he should be able to clear his decks by then and they could arrange a meeting.

It was Monday morning in New Zealand, and time for Jock Hobbs to meet with the All Blacks. By 10 o'clock, most of the New Zealand World Cup Squad was at the Wellington Airport Travelodge. The only significant absentee was Jonah Lomu, but he was at least represented by Debbie Tawse, who was acting as his agent.

Hobbs began by saying he was here to do business, and he hoped the All Blacks were in the same frame of mind …

They were. They were tired, emotionally wrung out, but the mood in the room was "let's get on with it".

Hobbs had with him the All Black contracts.

For the next two hours, the former All Black captain and the current All Black players talked.

The All Blacks wanted confirmation that there would be an absolute cast-iron guarantee that there would be no recriminations against them, from this moment forth, till death do us part.

You got it. I do.

Player representation in the way things were done from this point?

Absolutely. Consider the Players Committee re-formed, from this moment.

For his part, Hobbs wanted the players to understand that if they hadn't signed with the NZRFU by the end of the week, then they would not receive the advance lump-sum payments on their contracts.

And so it went. Discussion back and forth, to-ing and fro-ing, moving towards basic agreement that the All Blacks really would return to the fold — and the NZRFU would, in turn, honour their commitment not to seek revenge on these refugee revolutionaries from this revolution that never actually happened.

The mood that both sides sounded to the press outside the conference room was up-beat.

"I suppose you can say it was the business end of the contractual arrangements," Hobbs told the forest of microphones. "That was the focus of today's meeting."

Fitzpatrick ditto.

"I'd like to think everything could be tidied up by Friday," the All Black captain was quoted as saying.

After those pronouncements, Jock Hobbs moved back upstairs to see each of the All Blacks individually, to go over the terms of their contract. Like he said, everything was starting to fall into place ...

Ross Turnbull and Harry Viljoen were hopeful. Maybe today was the day that they could finally achieve the breakthrough that had always beckoned without ever quite materialising. All they needed in the first instance was to convince Johann Rupert to do the deal.

Rupert was now back at his Cape Town base, and at 8.30am sharp, this time, Viljoen rang.

"Sorry, Mr Viljoen, Mr Rupert is not here right now, but if you leave your number I'll see if he can get back to you."

Viljoen left his number. Again. And again.

Even though Rupert had not returned their call, Turnbull deemed it wise to make reservations to fly to Cape Town on the afternoon flight if Rupert should agree to meet with them. He didn't return their call the second time, and they put their flight back by an hour. When Johann Rupert didn't call back the third time they cancelled their flight.

Johann Rupert didn't call.

Never mind. Ross Turnbull went ahead with his plans anyway. At least some other good things had happened that day. The South African provincial players had formed themselves up into a Players Union under the leadership of Tiaan Strauss, and they were giving open support to WRC — stressing the inequity of SARFU having committed so much of the Murdoch money to the Springboks that there was going to be precious little left over for them.

That very day, as a matter of fact, Strauss had openly fronted the television cameras to say that the top 30 players in all the leading provinces bar Transvaal — making 150 in all — had signed with WRC.

"The players are still committed to go with what was signed with

WRC because we feel it to be the best available option," the former Springbok No. 8 and captain had said.

"We will appeal to our provinces to support us, and to at least meet WRC representatives."

It was good stuff, and despite the failure of Johann Rupert to come through, or even take their call, Turnbull was in a particularly ebullient mood in the early evening when he went on a nationally televised show, called *Talking Sport*.

Ross Turnbull, thank you very much for joining us this afternoon.

"Thank you, thanks for inviting me."

And they were off. It was a typically bullish performance from Turnbull, waxing enthusiastic about WRC and its tremendous prospects, not only in South Africa, but indeed around the world. He confirmed that WRC held 150 contracts of South African provincial players, and ventured that it really didn't matter that the Springboks had reneged, things were going flat-chat ahead anyway.

And hell, he'd be happy to let the Springboks back on board once it was all over, there'd be no hard feelings.

Ross Turnbull even had a few kind words for Rupert Murdoch.

"Rupert Murdoch has a fantastic vision for the media of the world. I hope we can meet with Mr Murdoch and do a deal with him in relation to this whole thing because we need people like Mr Murdoch to globalise our game."

"So why don't you and Murdoch meet?" asked the interviewer.

"We probably will," replied Turnbull, breezily as you please.

But time to open the lines to our callers. And here's one now. It was a Dr Louis Luyt, from Johannesburg.

Are you there, Dr Luyt?

He was indeed, and raring to go. What followed was the only time Ross Turnbull and Dr Luyt ever directly spoke to each other on the subject of WRC. The tension crackled as they spoke. South Africa watched as they went at it.

After Dr Luyt began quite aggressively by challenging Turnbull to come clean about what the judge had actually said in his ruling on the previous Friday — Turnbull had previously downplayed its significance — the Australian interrupted him.

"I think we are going to be wasting each other's time if we are going to talk about courts," Turnbull said. "What you and I should be doing together is having lunch tomorrow and trying to sort this out so don't go on with what happened in the court."

Louis Luyt did want to go on with what happened in court, whereupon Turnbull repeated the offer:

"Louis, I hope that you are in a position where you and your colleagues will be able to sit down and talk with us and discuss that track. It is very important for the future of world rugby ... "

The Chairman of the South African Rugby Football Union couldn't have been more direct.

"Let me be very frank, Ross," he said. "I don't want *ever* to sit down with you."

"Well look, there has got to come a time, Louis, when we have got to sit down and talk."

"Not with you," Dr Luyt fired back.

The journalist intervened, saying surely it was a good idea to at least *talk*, whereupon Dr Luyt came back stronger than ever, with what was by any measure a fair point.

"I'm very sorry you are taking that tack," SARFU's Chairman said. "We told you we are talking about a million players in South Africa, he's talking about 150 players in South Africa, 150 England, 150 New Zealand, possibly 90 in Australia. We are talking about the masses, we have to cater for the masses, he's not talking about that."

Turnbull demurred, but Dr Luyt kept going.

"The fact of the matter is, Mr Turnbull, we do not need you in our Currie Cup, we do not need you in South Africa. Let me tell you right now, that [while] Murdoch bought television rights, you bought the souls of the players, the bodies and souls of the players. You can tell them what to do, what they cannot do, when they can speak, when they cannot speak, what they have to wear, what they have to do, that's what you have bought."

Turnbull: "What it is about, is whether rugby is going to remain amateur and run in the traditional way. What we are saying [is that] to compete into the 21st century, and to protect ourselves from Super League, we must take the game global, we must become professional.

"The players must be professional like every other international sport you can ever think of. Rugby is just slow in keeping up and, Louis, I hope you join with us."

Dr Luyt made it very clear that he never would, and it was left at that.

Whatever the conciliatory mood that both New Zealand and Australia were in at that time, none of the millions watching in South Africa that afternoon could have been left in any doubt — Dr Luyt would *never* have anything to do with making peace with WRC.

Not that Turnbull wasn't getting support from some sections of the South African rugby community for all that. At around midday on the Tuesday, he took a phone call from Naas Botha, the recently-retired Springbok fly-half, who offered his commitment to help in any way he could.

Not at this stage, Turnbull replied, but thanks for the offer. He'd get back to him.

There is sleep, the sleep of the damned, the sleep of the dead, and then there is the sleep that Ross Turnbull was sleeping on that Tuesday night of August 15. He had, after all, moved again and again through every time zone in the world over the previous five months.

Geoff Levy remembers the phone ringing an unusually long time before Turnbull picked it up and when he did the voice sounded as if it was coming from the bottom of a very deep coal-mine, which is, figuratively, where Turnbull was, in terms of consciousness.

"Hello?"

"Ross, it's me, Geoff. Listen, we've had some more problems … "

And it went from there, Levy explaining that the end had finally come, that there was nowhere to go now but out. PBL had not only withdrawn its support, but they wanted to make an announcement to that effect as soon as the following day and there was no doubt that the whole WRC scheme really would be gone for all money, once it was known that Packer was out.

This time, Levy told Turnbull, they would simply have to accept that Johann Rupert was not going to come on board and make the best of it.

The good news, if there could be any in those circumstances, was that at least there would be the announcement of a compromise, that they had been talking with the ARU and they were prepared to announce in press releases and at press conferences that the Unions and the WRC had "merged" their interests in the name of peace.

"Ross, I know it's hard for you," Levy remembers telling him down the phone line to South Africa. "But, it'll read like 'Peace In Our Time!' They're going to hate it, it'll be like eating a shit sandwich for them."

The ARU would do this, Levy said, so long as WRC agreed to hand over the contracts in their possession.

Did Turnbull now, finally, accept the inevitable and call off the dogs?

Still not!

He forcefully voiced his objections to Levy about stopping now after everything they'd been through and, after hanging up, spent the rest of the night in his suite, making phone calls back to Levy and Nick Falloon at Channel Nine, trying to convince them to give him the time originally agreed upon.

"But," says Turnbull, "they were both absolutely *adamant* that we had to pull out in a few hours. Absolutely adamant. Nothing I could say would change their minds. I felt very strongly that another agenda was in play, that Packer and Murdoch had come to some deal without WRC being involved."

This is a contention, incidentally, which is outright rejected by Brian Powers.

"No, it is not true," he says flatly. "We did not proceed with rugby union for one reason and that is because the player unity, which is what attracted it to us, basically started to dissolve in South Africa. And it was our judgement that the game was going to be damaged, split at best for a while, and that was not in the interest of the game."

The following morning, as part of the peace process, Ferrier met with Geoff Levy and Nick Falloon from PBL, together with the two key player representatives in Wallaby forwards Tony Dempsey and Mark Hartill, the two leaders of the Players Committee which had been formed the previous week.

By some measure, it was an extraordinary scene, with the men of the World Rugby Corporation clearly all washed up, and yet still having the wherewithal to have input into what the terms of the peace document would look like.

After a long discussion, Ferrier put pen to paper on a document that would henceforth be known in Australian rugby folklore as the "Ferrier document".

On behalf of the ARFU and its three principal provincial Unions (collectively known as "the Organisation"), Ferrier agreed that:

In consideration of all The Players agreeing to relinquish their rights and obligations under their WRC contracts the Organisation shall:

(Paraphrased version:)

1. *Alter the Unions constitutions so that they could accommodate two players as directors on their boards.*
2. *Support the concept of a Players Association and make a loan of 10,000 dollars towards its establishment.*

3. Guarantee a 95 per cent share of the monies flowing from the
   Murdoch deal to the players.
4. Not discriminate or in any way bring retribution against any of
   the players who have signed a contract with the WRC.

The final four lines read:

*This offer shall not be revoked by the Organisation unless the
overwhelming majority of The Players refuse to relinquish their rights and
obligations under their WRC contracts.*

Yours faithfully,
Ian Ferrier.

There would be much criticism later at the generous terms of the
document, but Ferrier took the view that whatever the cost, "We
just needed to finish it, and make damn sure that WRC gave us back
the contracts the players had signed."

He also bridles at suggestions that have been offered since, that
the promise of 95 per cent of the television monies to the players,
was *particularly* over-generous.

"Our solid information at the time, and still," he says, "is that the
money that comes to the Union from sponsorship and merchandising, will very shortly outweigh the money coming from TV rights."

Whatever, it was done. *Signed.* Both sides had now come to
agreement about the terms under which the whole affair
could be finished. *Really* finishing it, though, would happen at the
press conferences that were due to be held that day in Johannesburg,
Sydney and Melbourne, where the Wallabies were preparing to play
in a David Campese "testimonial match".

To keep up the appearance of a "compromise" having been
reached, it had been agreed that in Sydney, at least, representatives
of the WRC and the ARU would sit at the same table, seemingly
happily together.

There they would go through the whole charade that while it might *look* like WRC had been defeated, in reality WRC had simply "merged their interests" with those of the national Unions.

In South Africa, Ross Turnbull was at his inimitable, irrepressible best. Before his very eyes, the whole dream had turned to ashes, but still, STILL he looked fine, sounded terrific.

"WRC has not fallen down," he said exactly as if he believed it, to the gathered media. "All that WRC has done in Australia and New Zealand is merge its interests into the Rugby Unions and we will assist the players in South Africa in achieving a satisfactory result with their Unions."

Still, he wanted to make it also absolutely clear that he held no grudge against the ruling national body, and he was also available to offer assistance to them if they required it. Magnanimity be thy name:

"The invitation remains open to any member of SARFU who cares about rugby and the players, to meet me at their earliest convenience," Turnbull said.

At both Australian conferences the tone was calm, quiet, seemingly without the slightest trace of retributive joy on the part of the ARU that WRC had been put to the sword after a long and mighty struggle.

In Melbourne, at the Wallabies tribute match to Campese, a clearly relieved ARU President Phil Harry spoke to the rugby press down there for the game.

"All the parties have agreed that it is over," he said, "and we now want to just get on with playing rugby. It is over . . . absolutely over."

It was at the Sydney press conference, though, that the most impressive show of unity and "compromise" between the two sides took place.

At a table set up in a room at the Sheraton Wentworth Hotel, and heavily attended by the Sydney and international media, Geoff Levy sat behind a table with Ian Ferrier and Wallaby captain Phil

Kearns, who was available to be there because an injury had kept him out of the Campese game.

All three strictly maintained the fiction that "a compromise" had been reached and that the interests of the two sides really had been merged.

When it was finally all over, Kearns turned to Ferrier and Geoff Levy and said, "Can I buy you blokes a beer?"

As a finish to the final whistle blowing, it was perfect. There is no more idealised part of rugby mythology worldwide than the notion that following even the most bitter battle imaginable, you should always have a beer together afterwards.

The Rugby War had, in the end, been a very rugby kind of war.

Epilogue I
May 1996

Dawn of a new era

It is a little over a year, at the time this book is released, since the whole World Rugby Corporation vision took shape in Geoff Levy and Ross Turnbull's imagination.

It did not succeed, but it nevertheless acted as a catalyst to changes to the code around the world that are of an enduring nature.

In Paris, on August 27, 1995, a meeting of the International Rugby Board declared that amateurism was no more, that the central plank on which the game had been built was no longer viable in the modern era. The former World Cup-winning Wallaby captain, Nick Farr-Jones, who was there when the gentlemen came out of the conference room to announce their decision, reports that "It looked like they had just come out of their own funeral."

Nevertheless, there was nothing to be done. Love it or hate it, the pressures brought by WRC, on top of the Murdoch deal, had ensured that rugby would be dragged kicking and screaming into the modern sporting era, a professional era.

As *The Times* of London declared in an editorial the day after the news was announced, "After all, there is an ethos for every age."

And people to profit from those new ethoses.

In terms of pure money earned, there is no doubt that WRC was also instrumental in getting a bigger share for the elite players. Whether this is the best thing for the code as a whole is a moot point still fiercely discussed by rugby people.

But to the key players of the Rugby War ...

Geoff Levy has returned to his law practice, and is doing well, his profile in the Sydney business community at least enhanced through the demonstration that he was capable of creating a whirlwind of change.

Ross Turnbull? He's out there somewhere, unsinkable as ever, and was last seen flitting between Sydney and Miami in pursuit of deals unknown.

Michael Hill has returned to running his successful legal practice in Newcastle.

Sam Chisholm, since the time of doing the SANZAR deal, has tied down many more deals with many more organisations and corporations. It's his thing.

Ian Frykberg remains at the head of CSI and has also completed some 10 deals since that time, some of them with News Corporation.

Of the principal officials who led the fight against WRC, nearly all remain in place, with two notable exceptions. In New Zealand, Jock Hobbs lost his place on the 19-man Council, when that body was slimmed down to a nine-man board in accordance with the recommendations of the Boston Report.

Richie Guy and Rob Fisher survived, with the latter narrowly failing to become the new Chairman at Guy's expense, when he had a tilt for the top NZRFU post. A newly-appointed member of the board is Kevin Roberts.

In South Africa, the head of SARFU, Edward Griffiths, fell out with Louis Luyt, and lost the position in March of this year. Leo Williams retired as Chairman of the ARU.

Which leaves us with the players and coaches, many of whom,

even as we speak, are driving around in beautiful new cars and moving into larger houses. Good luck to them all …

Of the New Zealanders, Mike Brewer has retired and is now living in Dublin. Laurie Mains has stepped down as coach, but was accorded the rare honour at the conclusion of the final Test he coached the All Blacks in — against France in Paris — of being chaired from the field on the shoulders of his players.

He was replaced in the All Blacks coaching position by none other than John Hart.

Sean Fitzpatrick remains as All Black captain, Phil Kearns will miss the '96 season through injury and thus cannot resume his position as Wallaby captain.

In South Africa, the policy of "no recriminations" has held absolutely firm and Francois Pienaar remains Springbok captain — though at the time of writing he has been struggling for form.

In Australia, after a difficult year which included his charges being knocked out in the quarter finals of the World Cup, Bob Dwyer has lost his position as coach of the Wallabies.

In England, both Brian Moore and Rob Andrew have retired from international rugby, the latter to take up a position as the first real professional guiding light of the Newcastle club.

And the exceedingly well-connected Will Carling? He has retired as England captain. For more detail on what he's up to, check out any women's magazine near you.

Which leaves us with the rugby game itself. It goes on, of course. It remains to be seen how such a traditional and soulful old thing as rugby will fare in the glittering professional sporting age. The jury is still out, unsure whether they like to see such a familiar well-worn face atop such sparkly and expensive new clothes.

But we'll see.

June 2003

The state of the union, and the unionistas, nigh on a decade later...

"*For a sport that just six years ago had the corporate finesse of a cauliflower-eared prop forward, rugby union is now a money-making juggernaut with the die-hard fanatics as stakeholders and the Wallabies themselves a prized commercial asset ... Since rugby's rapid rise from well-meaning amateurism to professionalism in 1995, the 15-man code has become a mass entertainment business.*" — Bernard O'Riordan, The Australian Financial Review, July 2001.

"*The All Blacks are no longer a team. They are a brand that is proving irresistibly attractive to international sponsors who can see the marketing value in the colour black. The players who, barely a decade ago enjoyed none of the trappings of full-on professionalism, are surrounded by an ever-growing phalanx of coaches, managers, media advisors, counsellors, psychologists, motivational experts, doctors of varying specialty and, of course, accountants. They are contractually bound to do this or not say that. They are on an endless conveyer belt from place to place, signing merchandise, posing for photographs, making television commercials and acting out the part as 'brand ambassadors', for Philips, adidas or the ubiquitous purveyors of alcohol."*—Chris Laidlaw, former All Black half-back and New Zealand parliamentarian in an article entitled "For Love And Money", published in the December 1999 issue of *New Zealand Books*.

"Every aspect of the [rugby] business has grown. We've certainly been commercially astute, but we've also had a winning product, the Australian Wallabies." —Brian Thorburn, Marketing Manager of the Australian Rugby Union, quoted in *The Australian Financial Review*, July 2001.

And so to the most recent update on where are they now, as of June 2003 ...

Ross Turnbull himself is still out there, still going and — as ever — *right* in the thick of it. The scene was set for his latest incarnation in the latter part of the 1990s, when the board of the enormous NSW motoring company NRMA devolved into a caterwauling cat-fight, with board members publicly screaming at each other, taking out writs, and engaging in a kind of corporate civil war on front pages everywhere. And that was on a good day.

This continued for four years until, in late 2002, out of a clear blue sky — and on the basis of his extraordinary network of contacts, and willingness to wade where the wary would not tread — one Ross Vincent Turnbull suddenly was appointed interim Chairman. There were howls of protest from all sides, but Ross did what Ross does best. He laughed off the worst of the insults and, rather in the manner of a hefty tugboat insisting on its right of way through light harbour traffic, got on with it. *Rrrrrrrramming* speed!

One of his first moves was to fill a vacant position on the board with his friend **Ken Rennie**, the Ernst & Young partner who had previously been heavily involved in the Rugby War. Though Rennie resigned from the NRMA board in the same week he was appointed when it became clear that there would be a conflict of interest — Ernst & Young were on the point of becoming the new NRMA auditors in place of KPMG — the brief outcry didn't appear to affect Ross at all. He carried on.

In February of 2003, the ticket led by Ross Turnbull won "a clean sweep" in the ballot held by the company to elect its directors — in part thanks to a highly controversial Ross scheme using proxy votes — meaning every member of the board now owed at least some allegiance to Ross. Certainly the subsequent Annual General Meeting was acrimonious, and there was shouted criticism from many NRMA members at the way Ross Turnbull had handled it, but the photo on the front page of *The Sydney Morning Herald* said it all: there was a smiling Ross emerging from the meeting, promising that a new era of peace had begun.

It was *vintage* Ross, not that any resurgent harmony was immediately apparent for all that. In early March 2003, Ross personally dismissed the Chief Executive of the NRMA, Rob Carter, immediately before making it public that the NRMA had lost 60 million dollars in the current financial year. In response to the outrage, Ross smiled broadly, and promised that all would settle down and the NRMA would soon be going on to bigger and better things. As we speak, Ross is writing his own memoirs, and I for one will be the first in the queue to buy.

Though he has no official role in rugby, **Geoff Levy** has done extremely well in his professional field. In 2001, the boutique corporate advisory firm of which he was one of three partners, Wentworth Associates, was sold to a South African merchant bank, Investec, for a price that was reported in the press as just a little over $A60 million. Geoff has stayed on with Investec as its CEO ... and

he is also a director of such heavyweight corporate crowds as
Network Ten and the Singleton Ogilvy & Mather advertising
group, as well as Chairman of the Film Finance Corporation
Australia.

Shortly after the first edition of this book was published in 1996,
Michael Hill became Chairman of the Newcastle Knights and
presided over a singularly successful period for the club, as they won
the rugby league premiership in 1997 and 2001. It is worth noting
that in the schism in rugby league which was wrought by Super
League, the Knights were on the establishment side of the
Australian Rugby League, and the first of their premierships under
Michael's stewardship was won when the competition was still split.
In early 1998, Super League more or less collapsed as its "vision"
proved entirely unsustainable, and it is regarded as one of the
greatest and most expensive cock-ups in the history of Australian
sport. When the two sides came together again Michael Hill was
one of the peace-makers, and in 2002 he was in fact the Chairman
of the newly-formed controlling body of rugby league, the National
Rugby League. Professionally, Michael continues as the principal
partner of the well-respected legal firm of *Turnbull & Hill* in
Newcastle. He remains on the board of the NRL and was also on the
winning ticket of the NRMA with his good friend Ross Turnbull.
They remain extremely close.

The peripatetic **David Moffett**? Like Ross Turnbull, he is above
all a *survivor*, and has had an extraordinarily varied career since the
time that rugby went professional. In 1997 he resigned his position
as the CEO of South Africa New Zealand Australia Rugby and —
amazingly, it seemed at the time — took up the position as CEO of
the New Zealand Rugby Union. In short order he was turning up at
All Black Tests in black blazers and trading pot-shots with his
former superior in the Australian rugby structure, John O'Neill. He
was still in the post of CEO of the NZRFU when — during the 1999
World Cup — the next thunderclap broke. David Moffett, a rugby

die-hard to beat all rugby die-hards, was the new CEO of the NRL back in Australia. He had been selected by a four-man committee which included ... Michael Hill and Ian Frykberg!

The International Rugby Football Board took quite a stern view of this "treachery". It was made clear that Moffett was no longer welcome at any of the remaining World Cup games, and he was shortly on his way to Australia to take up his new position. The irony that Moffett was now heavily engaged in boosting the commercial success of rugby league against the claims of the likes of the Super 12 and Tri-Nations which he had helped to create, was not lost on any of the rugby cognoscenti — or on Moffett himself for that matter.

In late 2001, Moffett left the NRL to go to England, where he became Chief Executive of Sport England, an organisation devoted to strengthening sport by the wise distribution of profits from the national lottery. After just one year though, David again changed course, this time to take up running the Welsh Rugby Union, which had fallen on exceptionally hard times — and was no less than $A132 million in debt. At last report David Moffett was meeting a lot of resistance to his plans to entirely transform the structure of the way the game is played there, including the forced merger of the nine premier clubs into five provincial teams, but he was pushing through regardless.

Generally, he still comes across as a resilient, happy kind of bloke who remains proud — and rightly so — of his role in forming up the Super 12 and the Tri-Series.

Louis Luyt fell on hard times, at least insofar as rugby is concerned, but it took some time in coming. For two years after the Rugby War was over, Luyt continued to run the South African Rugby Football Union in his bombastic style, but perpetually ran up against the extremely powerful and black-led National Sports Council, responsible for the administration of all sports in South Africa. As ever, Mr Luyt never backed off an inch, up to and including forcing President Nelson Mandela to appear in court to defend a planned government investigation into rugby. By 1998, the National Sports Council was so incensed they threatened to ban the use of the Springbok emblem, and re-introduce sanctions against both incoming and outgoing international tours. Did Louis back off? Did he, *hell*.

At a businessmen's breakfast at Ellis Park in early May 1998, Louis Luyt was at his inimitable best/worst, depending on the view you took of it. As reported by the doyen of South African rugby journalists, Dan Retief: "a whiff of fascism mingled with the smell of fried bacon, as Luyt addressed the throng".

"He was upbeat and aggressive," wrote Retief in South Africa's *Sunday Times*. "He launched a gratuitous attack on World Cup hero Francois Pienaar, comparing the blond one with 'Judas'. He said he bowed to no man other than God — he might have added 'and also not Nelson Mandela'. He drew some applause; some patrons even rose to their feet to signal their approval."

That afternoon though, he faced a SARFU meeting at the Sandton Hotel where his dominance was more than merely challenged. Four black board members resigned in protest at Luyt's actions against Nelson Mandela. By the conclusion of the meeting — and directly against the wishes of Louis Luyt — his own son-in-law **Rian Oberholzer** was reading out an official statement from SARFU apologising to Nelson Mandela. By the following Saturday, just four days later — with his own union, the key sponsors, the national government and most of the media standing united against him — Luyt's position was untenable, and he mercifully resigned. As Retief reported, "Luyt was fond of saying that he bowed to no man. Perhaps. But when he took on Mandela he was simply swept aside." He was replaced by Rian Oberholzer, with whom his relations were severely strained.

Within a year, however, the irrepressible Luyt was back in the news, this time as a member of the South African Parliament, the sole member of a newly formed party called the Freedom Alliance, with a political agenda which was not always easy to determine — but it was certainly based on the premise that South Africa had moved too far and too fast from the way it was before Nelson Mandela had taken over and it was time to redress the balance.

Richie Guy remained on the board of the NZRFU until 2001, when he stepped down and returned to his farm.

Rob Fisher became Chairman of the NZRFU in 1997 until 2000. He then served another stint in 2002, and that season proved to be the winter of New Zealand Rugby Football Union's discontent. The union went through a sustained period of deep instability resulting from the fact that the IRB considered that NZRFU was not keeping to the commercial undertakings it had originally committed to, in order to co-host the 2003 World Cup. When the NZRFU failed to react to the IRB's requests to fall in line, New Zealand did indeed have co-hosting rights taken away by the IRB, and Australia won the hosting entirely. A public inquiry as to how the whole gaffe had occurred was held, and when the highly critical report was tabled the entire board of the NZRFU resigned.

Who could New Zealand rugby look to in this time of crisis? The same man they had looked to during the Rugby War. Enter, once more, **Jock Hobbs**.

Since the days of the Rugby War, Jock had remained in the wilderness in terms of an official role with the NZRFU — his only contact with the game was watching his young son play college grade rugby — but now he suddenly emerged as Chairman of the board in the spring of 2002, regarded as something of a saviour of the game in New Zealand. His return to the board was hailed by *The New Zealand Herald* with an article beneath the headline: **HOBBS ASKED TO SAVE NEW ZEALAND RUGBY AGAIN …**

Francois Pienaar retired from the Springboks in 1996, and went on to become a player and then player/coach for the professional British rugby club of Saracens, with only mixed success.

Phil Kearns did not captain Australia again after the Rugby War — he was replaced in the post by **John Eales** — though he continued to play with great force and only retired after the successful 1999 Wallaby World Cup campaign, where he had to withdraw through injury. He is now a notably successful businessman in Sydney.

So, too, with **Rod McCall**, who continues to prosper in his Brisbane printing business, though his rugby days are also long gone.

Sean Fitzpatrick continued as All Black captain all the way until November of 1997, when a bad run of injuries pretty much finished him after having played 92 Tests, of which 51 were as captain. He remains one of the most respected figures in the game internationally and is currently the manager of the New Zealand Under–21 team and the [Auckland] Blues Super 12 team. As well as continuing his work as a high-ranking executive with Coca-Cola, he is busy on the after-dinner speaking circuit, though not nearly as busy as **Eric Rush**. Eight years on from the Rugby War, Eric continues to work in the marketing field, and is also one of the most highly regarded speakers in Australasia. And he is *still* travelling the world as the captain of the New Zealand seven aside team.

For his part, **Simon Poidevin** continues to work as a stockbroker and also as a rugby commentator, where his views on rugby remain widely respected.

Phil Harry retired from the presidency of the ARU in 2001, and was replaced in the position by former NSWRU President **Peter Crittle**. **Ian Ferrier** stood down from all administrative rugby posts in late 1999, and continues to work as one of Australia's leading liquidators.

Sam Chisholm? In the corporate world he remains "Sam the man". Though he left the employ of Rupert Murdoch and BSkyB just before the turn of the millennium with full intentions to retire to his farm in the NSW Southern Highlands (just next to Rupert Murdoch's) and his beach-house at Palm Beach (right beside Kerry Packer's), it was never a retirement that was going to last long. At the behest of Simon Poidevin, in early 2000 Chisholm dined at his favourite London restaurant with another of Simon's friends, Bob Mansfield, who was by then the Chairman of Telstra, and things moved quickly from there. Chisholm accepted Mansfield's proposal to get back in the game (Chisholm's wealth at this time was reported to be around the 100 million dollar mark, give or take a lazy twenty million, so he didn't need the money). In short order he had returned to Australia as not only a director of Telstra, but by July of 2001 also Chairman of Foxtel with a specific brief to sort out Australia's pay-television mess, and hopefully merge Foxtel with its smaller, though still debilitatingly troublesome competitors. That successfully accomplished, Chisholm took on another role as Chairman of John Singleton's Macquarie Radio Network, where he was instrumental in such colossal deals as luring radio broadcaster and former Wallaby coach Alan Jones away from 2UE to join Singleton's 2GB. Not for nothing was Chisholm described by the influential media watchdog website crikey.com.au as "the most powerful man in Australian media". Occasionally, given Chisholm's close association with John Singleton, he has dealt professionally with Geoff Levy and the two get on well. They have not yet discussed their opposing roles in the Rugby War. In April 2003, Chisholm had a successful double lung transplant.

And finally **Ian Frykberg**. He too, is still out there, still going. He continues to do deals across the world — albeit now for his own company — and makes a very handsome living via a frantic lifestyle: he lives life on the run. A former rugby prop forward of simple tastes and once simple means, he has come an awful long way and, after a fashion, Ian Frykberg is in himself an allegory for the elite end of the rugby game itself.

For the game, too, has come an awful long way since it went professional, with an extraordinary number of changes wrought upon it. The most crucial change has been the means of navigation.

In the purest of amateur days, union administrators steered by the star of "How do we get as many bums in muddy shorts as possible?" while the league administrators always set their compass by the shining star of "How can we generate as much money as possible?".

While it is an exaggeration to say that rugby union administrators now steer entirely by the latter star — because the vast bulk of rugby union players remain amateur, and they too must be administered — at the elite end of the game it is not too far from the truth. For since the advent of professionalism, the game at the top level is all but unrecognisable from the way it was ...

The most obvious visual change is that brand names now cover most moving parts of the game, including a huge swathe over once sacred international jerseys. Too, everything else is sponsored, from the balls, the referees, and the grounds right up to the goal-posts and the flag held aloft by the touch-judges. While some of these already bore brand names prior to professionalism officially being inaugurated, it is now endemic. Even the names of the teams themselves have changed, with the team once known as the All Blacks now officially "the adidas All Blacks", and as a matter of fact they play the "Bundaberg Rum Bledisloe Cup" against the "Vodafone Wallabies".

The names of those key sponsors came to be plastered in large type on jerseys which themselves had gone to the highest bidder. In 1997, the ARU changed the famous Wallaby jersey to a new design by Reebok which was described by this writer — for one — as "volcano vomit on a rag". So great was the outcry against the jersey that after a couple of years the ARU changed it to a jersey that was substantially the way it was before, but this was because it made good commercial sense rather than by cause of the outcry itself.

In the amateur days, a part of being in national teams involved doing a lot of signing of jerseys for the purposes of raising money for charities and the like. This was something everyone did without having to think about it, and no one ever complained. These days players are legally required to put their signature on a certain amount of memorabilia, and then the jerseys are distributed. While a certain number still go to charity, others are commercially marketed, with advertisements in the newspapers offering up framed copies of signed Wallaby jerseys for as little as 199 dollars a month for ten months.

Too, generally professional rugby players in these parts now play in stadiums that bear corporate names. The "HSBC Waratahs", for example, now no longer turn out at the Sydney Football Stadium, as it has been renamed "Aussie Stadium", after Aussie Home Loans, while the Olympic stadium once known as Stadium Australia is officially called "Telstra Stadium".

The famous Athletic Park in Wellington has been knocked down to make way for a retirement village and the Hurricanes now play home games at the "Westpac Stadium". Lancaster Park is no more for the young men of Canterbury, for they turn out at the newly named "Jade Stadium", which software company Jade has paid the naming rights for. And so on.

Because the players are now full-time professionals, the manner of their preparation has also changed. Not only are trainings held during the day, most days of the week but, at international level, the players now live at the one camp for the duration of their commitment.

It was an innovation brought in by Wallaby coach Rod Macqueen in 1998 when, under his guidance, the Australian team established a training base for themselves initially up at Caloundra, north of Brisbane, where they lived with their wives and families for three months of the year. It was a way of circumventing the constant travel to and from games and gave them the crucial time they needed to become the strongest team in the world — demonstrated by their winning of the 1999 World Cup. So successful has it been that many other national rugby teams have copied them. The greater amount of time spent together by professional players perfecting their rugby, and the greater importance which has been attached to finding new methods of winning, has meant that the game as it is now played at the elite level is all but unrecognisable from the way it was.

In the course of writing the biography of John Eales in the year 2000, John and I briefly discussed, among many other things, the defensive pattern of the game now. As a small example, he illustrated how it was very common in modern rugby to have three forwards lined up beside a ruck waiting for the next wave of attack to strike. In the old days, the tackler of the ball-carrier was simply whichever one of those three he ran at. But in professional rugby they had been told a different way. The Wallabies' defensive coordinator, John Muggleton, taught them that the man closest to the ruck was to be known as the pillar, the man next to him, no.2, while the third man out was to be known as the key.

Now, as John explained to me, "The pillar's job is to tackle the first man from the ruck if he runs directly at him, but if the runner drifts then the pillar lets the second man tackle him while he stays on guard for any inside pass from the ball-carrier. The second man has to watch for any outside runners off the ball-carrier, and any inside runners once the ball is passed to the next man. The key is set on the ball player alone. All three can only drift out when the ball has been passed beyond the key. At all times the three men must move forward before they move across."

It could get very complex.

So complex that John may as well have been speaking Swahili to me; I had simply not the slightest clue what he was on about — even though I was in the generation of the Australian second-row immediately before him. Together with the new-found complexity, there has been an explosion in coaching staff and sundries to help nurture it all. These days an international touring team does not merely comprise the players, a manager, a coach, an assistant coach, doctor and physio, but usually has extra people answering to such varied job descriptions as assistant manager, technical adviser, skills coach, conditioning consultant, athletic performance coordinator, rugby administration manager, kicking coach, media liaison officer, fitness trainer, coaching coordinator, video man, sponsor's rep and even — in the case of New Zealand — "throwing coach". The Springboks have even been known to travel with something called a "biokineticist"!

The oldest of all sayings in rugby is of course that "a rugby tour is a lot like sex, in that when it's good it is FANTASTIC ... and when it's bad ... yeah, well, it's still pretty good!" .

This may not necessarily still be the case at the professional end of the game. For the first thing, long tours by the Wallabies, Springboks, All Blacks *et al* are essentially a thing of the past. There is no more of the classic three-week warm-up campaign against strong clubs and provincial teams of the country visited before the climactic Test. This is for the simple reason that in the professional era *time is money*, and as those three weeks earned little in the way of money they simply weren't worth it. Now international teams tend to fly to the opposing country, have one warm-up game and then the Test match the following week.

The great former Wallaby coach David Brockhoff used to exhort his forwards to approach a maul in the same way they would put "crowbars through the Opera House windows ... we're in, we loot the joint, and we're out", and there is something of the same approach at the top level of the game towards Test matches.

And because it is such a serious affair now, players tend to "play up" a lot less. Now that it is their genuine livelihood, and the renewal of an extremely lucrative contract may hang in the balance, players are far more inclined to stay in their rooms rather than explore the nightlife of the country they're visiting.

This is not something which is discouraged by the coaches. When the Wallabies embarked on a brief tour to England in late 2002, they played a one-off warm-up game against Oxford University. They were invited to attend, after the game, a black-tie dinner in their honour at a 500-year-old hall. Team management declined on the grounds it was more important to get the team back to London in time for them to get to bed at 10 p.m.

Both the Super 12 competition and the Tri-Nations have been a great success in commercial terms, with the Super 12, particularly, generating enormous public interest across South Africa, Australia and New Zealand, and generally setting new records for attendance each season. As this book goes to press, the NSW Waratahs are drawing crowds of just over 30,000 to their home games, while the Wallabies drew an average of 55,000 in 2002, and across the Tri-Nations the graph of attendances has steadily risen since the game went professional.

Club rugby too — in Australia and around the world — has changed. Though it would be an exaggeration to say that clubs in Australasia are now mere "feeder teams" for the professional leagues, certainly that is a part of their role within the modern structure of the game. Many say that club rugby is now dead in Australia; a sure sign that *some* traditions go on unchanged. The happiest sign for Australian rugby, however, is that even though there has been a clear change in the star by which the game is steered, there still have been more bums in muddy shorts than ever before. The number of registered players in Australia has risen from roughly 100,000 when the game went professional to almost 150,000 now.

In the northern hemisphere the top clubs compete in an annual pan-Europe competition called the Heineken Cup, with massive prize-money for the winners, and it is in fact in Europe that elite rugby most resembles the vision put forward by the World Rugby Corporation. For in Europe it is the leading clubs who have often been taken over by rich entrepreneurial rugby-lovers, and it is these same clubs/franchises who are now the paymasters of the players with the national unions topping up the salaries. This model has had mixed success. While the famous Leicester Rugby Club went so far as to successfully form themselves into a public company — with their many devoted fans essentially becoming shareholders — other clubs have been less fortunate. At the time of publication the great Bristol club appears to be in financial trouble because the millionaire who has been financing them over the previous five years has announced his intention to withdraw. Club Chairman Malcolm Pearce had put in no less than £5 million and it is not screamingly obvious just who or what will be now able to match that level of generosity.

In the southern hemisphere, a different model of the relationship between players and their clubs and unions has grown. An elite player in New Zealand and Australia receives the vast majority of his money from the national union, a top-up from his province and usually nothing from his club of origin. (And though there has been some pay-for-play in the southern hemisphere at club level it is usually only at the very minimal level.)

Under this system it is no surprise then, that it is a very rare occurrence for a Wallaby, All Black or Springbok to turn up in a club rugby game. It is in part because they are "assets" of their unions and cannot be risked in minor encounters, and also because there are so many Tests and Super 12 matches that there are few free days left for club rugby anyway. In England, on the other hand, it is the reverse, where the paymaster clubs are less keen to release their star players for national tours that they might regard as being of minimal importance.

The fact that it was Rupert Murdoch's television interests that provided the bulk of the money for rugby's professionalisation has meant a change in the way the game has been viewed — and that has a meaning beyond the fact that Tests are now all but exclusively played at night, because that is when television can attract the most viewers.

Generally, keen rugby followers must cough up for one of Murdoch's pay-television services if they want to see important games live. In Australia in 2003, the free-to-air station Channel Seven announced that it would no longer be airing Super 12 matches, meaning that the only recourse for those who wanted to watch was to shell out around 50 dollars a month to subscribe to Murdoch's pay-television channel and watch it all as it happens.

Similarly, in New Zealand, the new force is Sky Television, which runs all the important games live, and even has a 24 hour rugby channel — but one to which the rugby public must subscribe. New Zealand's free-to-air TV3 still runs replays of the important games, but the bottom line is that because access is now restricted to those who are willing to add to News Corporation's bottom line, according to Joseph Romanos's book, *The Judas Game*, half the national viewing audience of New Zealand who used to watch every game religiously, is now no longer regularly watching.

In Britain, rugby was taken off the free-to-air BBC in 1997, meaning that rugby people had to front subscription fees for pay-for-view BSkyB Television. The result? One estimate, also reported in *The Judas Game*, has it that the television audience in Britain for rugby was cut by 90 per cent. No matter. The 10 per cent who could afford to pay, paid enough that both News Corporation and the rugby union were satisfied. Fortunately the situation in Britain has been rectified somewhat with major matches again showing up on BBC free-to-air, and BSkyB having the rights to play the games on delay.

Either way the money has indeed flowed in fortunate parts of the rugby kingdom, as never before. To take by way of example the growth in revenue across the board, we need look no further than the revenue of the World Cup. In 1987, it turned a profit of $A9 million dollars, not counting ticket sales. In 1991 that went up to 57 million dollars and then nearly doubled in 1995, when income apart from ticket sales was 93 million. In 1999 that more than doubled again to 210 million, and in 2003 the projection is that it will very likely double again to bring in profits, before ticket sales, at around the half-billion dollar mark. For the record, the estimate of Australian economist Tim Harcourt-Smith is that no less than one billion dollars will flow into Australia's public coffers by virtue of hosting the rugby World Cup.

Between World Cups, events like the twice-annual staging of the Bledisloe Cup generate something to the order of $A20 million, based on such things as sell-out crowds of just under 100,000 people (paying about 5 million dollars in total), sponsors (around 4 million dollars), plus television rights, merchandise sales, corporate boxes, corporate marquees, and all the rest.

Just before rugby went professional in 1995, Australian Rugby's revenue was to the order of $A10 million per annum, while in 2001 it was up to $60 million a year, and as this book goes to press the projections are $80 million for 2003.

This prosperity in rugby union is not universal, however. Strong rugby countries such as Fiji and Western Samoa, for example, which do not have large enough or affluent enough populations to be able to attract Rupert Murdoch's interest to provide pay-television services — and consequent big cheques to the rugby products to provide content — have been largely left behind.

And even in the far more prosperous nations of Wales and Scotland, things are very grim financially, with both of those national unions said to be struggling financially, as they have tried to keep pace with competing nations which simply have greater rugby "markets" and more industrial muscle. Each has huge stadiums they are finding hard to pay for, while Italy — now six years in the Six Nations — is not yet self-sustaining.

As to who gets the bonanza of money that rugby generates in the countries that are doing well out of it, the short answer is: those who operate within the professional realms of the game, starting with players, coaching staff, referees and administrators and extending out to a genuine industry which provides employment for *thousands*.

By way of example, back in the late 1980s there were three people who ran the ARU out of modest offices in the Sydney suburb of Kensington, and there were 19 working there when the game went professional in 1995. In 2003, at the time of going to press there are some 160 people working at the ARU's plush offices in North Sydney, and when the World Cup is at its height that figure will grow to 260 people taking a direct wage out of the administration of the game and its premier event.

The best of the Wallabies are now on salaries from the ARU in the vicinity of half-a-million dollars, with all professional players in Australia sharing in a revenue pool which is just under 20 million dollars. Overseas, the biggest star in world rugby — who remains All Black Jonah Lomu — earns a reputed $A3 million dollars a year when all his endorsements are counted. Today, when players file onto 747s to depart on their rugby trips, they all turn left from the entrance to make their way to business class, instead of right and then down the back to "cattle class" as in the days of yore.

Indeed, so dramatically have things changed in the financial returns of union and league that it is now the *league* players who are snaffled by union scouts. Three of the biggest names in the league game for the past three years have been Mat Rogers, Wendell Sailor and Lote Tuqiri. In 2003, all three were playing Union and all were good chances to make the Wallabies for the World Cup at the end of the year. Many other league players have also been recruited for provincial union teams.

The big money though, is not limited to the international players being paid by the unions. With the advent of professionalism there are now a serious number of South Africans, Australians and New Zealanders particularly, playing for clubs in Japan and Europe. In 2003, a very good club player in England could earn as much as £150,000 a season. This exodus of top players to where the money is has probably hit South Africa the hardest; with their weak currency of the rand the temptation for even top-notch players to take the Euro and run has been irrefusable. Ditto the majority of Argentina's internationals, who for the most part live and play in Europe. Most Georgian and Romanian internationals are now playing in the rich European leagues.

Beyond players, administrators and coaching staff though, there has been a great deal of employment provided in ancillary industries which have grown up around the professional game. These include caterers, security staff, player agents who take a percentage of the salaries they negotiate for their clients, not to mention pay-television commentators, journalists, authors and rugby after-dinner speakers. (I note particularly the last four roles, for it is only fair that I acknowledge that I have benefited as much financially from the professionalisation of rugby as most. And as an example of how much the rugby "market" of people interested in the game has grown, the biography I wrote of Wallaby World Cup winning captain Nick Farr-Jones in 1993 sold some 45,000 copies, while the one I wrote on John Eales released in 2001 sold well over twice that.)

While with this level of financial success and growth in following rugby union is now a serious competitor to rugby league, there is no doubt that the relationship between the two codes has grown a lot closer. This is not simply because many league players are now playing union, and many union players are having at least brief stints playing league. Nor because the modern way that union is played — with a brief burst by one player with the ball frequently followed by the ball being laid back for another player — sometimes resembles league. Rather, it is because now that both games are professional the huge cultural gap between the two has disappeared, and with it a lot of the distrust that used to poison the relationship.

Those of rugby union who were once described as "defectors" because they had left the amateur game to go to league are now practically considered "pioneers" in that they were among the first to force a passage between the codes. In both Britain and Australia there is more and more talk of both union and league teams turning out from the one club, with facilities shared. In Britain, the Wigan Rugby League Football Club was recently invited to enter a team in the Middlesex Rugby Union Sevens competition, and it is now common occurrence for league teams to play on union grounds and vicky versa.

In 2003 the gap is so small that many — including the former boss of British Rugby League, Maurice Lindsay — believe that the codes will soon merge. Short of an outright *massacre* of rugby league, this will not happen. For while rugby league remains a genuinely strong game in Australia, in most other countries it is a parish pump game at best, and there is simply no chance a hybrid version of union and league would ever be accepted in a country like France or say, Scotland, or other countries which make up the International Rugby Board.

Attitudes have changed too. While in 1990 I found it very odd that the ARU should examine whether my first book *Basking in Beirut and Other Stories* was about rugby, which would have breached strict amateur regulations — it included many other subjects as well, so I was okay — I now find it extraordinary that something like that could have been an issue in such recent times.

And as a rugby commentator I look back on a couple of columns I wrote in the mid-1990s — where I said that rugby union must *not* allow players who left to go to rugby league come back again — and find them extraordinary in their own rough fascism. How could I have been so supportive of civil liberties in every other field, but want to blackball for life a bloke who simply wanted to play rugby league? How could I, who'd been such a loud-mouth supporting sanctions against racist South Africa, have supported a veritable sporting apartheid in my own country?

Ultimately though, the game goes on and well away from the revolution that has been wrought on the elite end of rugby; down at the grass-roots level rugby players continue to delight in running into each other on the weekends, much as they ever did.

Oft times, the grass-roots troops look with a certain bemusement at the way the elite rugby people carry on and this was best illustrated in a story told by my old rugby coach, Peter Fenton, in the NSW–Queensland match program of 2003. Fenton, who was a successful club coach before coaching the Sydney representative side, recounted how the former St George coach Butch McDougal once expressed astonishment at a national coaching seminar when a man with several degrees in physiology was attempting to explain the difference between "aerobic" and "anaerobic" fitness.

"Geez, this fitness thing has got complicated," Butch said. "I just run my blokes till they spew and then take 'em down the pub."

The point is that across much of the land teams still are coached that way, and nothing has really changed.

As to the older players, the ones who came to maturity in the fully amateur era, absolutely NOTHING has changed at all, and they are behaving much as they ever have.

By way of example, some seven years into the professional era of rugby, the old and the bold from Sydney's Hunters Hill Cats Golden Oldies Rugby team were on a flight bound for some rugby revelry on the Gold Coast. The fact that the airline had not spotted them as a rugby team was likely due to the fact that they had booked as lady bowlers and therefore were all seated together. The stage was thus set. The flight attendants on that day were headed by the truly gorgeous and shapely Brenda and ...

And as the drinks trolley did its job and the Golden Oldies focused progressively more on her lovely form, they soon forgot their baldness, creaking joints and obesity and were taken back to their youth, back as far as 1977, when they had gone through the entire season undefeated. The more they gazed at Brenda, the more they remembered, until, somewhere over Tweed Heads, it happened ...

From the midst of the drooling mob came: "Hey, Brenda, what's ya muvva's phone number?"

The game goes on.

Index

Photo credits

First photo section
Geoff Levy, News Limited; Ross Turnbull, News Limited; Simon Poidevin with Willie Ofahengaue and Tim Gavin, News Limited; David Moffett, News Limited; Sam Chisholm, News Limited; Phil Harry with Ian Ferrier, News Limited; Rob Fisher, Sport the Library photo by Andrew Cornaga; Jock Hobbs, *New Zealand Herald*; Leo Williams, Dr Louis Luyt and Richie Guy at press conference, Associated Press; Laurie Mains, Sport the Library photo by Clifford White; John Hart, Sport the Library photo by Joanna Caird; Richard Loe battling Phil Kearns, Getty Images; Eric Rush, AAP Photo Library; Rod McCall, Getty Images; Troy Coker, Getty Images photo by Joe Mann; Sean Fitzpatrick with Jonah Lomu, Craig Dowd and the Bledisloe Cup, News Limited; Phil Kearns, News Limited.

Second photo section
Francois Pienaar being chaired around Ellis Park by Hennie Le Roux, Sporting Pix Australia; Rob Andrew dropping dramatic last-minute goal, Getty Images; Rob Andrew diving at the ankles of Jonah Lomu, Getty Images; Bob Dwyer flanked by Bob Templeton and Glen Ella, News Limited; Jason Little, News Limited; Michael Lynagh, News Limited; Jeff Wilson, Sport the Library photo by Andrew Cornaga; Josh Kronfeld, AAP Photo Library; Chester Williams, Touchline/Australian Picture Library photo by Tertius Pickard; Will Carling, Getty Images; Richie Guy and Rob Fisher looking on as Sean Fitzpatrick signs contract, *New Zealand Herald*; Phil Kearns leaning behind Ian Ferrier, News Limited; Ross Turnbull on the steps of the Cape Town Supreme Court, Associated Press; Steve Merrick, News Limited.